AF201885

Julia Hildermeier

How Ideas Change Markets

Mobilität und Gesellschaft

herausgegeben von

Weert Canzler, Stephan Rammler
und Oliver Schwedes

Band 8

LIT

Julia Hildermeier

How Ideas Change Markets

Social and Semantic Construction(s) of Automobility
in 21st century Europe

LIT

Umschlaggestaltung: Niels Schröder

Gefördert vom Ev. Studienwerk Villigst e.V., gedruckt mit freundlicher
Unterstützung der Humboldt-Universität Berlin

Dissertation an der Humboldt-Universität Berlin, Kultur-, Sozial-
und Bildungswissenschaftliche Fakultät, und an der Ecole Normale
Supérieure Cachan

This book is printed on acid-free paper.

Bibliografische Information der Deutschen Nationalbibliothek
Die Deutsche Nationalbibliothek verzeichnet diese Publikation in der
Deutschen Nationalbibliografie; detaillierte bibliografische Daten sind
im Internet über http://dnb.d-nb.de abrufbar.

ISBN 978-3-643-90832-2
Zugl.: Berlin, Humboldt-Universität, Diss., 2015

© **LIT** VERLAG GmbH & Co. KG Wien,
Zweigniederlassung Zürich 2016
Klosbachstr. 107
CH-8032 Zürich
Tel. +41 (0) 44-251 75 05   E-Mail:
zuerich@lit-verlag.ch   http://www.lit-verlag.ch

Auslieferung:
Deutschland: **LIT** Verlag Fresnostr. 2, D-48159 Münster
Tel. +49 (0) 2 51-620 32 22, E-Mail: vertrieb@lit-verlag.de
E-Books sind erhältlich unter www.litwebshop.de

Meiner Familie

Contents

Introduction

In autumn 2015, one of the world's largest car makers, Volkswagen AG, broke the largest global scandal in the automotive industry's recent history when the company admitted to having manipulated emission measurements to display lower emission values. The scandal showed how deeply Europe's automotive industry is linked with politics on different decision-making levels. Those that started researching the reasons for which this interdependence could be ignored for so long, dived into the institutional complexity of a multi-layered European government in a sector that transcends national borders and imposes its own power structure across 20th century history, melting institutional influence through market dominance, employment and lobbying power, the impact of technological developments and consumers' changing mobility patterns. Those that looked for solutions discovered that these would need to be embedded in a context of given environmental regulations such as emission and air pollution standards for vehicles, and that every company weighs the cost of improving existing technology against the innovation potential of less polluting alternatives to the combustion engine, such as electric cars. In short, many practitioners are currently confronting the two questions that this book is about: Why do institutional paths endure? And how can new paths emerge?

The automotive industry has often been described as 'path-dependent'. Throughout the 20th century it has been considered an economic pillar of growth in the industrialized economies of Europe, the US and Japan. Along with other manufacturing industries such as steel, chemistry or machine tools, Fordist mass-production of combustion-engine cars guaranteed jobs and export revenues in affluent post-war societies. With the beginning of series production a century ago (Ford started to produce its Model T in series in 1913) a complex institutional structure emerged, based on user demand, political regulation and production organization, commonly referred to as the automotive industry.

The decades of stability are linked to a stable organizational pattern of mass production and consumption (Chanaron/Lung 1995; Boyer/Freyssenet 2003), embedded in automotive countries' national economies. The car market has survived various (cyclical) economic crises. Research on the transition of socio-technical regimes has explained the automotive sector's stability by an automobile 'paradigm' or 'regime', rooted in cultural patterns of mobility behaviour, consumption patterns, infrastructure use and planning, as well as the continuous development of technological innovation (Geels et al. 2011; also Canzler et al. 1993). This paradigm is expressed by a simple fact: Today, most vehicles are passenger cars, run on gasoline and are privately owned. Car sales have been growing. Forecasts expect 1.5 billion cars to be in use by 2030 (ICCT 2012:6). Road transport, mainly consisting of passenger cars, has become a major source of environmental pollution. Cars are responsible for about 12% of Europe's total CO_2 emissions; and they are the single largest source of emissions in the transport sector (EU 2014).

With the 2008/2009 economic crisis and its repercussions, this study argues, a possible rupture arises in the sector's path of global expansion and stability. The crisis, the following chapters will show, merely revealed an underlying structural change, bringing the European automotive industry to a historical bifurcation point: the end of combustion-engine-based private mobility. The development of alternative engine technologies, and increasing shared car use have started to question the dominant individual ownership model, and with it, car makers' oligopoly on global markets. Facing more urgency to cut transport emissions, fuel-efficient cars have already becoming a priority for firms, policy makers and consumers (Calabrese 2012). In this context, the development of the electric car, an energy efficient, (at tailpipe) non-polluting alternative, could start no less than a 'second automobile revolution', after the first one of Fordism a century ago (Freyssenet 2009). Other observers are more cautious, arguing that technological change does not automatically induce path change. "At present, more activities, beliefs and resources are oriented towards a 'greening of cars', which sustains the existing car-based system, than towards more comprehensive system innovations based on combinations of different forms of transport" (Kemp et al 2012: 26f). Representatives of a powerful oil and gas lobby, fearing losses in the fossil fuel transport, have recently invested 10 million dollars per year to discredit the electric car and prevent the transition to electrified transport[1]. How can we distinguish a temporary phenomenon from a profound institutional restructuring, starting with the creation of a new (fossil-free) path (in transport)? Two challenges emerge for researcher in order to understand and identify conditions of path change.

Research objectives

The empirical question is: Which forms of automobility will appear in the 21st century? In the context of climate change, increasingly scarce petrol resources, the shift to post-fossil transport is one of the pressing political issues on a global and local scale (Canzler/Knie 2014). Growing urbanization and populations' increasing needs for mobility provide new challenges for existing public and

---

[1] The Kochs are plotting a multimillion-dollar assault on electric vehicles. A new group could spend $10 million a year on the campaign. URL: http://www.huffingtonpost.com/entry/koch-electric-vehicles_us_56c4d63ce4b0b40245c8cbf6

private transport. The question which patterns and visions of auto-mobility will prevail in the future is crucial to adapt and prepare tomorrow's resource-efficient and intelligent transport systems, replacing today's "high carbon mobile lifestyle" (Grieco/Urry 2011). The role of today's dominant means of transport - the car - and its possible electrification plays a key role in this ongoing debate. The theoretical challenge for different approaches in social sciences dealing with path rupture and change is to qualify the industry's future trajectories. How to determine if we are witnessing a moment of path rupture in a century-old industry that has shaped our lives and cultures as only few others have? Identifying conditions of path rupture is necessary for understanding processes of path creation: How and why would the automotive market, the product, regulations and its forms of use change? How can we explain the emergence of new institutional configurations?

Existing approaches struggle to accurately analyse causes and impacts of this potential shift. Political economists identified why path-dependent configurations only change at high cost from their different national patterns (Crouch/Farell 2004). Historical comparison with other industries shows that different political imperatives such as environmental regulation are reinterpreted as specific sectoral problems and negotiated in a complex hierarchy of actors (Jullien/Smith 2014). The character of transitions identified in such analysis is therefore likely to reflect the industry's structure rather than explain radical change. As a result, 'structuralist' institutionalist literature, focusing on the way economies and sectors are organized, despite its merits of taking into account characteristics of the automotive industry, could not yet satisfactorily explain its transformations. Other culturalist approaches have investigated the transitions of the 'automobility regime' (Geels et al 2012) from a user- and behaviour-centered perspective. Describing a shift away from individual automobility towards shared and collective use of transport means, authors observe "cracks under the surface...that create opportunities for wider system change [...]" (Kemp et al. 2012: 3). System change could signify the emergence of a new path. However, lacking concepts that describe the interaction of companies, politics and users and how they collectively make sense of these phenomena, authors cannot explain how possible factors of transition actually operate. Their diagnosis of a possible regime shift therefore falls short of identifying new path options. As a result, paradoxically, there is consensus among scholars that "the automotive industry is currently changing more profoundly than over the last 50 years"[2], but existing theories can neither explain its causes, nor seize

---

[2] "Die Automobilindustrie verändert sich derzeit mehr als in den vergangenen 50 Jahren" (Lars Thompson, trend researcher, interviewed in: Die Zeit, 2013)

the impact of this transformation. This study suggests a third way in approaching the question of path creation in recent automobile history. By joining both perspectives, it can be explained why and how an institutional path can emerge, based on new but coherent organizational and semantic patterns.

The study's objective is twofold, meeting both the empirical and theoretical research challenge. First, it aims at empirically identifying and characterizing possible alternative institutional configurations to the current automobile path, based on a qualitative case study exploring principal environmental conflicts and their institutional impacts in the sector since the 1990s. The second aim is to develop and apply elements of a theoretical framework that can account for existing shortcomings in institutional literature and facilitate the study of path creation. The study suggests how sociological micro-foundations, based on existing concepts such as framing, can be combined with the idea that policy-instruments translate actors' judgements and strategies and thus can have institutional (semantic and structural) impacts. On the macro-level of observation, institutional shifts can then be explained by endogenous factors instead of external crises. As a result, possible futures (of automobility) emerge from actors' collective solutions of present (environmental) conflicts. Current trends in mobility such as (public) vehicle-sharing, electrification of transport and intermodal connectivity between public and private transport can be explained in the context of changes in the automotive market's hierarchy, regulation and the patterns of governance on different decision-making levels. Merging the empirical with the theoretical objective, the study's outcomes allow conditions of path creation to be identified more generally.

Overview of the study

By means of a brief historical introduction, **Chapter 1** illustrates the structural and semantic reasons of the European automotive industry's stability and growth. The theory **Chapter 2** explains why existing approaches struggle to explain path change and suggests an analytical framework to understand path creation. The research design in **Chapter 3** details how these theoretical categories apply to the empirical case study in an inductive research design with qualitative methods of data gathering and interpretation. **Chapter 4** is the first of two empirical chapters, presenting findings of the case study in a historical reconstruction. By reconstructing interactions between different sector organizations such as corporations, lobbies, environmental groups and public authorities, the chapter analyses the preconditions of path change and the first sequence in the industry's environmental conflict on CO_2 regulation in the 1990s. This micro-level analysis describes how an alternative framing of companies' environmental responsibility emerged, mainly through advocacy of civil socie-ty representatives and a growing critical public. Transparency and environmen-tal performance were institutionalized as new criteria of legitimacy for players in the market. The seeds of transformation this regulation instrument planted would unfold with the crisis in 2008, when a broad debate on electric cars as a solution to emission problems emerged. **Chapter 5** shows that on this historical ground, parallel to the continuing investments of car manufacturers in the op-timization of diesel and petrol engines, electric vehicles would quickly become a major strategic challenge for the manufacturers and national governments across Europe. Contrarily to the industrial path, the electric vehicle's benefits for the sector's structural problems developed into a shared solution narrative before its market had been taken up. The resulting wave of Research, Devel-opment and Demonstration funding, and companies' subsequent investments, produced institutional effects, setting the conditions for path creation. **Chapter 6** identifies two different new paths that could emerge, articulating new forms of sustainable (auto-)mobility.

1. The automobile 20th century in Europe

""The Machine that Changed the World" (Womack et al, 1990)

Automobility, the individual possession and driving of a car, has been the dominant representation of mobility in the 20th century. As an economic and cultural characteristic of industrialized societies, it has become a symbol of individual freedom and modern capitalism. Throughout the 20th century, the combustion engine car has become "a paradigmatic product and integral part of a society of fossil mobility" (Altvater 2006: 175[3]). The idea that people drive freely whenever they want, where they want, is closely linked to the individual combustion engine passenger car and the way it is fuelled. The petrol-based mobility and infrastructure and growing engine power helped realize social, cultural and geographic aspirations. The car has been "a symbol of social status, affluence, freedom (to move), dynamism and progress" (Buhr et al. 1999: 11). Decades of advertisement for ever new brands, segments and models have successfully reinterpreted the car from a means of individual transport meeting necessity (to move) into a symbol of social distinction and personal accomplishment.[4] As the objectification of social status, the car engine in particular has remained the core value of the car. Economically, the engine as a technical artifact guaranteed speed and power of the vehicle (the diesel or Otto engine, are continuously improved by competitive engineering teams in different car companies). Symbolically, it incarnated the driver's *and* owner's social status.[5]

Shaping automobility as a culture, the car also created a highly differentiated economic and organizational structure in its main markets worldwide. Rising vehicle sales and production conditioned economic growth periods after the

---

[3] Cited from Aigle et al 2007:3. Altvater further identifies fossil energy, fuelling the car, as the third institutional pillar of contemporary capitalism with European economic rationality and corresponding dominant social organization in capitalist societies.

[4] Examples are: "The power of Dreams" (Honda), "Engineered to move the human spirit" (Mercedes-Benz), "Freude am Fahren" (BMW), "The art of performance" (Jaguar), "Don't dream it. Drive it" (Jaguar), "Infiniti. Accelerating the Future" (Infiniti), "It's not a car. It's a Volkswagen" (Volkswagen), "Welcome to the State of Independence" (Saab). Source: http://www.thinkslogans.com/slogans/advertising-slogans/car-slogans/, accessed: 10/2014. Communication strategies in car advertisement are also a subject of scientific research (Leithäusl 1997).

[5] Until today, the size of the car, its engine power, is determined as corresponding to different social strata. Car segments are referred to 'classes' in German, English and French ("Mittelklasse, Kompaktklasse",...).

Second World War. The economic miracle (Germany) or the trente glorieuses (France) witness this development in Europe, a similar development shaped the success of the 'Big Three' US car makers and the central role of the car industry in Japan supplying cars for the entire Asian market. Today, the industry constitutes a highly differentiated value chain. In Europe, 12.9 million jobs depended directly and indirectly on the car industry in 2012 (ACEA 2013). Car makers as integrators, as companies that assemble a car of a complex chain of pieces and parts, have dominated the value chain since the first assembly lines were built by Henry Ford. Since the 1950s, a movement of concentration through mergers, acquisitions and bankruptcies can be observed, which leaves the current global market with a powerful oligopoly. Few multi-national companies dominate the global market today through selling a product, providing a lifestyle, nourishing aspiration of social advancement or status and reproducing respective demand. Emerging and rapidly motorizing markets such as China or India will become beneficial if as many cars as possible can be sold. To secure new markets while 'old' triad markets are in decline, the automotive industry is interested in reproducing the cultural model of car ownership in these societies. In sum, "since Henry Ford's push towards industrial car manufacturing more than a century ago, selling cars to private owners has been a successful and stable business strategy" (Firnkorn/Müller 2012:1).

Institutionalist literature has explained the industry's stability - the reproduction of an institutional configuration over time - by path dependency. The concept is derived from the observation that technologies diffuse against rationalist ideas of efficiency by constituting their own paths through convenience or repeated use.[6] Historical institutionalism observed that path dependent macro-configurations such as nation states (Streeck/Thelen 2005; Pierson 2004), (Hall/Soskice 2001) and industries (Jürgens/Sablowski 2008) tend to reproduce their dominance, i.e. the path, against all historical and rationalist probabilities suggesting more efficient evolution. The power of self-legitimating mechanisms outweighs the possible change to less costly alternatives. This leads to the problem of lock-in: the longer a path continues, the higher the cost of change. Actors are caught in institutions, i.e. in organizational ways of doing and their legitimate patterns of reasoning.

One question has remained unanswered so far: Why do paths rupture and how can new paths emerge? In order to identify path creation empirically and theoretically, we need to understand the historical reasons for the car sector's stabil-

---

[6] Artur (1984) gives the example of the irrational diffusion of the QWERTY computer keyboard which was adopted from the typewriter instead of being ergonomically shaped. It persists to this day because it has shaped the typing styles of generations of PC users.

ity. The remainder of Chapter I identifies historical reasons of stability of the automobile trajectory (I.1.). It highlights that the industry's path continuity actually had never been unquestioned. Instead, efforts to introduce different technologies (such as the electric car) and different patterns of use (car-sharing) have already started to question the prevailing *conception of control*. However, none were able to transform the rules of path reproduction (I.2.). My study will explain why the situation is different in the first decades of the 21st century.

1.1. Structural and semantic conditions of path dependency

"Every German should have the right to purchase his own car. And we want to build the roads for him." (Helmut Schmidt, 1965)[7]

"Free citizens want free roads" (German Automobile Drivers' Club, 1974)[8]

Historically, the conception of 20th century automobility is rooted in three unquestioned assumptions in the area of technology, politics and the market.

- Technology: Combustion engines will prevail due to their technological superiority, and original equipment manufacturers (OEM) as integrators dominate the value chain and demand.

- Politics: Decision-makers respect the economic power and employment creation capacities of the car industry.

- Market: Consumers seek to possess and drive cars and are able and willing to pay for individual motorized mobility.

The following overview shows that one of the main reasons for the industry's stability has been the coherence between these spheres of action. Coherence can be understood as shared assumptions firms and policy makers reproduce when solving different conflicts such as environmental ones. The European automotive history shows how the social and semantic structure of the sector has emerged and stabilized in these three dimensions[9]. Roughly chronological,

---

[7] Cited in Der Spiegel "Mehr Strassen, weniger Wohlfahrt", 14/1978, http://www.spiegel.de/spiegel/print/d-40616854.html
[8] Cited in "Ausweichen, Abwarten", Der Spiegel, 31/1975, online archive: http://www.spiegel.de/spiegel/print/d-41458151.html.
[9] European automotive history is necessarily bound to national borders in its early phases from 1970-1990, as the technological development, politics and markets were organized within the borders of national markets, until the integration into the Single European Market in 1993. The

the overview reveals that the characteristics of the automotive sector's three institutional pillars have remained stable despite many events, arguments and expectations that could have undermined this stability a long while ago.

Technology

Organisation of production and gradual innovation patterns explain the sector's longevity. Producing car parts and assembling these to a vehicle requires a diversity of processes in a highly differentiated but embedded value chain. For this reason, the car has been called a product-system, embedded and linked through multiple ways to the national economy (Chanaron, Lung, 1995). The debate on car manufacturers' production models (Boyer and Freyssenet (2003) contend that companies diffuse different production systems that compete globally) revealed that car makers' dominance of global value chains was founded in ways of organizing production but also in the creation of shared narratives. Toyota in particular advocated its system of efficient and on-demand lean production in the 1980s as the new 'one best way' to assemble cars after Fordist mass production. Pardi (2011) points out that this organizational model implied not only a way of organizing production, but also produced an ideological consensus justifying the industry's cultural importance: It was backed by widely diffused advocacy on the car as 'the machine that changed the world' (Womack et al. 1990).

Embedded in this production system, the stable and gradual technological amelioration of Otto and diesel combustion engines constitutes a core feature of the automotive sector's path-dependency. Innovation research observes that despite the manifold organizational transformation of production and car makers' global oligopoly, the sector has never undergone a technological rupture (Christensen, 1997). In other words: no technological alternative to the combustion engine car was mature or even competitive enough to set up market dynamics to force the old system to adapt to changes or make place for the new one. As Jullien, Lung and Midler (2012) argue, automotive companies clearly

---

overview mainly draws from decades of car-industry-related research conducted by the main global research network on the automotive industry, Gerpisa. Understanding the reasons for the global car industry's specific durability and longevity has been one of the programmatic objectives of the Gerpisa's research network on the automotive industry. Gerpisa's interdisciplinary researchers mainly take an 'institutionalist' perspective focusing on the supply of cars, market structure and technology development. Founded in 1992 by Freyssenet and Fridenson, its past research programmes provided a detailed historical understanding of the consequences of the organization of production (comparing corporate-made productive models, 1993-1997), and markets (comparing 'varieties of capitalism', 2004-2007).

followed an incremental strategy to integrate technical innovations to an existing technological and economic system, rather than allowing radical innovations. Especially if developed by competitors, radical innovations would risk
changing the balance of power in the sector, enabling companies to define the
industry's future path. Christensen defined the electric vehicle as such a radical
innovation: "[...] the electric vehicle is not only a disruptive innovation, but it
involves massive architectural reconfiguration as well, a reconfiguration that
must occur not only within the product itself but across the entire value chain
[...]" (Christensen 1997: 252). His argument is that by definition of its innovation pattern, the industry *is not prepared* for a technological path change.

Politics

Industrial policy, in the sense of public regulation sustaining or seeking to improve the production organization and system, has been the second institutional
pattern stabilizing 20st century automobility. Many examples can be given on
national level, especially in Germany and France, where the car industry had
become a synonym of economic growth after the 2nd World War. Germany's
support of mass production and consumption dates back to the 1950s in Germany, laying the foundations of an automobile society. Jürgens et al. (2010)
illustrate the process of car ownership diffusion: "Due to Fordist mass production, employment in the automobile sector increased more than eightfold, from
around 44,000 in 1948 to 358,000 ten years later. The output of cars plants set
new records each year. Already in 1963, one in four families owned a car. The
automobile penetration was supported by the idea of the car friendly city between 1963 and 1973. In the middle of the 1970s one in two families had an
own car" (Jürgens et al. 2010: 240). In order to raise consumption, production
and national gross income, the Social Democrats decided on a historical sum-
mit[10] in 1959 to support investments in car production, and all other political
parties followed. The spirit of pro-automobile politics is well summarised by
social democrat chancellor Helmut Schmidt (1965): "Every German should
have the right to purchase his own car. And we want to build the roads for
him." Infrastructure building and city planning were adapted to the unquestioned assumption of universal car ownership and use. Until the early 1970s,
along with other manufacturing industries such as steel or machine tools pro-

---

[10] With the Godesberger programme, valid from 1959 until 1989, the German Social Democrats
decided on supporting capitalist market economy and no longer supported socialist economic
ideas.

duction, the automotive sector guaranteed wealth through employment and exportation in core European countries such as Germany and France.

The first severe recession following the oil crisis in 1974 gave birth to emission regulation on European level. The influential Meadows report of 1972 on the "limits of growth" made decision makers and the general public realize that resources for petrol-based transport were limited. The consequent trade-offs between environmental and economic objectives produced first structures of political coordination between industry and authorities on European level. Business historian Morguen-Toursel (not dated) shows that the member states of the European Community had committed to rationalize the use of petrol energy and tried to oblige the transport sector to contribute to these objectives since the 1970s. The then arising conflict of interests between car makers, who wanted to keep control over their (loose) emission reduction efforts, and environmental organizations or environmentally ambitious governments who want to see standards tightened as to reduce emissions of all cars, has been ongoing for almost 40 years. It provided fertile ground for consequent structural and semantic changes nourishing discussions on sustainability, electromobility and vehicle-sharing in later decades.

The early environmental conflict stabilized, rather than opened, the existing automotive industry's path. European air pollution norms for vehicles, concerning the reduction of toxic gases such as carbon-monoxide and nitrogen oxides (NO_x), until 1986, could only be agreed upon in principle among member states on European level, because Denmark opposed the compromise and asked for more ambitious norms (Morguen-Tousel 2009:14). But car manufacturers secured their dominance as market leaders by offering a technical solution: the catalytic converter. This pattern of industry providing technical solutions to political conflicts, as the case study shows, will be repeated later on with regards to CO_2 reduction. As Morguen-Tousel points out, authorities supported the catalytic converter to reduce combustion emissions from conventional cars at the expense of investing in research and development of other alternatives that would have questioned the consensus on the automobile path at an earlier stage, such as speed reduction, fully clean engines, electric engines or producing less polluting fuels. The Commission would repeat this pattern in the late 1980s in other directives to the benefit of German producers of catalytic converters. "The Commission's choice (in particular for the catalytic converter) are beneficial to the Germans and to a lesser extent to other European car makers. The French suggestions (speed reduction, clean engines, electric cars or improving fuel quality) found little understanding in the Commission" (Morguen-

Tousel n.d.:4).[11] In the conflict, the German industry opts not by coincidence for the incremental technical improvements (catalytic converter) and thereby against adapting the 'automobile compromise' embedded in society of unlimited speed on highways, combustion engine technology and fossil fuels. Parts producers for the converter, but also car makers appear to have had strong political weight, and opted for path continuity.

Public authorities emerged as an autonomous actor in the car sector when environmental-economical trade-offs had to be managed and regulated. The increasing need for negotiation at the European level set the basis for a coordinative legislation pattern since the 1990s. In the automotive sector, policy instruments were jointly created, for example emission standards, by firms and authorities. "Norms are established by and for the interested actors. Their use as a reference in legislation, even voluntary, is part of a co-regulatory process" (Morguen-Tousel n.d.: 2). Since the coordinative approach on EU-level emerged, historically, environmental politics in the car sector, especially emission regulation, are thus intrinsically linked to the supra-national level of decision-making. The early conflicts on emissions set important preconditions of stability in terms of governance in the automotive sector. 'Co-regulation', as Morguen-Tousel puts it, emerged as a governance pattern by which actors tried to deal with trade-offs between growth objectives and that of emission reduction. In this sense, the emerging compromises had an additional stabilizing effect on the industry since the late 1980s regarding the way how decisions were taken: they included and increasingly institutionalized car makers as co-decision-makers. Vice-versa, co-regulation and compromise contributed to institutional stability and thus the continuation of incremental innovation and path dependency, instead of change.

---

[11] The introduction of the catalytic converter is an example of increasing competitive negotiation in the field of environmental politics. The German government had pushed for the introduction of the converter for two economic reasons. First, the majority of firms involved in the production of the catalytic converter were German. Second, Volkswagen had gained significant market shares in the US where strict environmental norms were already applied. Replicating these in Europe would be beneficial for sales. The introduction of the catalytic converter implied, however, higher cost of production and consumption that would hit especially the French, Italian and UK volume producers of small vehicles. Regulation finally gave reason to the German industry. Morguen-Tousel rightly hints at the fact that the German car manufacturers in general had been rather reluctant to introduce strict environmental regulation (except for the catalytic converter), and that there were internal struggles between an ambitious environmental ministry and a conservative transport-ministry to which car manufacturers were allied. The largest car market and industry, as will be shown throughout the analysis, has been both driver of and obstacle to environmental regulation.

Markets

The dominant pattern of vehicle demand, the third institutional pillar of 20th century automobility, has remained largely stable throughout the oil crises and first environmental conflicts. This is due to the extremely supply-oriented character of the car market. Car makers had become market shapers. Expanding the product offer through technological improvements they created, stimulated and continuously recreated demand. The stability of consumption is also rooted in the reproduction of semantic structures, i.e. collectively shared meanings which market actors build, verify and share through communication. As such, the car as a technological artefact to move people does not require a specific form of use: it can be shared or individually owned, rented or leased, publicly or privately. But shaping demand car makers reproduced what Beckert calls a 'rationality fiction' (Chapter 2), i.e. a normative representation of reality based on which market participants interact. Consequently, individual car ownership thus emerged as the socially most valuable and desirable mode of car use. *As a shared collective understanding* it inspired and reproduced a whole product-system because neither suppliers nor users questioned its legitimacy.

This and other shared collective understandings that founded the semantic content of 20th century automobility were institutionalized through dedicated communication channels. Drivers' clubs communicate with their members through specialized magazines. Motor shows in Paris, Geneva and Frankfurt attract millions of visitors. Membership in car clubs promoting car use such as ADAC[12] in Germany had been growing continuously. Between 1964 and 1973, membership tripled from 800,000 to 3 million. Public investments in road infrastructure facilitated car use to reach larger distances and realize dreams of mobility, freedom and modern lifestyle. As long as the automobility path remained unquestioned as a social asset, there was no reason not to inspire demand by an ever larger offer of cars in increasingly diversified product segments. The cultural and social definitional power of car makers resulting from this configuration ensured market control. As their technological investments reproduced a specific narrative of consumption, they controlled the generative rules of the sectoral configuration, making and reproducing its institutional coherence.

The brief overview illustrated that car makers had secured their share in the shaping of the future of mobility by controlling rules of the production of supply, regulation and demand in the industry. The sector's coherent structural

---

[12] Allgemeiner Deutscher Automobilclub. In Europe, the ADAC, with more than 18 million members, is the world's second largest such organisation after its US equivalent.

order reflects and is reflected by a semantic order: If cars as products guarantee freedom, independence, and social affluence, production was considered securing employment and economic well-being. Within this coherent narrative, requests for transforming this order (such as environmental concerns to reduce emissions) were answered by firms by placing technological innovations on the market, mostly supported by governments seeking to secure employment and value creation. The strength of car manufacturers as the dominant actors, especially from the environmental point of view, unveils a weakness regarding the costs of path change: Once the coherence between these dimensions and thus the path's stability would be questioned, their definitional power on shaping the future is compromised. This subchapter has hinted towards some incongruencies in the automotive industry's conception of control concerning early regulation of car emissions and the empowerment of the European decision-making level. With the harmonization of the EU market in 1993, the transfer of decision-making power starts to impact companies' strategies (Stone Sweet et al 2001, Fligstein 2001). Politics start to play a larger role as a destabilizing factor. The following subchapter illustrates the degree to which alternative patterns of technology, regulation and consumption could develop, setting the context for this case study of path rupture and creation.

1.2. Conflicts and renegotiations of the automobile path

Despite its path-dependent trajectory from a macro-level point of view (I.1), the path of automobility has never been fixed. This subchapter reveals from a micro-level perspective that the automobile path can be described as a temporary compromise between sectoral actors. Its history can be divided into sequences of conflicts in which different shared organizational structures and narratives of automobility were constantly renegotiated. The solutions to these conflicts, i.e. specific policy instruments and interest constellations provided the basis of an overall stable institutional macro-constellation. This is because they repeated the technological, political and market-related rules of rule-making. While the study will fully explain this mechanism later in more detail, this chapter briefly explains why several early attempts to introduce a different technology – for example electric cars that reduce local emissions – were doomed to failure.

Historians of technology confirm that vehicles with electric traction are older than that of the combustion engine itself. The electric car was at its first peak around 1900, during which some prototypes found public attention (Mom 2004). However, electric cars were soon overruled by petrol-based propulsion technologies, which then developed into the dominant path for more than a century. In the second half of the 20th century, first attempts to reintroduce the electric car in France in 1973 did not develop into a larger market phenomenon (Callon 1986). EDF, the country's national utility, had presented a prototype which could not attract confidence, investments or a collectively shared understanding about its relevance among markets and political observers. Despite the fact that these early debates set a small network of actors and elements of narrative framing around this innovation, often connoted with innovative technology and environmental improvements, it did not attract the interest of politics and dominant corporations such as car manufacturers so as to mature into a convincing alternative.

The political context changed in favour of the electric car after the oil crisis in the 1970s and the realization of peak oil. The US state of California reacted by setting ambitious emission regulations and promoting the first electric car prototypes. Confronted with particularly severe problems of air pollution, the Californian Air Resources Board (CARB) extended its competences for the regulation of car emissions through the Clean Air Act Amendments in 1970 (Weider 2007). These acts set the preconditions for fostering the introduction of electric and low carbon vehicle technology through ambitious emission standards for cars – an instrument aiming at technology forcing. In 1990 CARB published its Low Emission Vehicle and Clean Fuels Directive imposing gradually stricter limits for new cars' emissions by car maker. Part of this regulation was also the Zero Emission Vehicle mandate which introduced an obligatory sales quote for those for the years of 1998, 2001 and 2003. Car makers reacted and accelerated technological innovation: General Motors had presented its electric concept car 'Impact', the first vehicle which was to be produced in series under the name of 'EV1'". But even though EV technology was being developed, car makers did not consider it mass marketable. [13] In contrast, the fact that CARB was aiming, with technology-forcing measures, to develop the niche technology into a larger market, provoked the resistance of car makers and several law suits followed. Despite these backlashes, California's regulation produced one of the leading early markets for electromobility. The Californian example also inspired European legislation on clean and energy efficient cars which would affect technology paths in Europe (Jöhrens/Hildermeier 2015). The US example shows that electric cars had already been part of corporation strategies and governments' repertoire of solutions since the 1970s when it came to conflicts

---

[13] GM's failure to commercialize its first electric car EV1 is well documented in the film "Who killed the electric car?". GM, stating that the vehicles would not sell, destroyed its own first electric cars series at considerable cost. The film blamed the lack of political support and consumer information, cf. Shnayerson, Michael (1996). The Car That Could. New York: Random House

on vehicle emissions. Pushed by the Californian example, this potential alternative had started to question the given automobility in the early 1990s.

Early Electric Vehicle demonstrators - niches without a narrative

In the same years, in Europe, political authorities and automotive firms launched the first wave of demonstrators testing the technological potential and consumer acceptance of electric vehicles. In Germany, several demonstrators were run, which all remained at a "declared pre-competitive status" (Prätorius/Lehrach 1998: 46). The project on the peninsula of *Rügen* (Baltic sea), run from 1992-1996, was the most ambitious and until then the world's largest one. Between 36 and 60 converted electric cars from brands including BMW, Mercedes-Benz, Opel, VW, Neoplan and Fiat were tested on the island, with different batteries and charging technologies. The approximately. 30 million Euro (60 mill. DM) trial proved that electric vehicle transport was principally feasible: electric cars could be used in day-to-day conditions equipped with the battery technology at the time. However, ecological and technical results proved disappointing for the companies. Due to the high carbon energy share in the country's energy mix, the cars' overall emissions scored higher than that of conventional engines. Noise problems emerged because of the heavy batteries cars had to carry. Other technical problems only affected the availability of vehicles so that only 1 to 14 cars could be used at a time. As a consequence, the project was closed down after four years, lacking public and political interest to develop it beyond a strategic niche. Hoogma et al. critically point out that project closure was not only due to technological insufficiencies and that the project was not promoted in order to preserve the combustion-engine-based automotive compromise rather than develop potential alternatives at least technologically. Participation in the project was limited to major, established market actors "whose opinions about the electric vehicle niche were already formed. The dissonant voices of small start-up firms, environmental movement adherents, and critical scientists remained outside the project. [...] Most of the small firms subsequently went bankrupt" (Hoogma et al. 2002: 74f).

Another demonstrator was set up by national mail company Deutsche Post in Bremen as part of the company's commitment to environmental sustainability (Chapter 5). The company originally aimed at significantly reducing the vehicle fleets' emissions through integrating alternative powertrains (Prätorius/Lehrach 1998: 25). However, achievements were limited due to delivery and technical problems. Throughout the 1990s, national mail companies had emerged as a key actor in implementing the mass commercial use of electric vehicles. Their calculable and short- to medium-range delivery activities are an ideal testing territory for EV technology. Strategically, state-owned companies lend themselves to exploring the comparative advantages of innovations for national industries. As Chapter 5 will show, especially the French mailing company La Poste will play a significant role in implementing the French launch plan for electric vehicles in 2011. [14]

Early demonstrators were not only progressive in technological terms but also by promoting alternative forms of vehicle use. A demonstration project by car rental company Sixt, together with Deutsche Bahn AG, offered electric car *rental* at central railway stations in different cities, an *intermodal* service connecting different means of transport for one journey. However, limited technical feasibility, high battery prices and limited customer acceptance are again problems that prevented these experimental projects from developing beyond the niche. Inciting electric car use in combination with car-sharing, in contrast, seems to have had market potential since an early phase. A rare survivor is the French project LISELEC, which combined the idea of car-sharing with the introduction of the electric vehicle. Launched on the island of La Rochelle in 1999, it was run with Peugeot (PSA) cars in cooperation with local transport companies. [15] Successful until this day, it was bought in 2006 by Proxyway, a branch of the environmental infrastructure group Véolia. The service is still active today and shows that local configurations helped the project survive.

This short historical overview shows why EV demonstrators did not unfold sufficient conflicting challenges for car makers to question the dominant path. First, there was no political coalition of interests. Most EV demonstrations were carried out as research and development projects, focusing on technical characteristics under laboratory conditions. Second, dominant forms of car use were not questioned: Demonstrators were not intended to question the fact that the majority of users own and drive cars. Even if some of them such as LISELEC and the Rügen project proposed a new consumption pattern, this did not affect mass consumption. Third, they were not part of a larger ecological, economic debate that contextualized these experiments in a larger thinking of societal or market change. Fourth, EVs did not become part of car makers' product strategies. As a result, these potential alternatives were not embedded in any coherent narrative that could have been developed further. As the next and last section will highlight, the paradox between dedicated engineers' enthusiasm for radically different technologies, and the fact that the dominant ownership model was not publicly questioned persisted until the late 2000s.

---

[14] The Deutsche Post, however, so far has not been prominently involved in EV testing activities in Germany, although it could emerge as a market-shaper, given the size of its fleet.
[15] Others were TULIP and PRAXITEL

Existing explanations for rupture: behaviour or technology?

There are different explanations for the car industry's ability to solve conflicts on innovation and environmental regulation by resuming the dominant (fossil) rather than alternative (electric, intermodal) solutions. Geels et al. insist on the fact that the "fundamental issue of change and stability" (2011:3) in the car industry needs to be explained by more than one factor. "On the one hand, automobility faces a need for change to address persistent problems such as increasing traffic congestion and atmospheric pollution [...]. On the other hand, automobility is deeply embedded in western lifestyles and stabilized through sunk investments, interests vested in its continuation and taken-for-granted beliefs and practices" (Geels et al. 2011:3). In an edited volume on the automotive society's future, Geels et al. identify emerging niches of new practices and technologies, such as sharing electric cars, which could change existing regimes of automobility. In the long-term, this could affect the landscape, a term referring to the broader social, cultural and technological context of an innovation (Geels et al. 2011), for example the fossil-based lifestyle of developed economies. Their explanation has the merit to shed light onto the pillar of automobility that had not been questioned by many of the 1990s experiments: users' behaviour and cultural expectations that translate into specific demand patterns. It emphasizes that car sales are tightly linked to previously unquestioned practices of car use. It takes into account "the emergence of new cultures of mobility" (Sheller 2012; Grieco/Urry 2011), in particular "intermodal personal mobility" (Parkhurst et.al 2011), "the electrification of automobility" (Orsato et al 2011) through battery and fuel cell technology, and embedding these cars in intelligent communication systems (Pel, Teisman, Boons 2011). All these trends contribute to the diversification of car use and technologies. The multiplication of use options and the rise of mobility could discredit the automobility regime, providing transition opportunities. The essential shortcome of such cultural, behaviourbehavioural and policy-based explanations, however, is that they cannot explain if and how an automotive industry will transform in the same manner as behaviourbehaviour is predicted to change. Assuming that automobility is likely to change, authors refer to socio-cultural patterns of car use that adapt and change with technologies provided. The underlying conceptual link from representations to structures remains underexplored, just as production-system approaches (Boyer/Freyssenet 2003) inversely tend to ignore the fact that technologies shape cultures.[16]

Innovation research has instead focused on technological change and examined the chances of rupture of the combustion engine technology paradigm. The term paradigm can be understood as a conceptual equivalent to what Geels et al. characterizes as regime: a long-existing historically stabilized institutional path, featured by technological and cultural elements. Aigle et al. (2007) suggest a systematic approach to classify alternative technologies that could challenge the dominating combustion-engine paradigm, more or less prone to be integrated into a path-dependent system depending on the degree of radicality of the innovation (Aigle et al 2007: 15). Authors classify electric vehicles, driven by batteries or fuel cells, as radical innovation that potentially changes a given socio-technical regime due to its systemic and destabilizing character.[17] This literature suggests clearly that the paradigm shift in automobility is not blocked by technological or engineering problems, but rather by cultural and organizational factors that the new technology needs to be embedded into. Sociology of innovations has identified these as "deficits in coordination, adverse interests and social barriers to innovation" (Braun-Thürmann 2005, cited from Aigle et al. 2007).

Between culture- and technology-focused explanations of the destabilizing impact of alternative technologies there is room and material to argue for a joint perspective. This study argues that an explanation of ruptures in the path of automobility and the creation of possible alternatives needs to take both areas into account. Launched and nourished by an interdisciplinary research group at Wissenschaftszentrum für Sozialforschung Berlin, researchers from fields of science and technology studies and sociology of technology and mobility observed that the fast, long range sedan ("Rennreiselimousine") had lost its attractiveness as a collectively shared narrative since the 1990s (Dierkes et al. 2009, Canzler/Knie 2009, Canzler 1996, Canzler/Knie 1994)[18]. Authors

---

[16] Notable exceptions are Wells' (2010) account asking how both dimensions of automobility, supply and demand, change through the industry's phase of 'eco-austerity', and Mitchell et al. (2010), describing how personal urban mobility in the 21st century 'reinvents the automobile'.

[17] The research of Aigle et al. anticipates the electric car's path creation potential by differentiating between types of innovations: its type ('stagnovative' = improving existing technology and thus stabilizing it or non-stagnovative = destabilizing existing technology through different fuels or engines) and secondly, its degree: incremental or radical. A third criterion to judge the potential path-breaking impact of automobile innovations is, if it is modular or systemic. While modular innovations concern single vehicles, systemic innovations such as the electric car concern an entire institutional configuration of practices and products.

[18] It is the department 'Innovation und Organisation' that would co-found with Deutsche Bahn, Telekom, DLR and other industrial partners a small Think Tank on Mobility research in 2006.

state that both the given culture of automobility *and* its socio-technical objectified structures need to be studied when examining options of path change. A new conception of control, a new set of problem solutions, this study argues in the following chapters, would then replace the existing link between semantic and organizational structures ensuring a new path's legitimacy.

The introductory chapter has shown how the sectors' governance, i.e. the practices, processes and organization of decision-making, has been questioned through new technological alternatives and their demonstration, fostered by increasingly strict environmental regulation. It has also shown that the Europeanization of policy making networks is a probable common condition in which environmental conflicts had to be solved. What are the consequences of these conflicts on the automobile path, its embeddedness in the structural and semantic institutional order of the sector and more broadly, in European economies? This question has not been researched yet. The present study attempts to contribute to fill this research gap. The remainder of this study thus analyses if a new institutional trajectory is emerging in the automotive industry. Can new ideas of mobility, collective understandings of economic rationality change existing markets? How could we investigate and explain a potential creation of a new path? The potential for path rupture cannot be judged by looking at the radical character of the innovation and corporate strategies only.[19] Rather, we need to look for coherent alternative narratives that emerge in the same market context, put forward by new players or authorities. This analysis argues that narratives on the coherence of demand, supply and politics can transform the architecture of the automotive market. The following chapter introduces the theoretical framework of this study.

The Innovation Center for Mobility and Societal Change (Innnovationszentrum Mobilität und Gesellschaftlicher Wandel, InnoZ) started out with 10 employees to elaborate and implement electric car based mobility projects. With almost 100 staff in 2014, it has become one of the major Think Tanks on sustainable mobility projects in Germany. As both, an observer and actor in the market of new mobility solutions, it will guide and co-develop alternative electric mobility projects, co-financed by the government, and encourage the emergence of a new mobility path discussed in Chapter 5.

[19] After a few years' interval, the assumption of a radical "Second automobile revolution" (Freyssenet 2009) proved wrong. Villareal (2014) has shown that actors and technology, supported by political investment programmes and media attention, do not bring about a revolution, but at most a temporary and uncoordinated destabilization of permanently negotiated power relations.

2. Micro-foundations of path creation: an embedded policy analysis

This chapter elaborates the book's theoretical framework to explain how institutional structures of (European) markets or sectors emerge and change. It develops the basis of what I call 'embedded policy analysis', an analysis of markets as institutional configurations, their emergence and conditions of change applicable to different European political spaces. This framework will then be applied to the case of European automotive sector and emerging mobility markets (Chapters 4 and 5) and then be refined for future research (Chapter 6) in other cases.

By ways of introduction I outline why theories on the development of institutional paths can be found in two parallel theoretical discussions: institutional political economy and market sociology. Literature in institutional political economy seeks to understand how firms or market practices contribute to economies institutional trajectories and create more or less stable institutional orders. Looking at the history of economic institutions from this perspective, Fligstein states that capitalist economies reproduce themselves over time through *conceptions of control*. These conceptions can be understood as semantic patterns of legitimacy by which a specific institutional hierarchy is maintained (1991, 2001). Inspired by Bourdieu's theory of the economic field (Bourdieu 1997), Fligstein insists on the fact that these shared meanings are tied to the market structures in which corporations, but also other organizational entities such as public authorities, interest groups and consumers, interact. Hierarchies and symbolic power structures dominating the economic field or that of a specific industry, Fligstein suggests, determine the ideas that actors develop and share to make the system evolve. "Conceptions of control refer to understandings that structure perceptions of how a market works and that allow actors to interpret their world and act to control situations." (Fligstein 1996: 658).

Assuming that sectors are based on specific control conceptions seems straightforward. But this explanation runs into problems when we try to understand how any institutional configuration, such as the European automotive industry, based on specific control conceptions, emerged or changed, when taking into account vehicle emission legislation for example. Following Fligstein's reasoning, different control conceptions emerge throughout economic history and path-dependent development is the logical consequence as controlled hierarchies are reproduced. This finding is also representative of literature in institutional political economy. Scholars can convincingly explain how institutional systems such as economies, nation states, industries (Hall/Soskice 2001) or 'political cultures' (Schmidt 2002) remain dependent and tend to reproduce previous existing patterns identified. But they struggle to conceptualize how new ideas, visions or newly valued factors – such as that consumers' transport behaviour or the innovative potential of electric cars – transform existing institutional orders and eventually produce new ones. As a result, the concept of path creation, designating the emergence of new a technological, institutional and economic institutional trajectory, has been little specified[20].

First attempts to overcome this problem can be found in market sociology which, in contrast to institutionalist accounts of economic development, focuses on the expectations market actors attach to products and institutional development, and therefore to the visions that reproduce or change industries. This literature is the second strand of research feeding into my theoretical framework. Individual market or governmental actors' representations of the future can take the form of shared narratives, stories or 'fictional expectations' (Beckert 2013), i.e. expectations on a future (desired) state of the present that guides actors' seemingly rational behaviour. These concepts in market sociology build on the assumption that actors' rationality regarding markets is always embedded in an institutional context and therefore 'bounded' (Simon 1959), as opposed to economic theory which tends to ignore this context and understands these ideas as utilitarist expectations of future profit that aliment constant competition. Shared narratives in specific institutional contexts are the actors' very motives to interact and make sense of what they do. They usually describe a desired state of present configurations, motivating actors in markets to interact, and build institutional orders within capitalist societies (Beckert 2014). These ideas can be visions of future state of economies and societies in general, or precise expectations of outcomes of certain policy or market processes such as the introduction of innovative products.

Any framework that describes the institutional roots of path development of different fields such as the automotive and related markets needs to take into account economic imperatives as well as political negotiation of actors' expec-

---

[20] The academic debate on different 'varieties of capitalism' in the 2000s, inspired by Hall's and Soskice's volume (2001), further contributed to theory-building on path-dependency. Contributors compared the trajectories of different national economies, especially Germany and the US, showing that there is no one best (neo-liberal) way of running an economy, but different policies as each system has its comparative advantage against the others. As Jullien and Smith criticize, "Varieties of capitalism scholars have given analytical priority to strategic interactions which link firms, states and other parts of political systems in the definition of major institutions. In so doing, they often fall into the trap of considering that there is an 'institutional isomorphism' between the institutional characteristics of each type of capitalism and the types of organizational features that structure 'their' firms." (Jullien/Smith 2010:6).

tations and interests. It should be able to model the emergence and transition of institutional structures of a sector as a single political space, without reducing its empirical complexity. Therefore, drawing from both political theory strands above, my study explores the assumption that actors' ideas about the future impact the institutional development of different sectors and economies. Change of institutional paths can come from within.

A theory of path creation in different policy areas thus needs to explain how institutional paths emerge and change, taking account of conceptions of control at work and actors' shared narratives backing or contradicting these. To build this theoretical framework, I first critically review literature on path change and identify main research gaps (Chapter 2.1) i.e. lacking micro-foundations of action and the lack of imaginable futures different from variants of past patterns. The following subchapters address these research needs, developing a model for interaction on the micro-level (Chapter 2.2.) and how these impact future institutional paths (Chapter 2.3).

2.1. The research gap: micro-foundations of institutional change

Existing literature can explain stability of institutional configurations, but not change. This is illustrated by Fligstein's history of the United States' economy throughout the 20th century (Fligstein 1990), explaining how different conceptions of control stabilized different types of capitalism. He identified four different historical periods, leading to the current form of finance capitalism, in which corporations control other players by accumulating power through financial instruments. The evolution of different trajectories (of capitalism), he argues, can be seized by a historical analysis of firms' conceptions of control. Control conceptions act like a Bourdieusian 'doxa' in the field of the market, representing the core legitimating narrative that reproduces rules of interaction by which actors legitimate their choices. Ensuring legitimacy and thus stability of other market institutions, this shared narrative describes "how firms ought to solve their competitive problems" (Fligstein 1990:12) at different points in time and in different regulative contexts.

It is therefore all the more astonishing that Fligstein does not emphasize more the role of ideas in order to explain the emergence of new historical trajectories, i.e. the change between different conceptions of control and according types of capitalism. One reason may be that it would require a sociological analysis of how decision-makers in firms put ideas into action, and justify market or political decisions. Instead of conducting a qualitative study of how actors' visions could change markets, or government of capitalist economies, on the micro-level, Fligstein opts for a quantitative analysis of ownership relations and other macro-variables of the market throughout its different historical periods.[21] He therefore does not extend on an analysis of interpretive action in markets, especially of how sectors function in the most recent financial form of capitalism. Such an analysis would need further theory, detailing his assumption that managers in firms are endowed with reflexive capacities about what overall objectives their company should pursue to shape their market in a certain way. Without looking further into micro-foundations of control conceptions, we only learn that market actors reflect on their own and fellow actors' strategies (in homologue positions) and constantly mirror the market as a set of actors shaped by their practices.

Despite these shortcomings, Fligstein's work is rightly appreciated by sociologists and heterodox economists for including power relations as an explaining factor to the emergence of institutional configurations such as the European government of different industries (Jullien/Smith 2008, 2014). Fligstein's theory provides us with some more elements for a theory of path creation – and subsequently creation of (European) government spaces. A conception of control contains a shared narrative that justifies why incumbents are the dominant players. For changing it and creating a different path, consequently, those firms or other actors Fligstein refers to as 'challengers', play an essential role: companies that seek to change existing narratives and organized ways of market interaction in order to enlarge their market share and to gain power to define the markets' or sector's future development.[22] While Fligstein's analysis remains centered on how dominant players ensure control, this study argues that we can understand possibilities and roots of path creation only by looking at how challengers resist to control and suggest alternatives.

Tracing challengers, the way they are organized, and their shared narratives can reveal how organizational micro-structures change *despite* their being embedded in hierarchical relations. In order to do this, an analytical framework needs to understand how the "control" of a market is exerted, and how it can be criti-

---

[21] In order to cover a large period of time, Fligstein opts to remain at the macro-level of analysis. Because of this methodological choice, results remain general: "The sales and marketing conception of the firm began with the marking revolution of the 1920s and came to dominate the largest firms in the post-world War II era. This conception of control emphasized that the key problem for firms was the selling of goods and therefore the solution was to expand sales." (Fligstein 1990: 14). "The finance conception of the modern corporation, which currently dominates, emphasizes control through the use of financial tools with measures performance according to profit rates." (Fligstein 1990: 15). This transformation into a shareholder value-based finance-capitalism disconnects the firm of its adherence to only one industry (15), but considers it as a collection of assets valuable in many.

[22] Fligstein uses the terms 'markets' and 'industries' interchangeably. I will define what I refer to as 'industries' in Chapter 3.

cized. How do market actors interpret what other market actors do? Sociologists assume that ideas in general, and control conceptions in particular, emerge and are being reproduced in markets through communicative interaction. They criticize that institutionalist accounts, such as Fligstein's, lack micro-foundations, concepts to describe individual action and how actors (collectively) make sense of their understandings. Knoll (2012) suggests that this short-coming is linked to the fact that an interpretive understanding of institutions has never been agreed upon in institutionalist research.

'Institutions' are interpretive processes, not outcomes

Although DiMaggio (1988) argued that institutionalist analysis also needed to explain why and how actors follow organizational norms or ideas of rationality, ethnomethodological approaches to institutions that Zucker (1977) developed to meet these criteria were never accepted in organizational theory. She suggests instead focusing on cognitive processes that create and transmit institutions. Following Zucker, common understandings institutionalize through objectivation and externalization from what actors say. "Institutionalized acts (…) must be perceived as both objective and exterior. Acts are objective when they are potentially repeatable by other actors without changing the common understanding of the act, while acts are exterior when subjective understanding of acts is reconstructed as intersubjective understanding so that the acts are seen as part of the external world." (Zucker 1977: 728). As a result, Zucker considers institutions "as a qualitative process instead of a (quantifiable) outcome" (cited in Knoll 2012: 58). Zucker's definition thus assumes the building of shared frames of meaning as collectively objectified legitimate ways of doing and thinking. It builds the first element of sociological micro-foundations of collective action I will further describe in Chapter 2.2.

Struggling to explain crises and sequences of conflict in an institutional trajectory, historical institutionalists realized that they lacked concepts of micro-level action in recent years. Scott (2008) argues that "institutionalism had matured" with "the recognition that laws and regulations could be resisted and reinterpreted by those to whom they were applied" (cited in Aldrich 2010: 340). He suggests that today formerly marginal constructivist understandings of institutions, such as Zucker's, should be taken into account: "Structures only exist of and to the extent that they are continually produced and reproduced." (Scott 2008:438). This also allows us to consider crises and conflicts as parts of an institutional trajectory, eventually produced by actors, instead of understanding them as external 'non-explicable events: "Just as 'exogenous' changes could come from shocks and jolts and from invasions of 'foreign' ideas from other fields, endogenous changes could come from conflicts between levels within fields, mismatches between juxtaposed elements of different fields, and organizations' failures to achieve their claimed goals." (Aldrich 2010: 341). Several ideas on how to make sense of actors' practices in institutional environments have emerged in this debate, briefly discussed below. [23]

The concept of 'institutional entrepreneurship' was used to describe how start-ups change a given market constellation and thus, eventually, a trajectory. It shows that "changing attitudes about the environment motivated some entrepreneurs to create new firms for ideological reasons, reflecting the new cultural schema" (Aldrich 2010: 342). But analyses of how institutional entrepreneurs act so far have failed to take into account the complex environment of an institutional sector and explain how entrepreneurs become a challenger for an entire conception of control. Mobilizing institutional entrepreneurship to describe, for example, new successful business concepts such as electric car makers (e.g. US car maker Tesla) or electric car-sharing services (e.g. French service Autolib') would ignore that both firms were significantly supported by public authorities in California and Paris to set up their businesses (cf. Chapter 5).

Building on DiMaggio's term of 'institutional work', Lawrence and Suddaby (2006) suggest analysing practises of firms and policymakers as "the knowledgeable, creative and practical work of individual and collective actors aimed at creating, maintaining and transforming institutions" (Lawrence/Suddaby 2006: 219). Different categories of institutional work characterize how actors could solve potential conflicts between interests and prevailing control strategies of others. [24] 'Mimicry', for example, could be an explanation for seeming-

---

[23] Following these debates, the definition of 'institution' is constantly debated. "The prevailing emphasis on institutional stability even in the face of indisputable and important change points to a general problem in contemporary institutional analysis, which has always emphasized structural constraints and continuity" (Thelen/Mahoney 2010: 6). They observe that change has been described mostly as exogenous disruption. Gradual and incremental phenomena such as liberalization of Western economies, they argue, need to be described by a more procedural analytical vocabulary. Arguing that "the practical enactment of an institution is as much part of its reality as its formal structure" (18), they tie the notion of 'practices' to that of institutional change. However, their own proposals remain insufficient and rather descriptive. Streeck and Thelen argue, for example, that "fundamental change ensues when a multitude of actors switch from one logic to another" (Streeck/Thelen 2005:18). What a specific logic of action is, however, remains unclear. This invokes that the analysis of transformation and emergence of new institutional orders needs a theoretical foundation on micro-level.

[24] In a systematic literature review, Lawrence/Suddaby (2006) identify first forms of creating institutions. In addition to mimicry, they identify advocacy, defining, vesting, constructing identities, changing normative associations, constructing normative networks, theorizing and educating. In order to maintain institutions, actors create enabling rules, police them through ensuring

ly non-rational funding practices. Applied to my empirical case, it could explain the European Commission's problems to articulate a coherent strategy for electric vehicles in Europe: mimicry would suggest that the responsible officers simply mirrored the innovation strategies of national governments and corporations in order to stay within the game, to ensure a minimum control over new market developments, i.e. stay informed about other actors' practices. The conceptual problem remains that Lawrence and Suddaby (2006) do not suggest how mimicry – and other forms of institutional work they identify – should be empirically observed or distinguished in practice from other forms. It is used rather as a descriptive term to designate an observed practice in reference to its institutional context.

The critical review of recent institutionalist literature has shown that micro-level cognitive processes do play a role in shaping institutional configurations. However, lacking a definition that includes a concept of interpretive action on the micro-level, institutionalist scholars and political economists struggle to explain how actors find, share and enact these ideas in practice, either to ensure market control, or to transform control strategies and, eventually, existing orders.

Epistemological lock-in?

The second reason why existing institutionalist literature on path rupture cannot explain path creation, is that current methodological choices do not allow researchers to observe the market actors' role in it. This shortcoming has been pointed out by constructivist political scientists. Smith suggests that institutionalist research is 'locked-in' epistemologically, through the choice of the unit of analysis. This has been true, especially in comparative literature, in the case of the nation-state (Dobbin 1994, Thelen/Streeck 2005, Hall/Soskice 2001). "Among the followers of the VoC approach [Varieties of Capitalism, J.H.], the nation state remains the starting and ending point of all research. With this, this approach suggests a mode of comparative analysis and a form of institutionalism which is too static...." (Jullien/Smith 2012: 2).

From a market sociology point of view, Beckert has suggested an additional reason for epistemological lock-in: political economists (Thelen/Streeck 2005) and economic sociologists (Fligstein 2001) orientation towards past historical patterns of markets to study current market phenomena or forms of capitalism.

---

compliance, deter, valorize, mythologize or routinize normative foundations of institutions. Finally, in order to disrupt institutions, they disconnect through sanctions, they disassociate moral foundations or undermine assumptions and beliefs. All these ways of influencing institutions are part of the actors' "scope of action" to influence conceptions of control in industries.

However, without analyzing how actors make sense of their own institutional environment at a given point in time, Beckert argues, they cannot explain how new paths have emerged. Institutionalist accounts of capitalist development necessarily remain descriptive. While Fligstein hints to the fact that each form of capitalism has emerged on the basis of a previous one, he does not explain which elements have remained and why others, for example the importance of investment capital, have inspired the emergence of new forms. The regulative context, government action, new laws, public authorities' reactions to financial crises or other elements are part of the answer. But they are not necessarily the cause. Considering policy instruments as results of interpretive action, new regulation or changes in consumer attitudes can also be seen as reactions to perceived ways of making sense of a product or a market.

The insight of market sociologists that the future (profits, strategies, impacts, actions) is unknown to actors in capitalist society, implies a different understanding of the 'historicity of institutionalist trajectories'. Instead of anticipating present and future paths as the repetition of an existing path, actors' representations of the given institutional context, and of its possible future, can be studied as a source of creativity. They can create new ideas, or act out shared visions into new institutional configurations. If these stabilize, new institutional paths emerge. "Actors, whether they are companies, entrepreneurs, investors, employees or consumers must orient their activities towards an open and uncertain future." (Beckert 2014: 4)[25]. This perspective, starting point of a recent research program yet to develop, implies that the micro-foundations of interaction between corporations, public authorities and consumers in the sector should be analysed. This will allow us to anticipate if their shared imagined futures will become paths, and what these would look like. Ideas about the future can be individual expectations, ideas and evaluations attached to a future state of the markets, society or politics. Collectively shared, they can become narratives that can challenge present narratives and therefore given conceptions of control and market hierarchies.

In sum, two shortcomings, lacking concepts of interpretive action in institutionalist research and epistemological lock-in producing 'closed futures', prevent studying path creation. The role of shared ideas, however, seems to be crucial in explaining new institutional orders emerge and how they can look like. It would open valuable research possibilities on imagined futures in dif-

---

[25] Introducing the concept of fictional expectations, he suggests bridging two strands of research: the market sociologists' argument for the non-rationalist character of economic action and the institutionalists' quest to explain the persistence of historically contingent patterns in modern economies.

ferent institutional trajectories and provide elements to explain how new path and markets emerge. In those trajectories that are linked to socio-economic models of Western economies, such as the automotive industry, this perspective can allow future developments to be more easily anticipated – and finally derive possibilities to adjust or impact these developments for political actors. The following subchapters explain which micro-foundations are needed and how they act as openers for the understanding of present and future institutional trajectories.

2.2. Framing collective narratives

Sociological theories of interaction on the micro-level explain how individual actors produce semantics that can be shared among several people. Goffman established that continued communicative interaction between individuals produces frames, i.e. collective references within which action makes sense for individuals and can be interpreted by others. Any relationship between individuals is thus built on a collective frame of meaning in which two individuals define their position towards each other. Goffman (1974: 21) denoted frames as "'schemata of interpretation' that enable individuals 'to locate, perceive, identify, and label' occurrences within their life space and the world at large" (Goffman 1974, cited in Benford/Snow 2000:614). Framing describes the actors' capacity to ascribe qualities to their environment and thus produce meaning in social contexts. These qualities can oppose existing credible ascriptions, promoted by dominant actors such as car makers. Accordingly, the interactionist micro-level concept of framing also allows collective communicative practices to be observed as a purposeful re-interpretation of a public issue.

How can these collective framing processes on the individual level aggregate into collective narratives that underlie control conceptions and thus institutional orders such as the EU's automobile path? Social movement theory has used the framing concept to explain how the setting of collective action frames helps social movements to succeed in contesting mainstream perceptions of societal problems (Snow et al. 1986). If they succeed, alternative framings impose a different interpretation of societal problems through convincing public opinion or dominant actors to adapt their problem interpretation. In reference to Goffman, Snow and Benford accordingly define framing as interpretive communicative action oriented towards a problem; as a process in which "frames help to render events or occurrences meaningful and thereby function to organize experience and guide action" (2000: 614). This is possible because framing has a legitimizing function "in that collective action frames are action-oriented sets of beliefs and meanings that inspire and legitimate the activities and campaigns of a social movement organization" (Snow/Benford 2000:614). They can thus be used intentionally, as interpretations "intended to mobilize potential adherents and constituents, to garner bystander support, and to demobilize antagonists" (Snow/Benford 1988:198). Social movements aim to change dominant practices accordingly, i.e. to change the rules, and not just temporary outcomes. If they are successful in diffusing new frames, these views will constitute legitimate patterns for all actors in a sector. They will change its institutional configuration.

Framing ideas into collective issues or problems is part of the activity of interest groups, public policy makers and firms. Each actor frames a collective issue with the intention to provide a solution to it that accommodates their own market – or policy – interest. Probably due to its interactionist origin, the concept of framing has been rarely applied to market settings, although it is relevant to explain institutional change on markets and the emergence of new markets. The potential of this conceptual transfer has not been fully explored yet[26]. As Hellmann (2007) noticed, Fligstein hints to links with macro-level institutionalist study of markets as institutional configurations: "In new markets, the politics resemble social movements. Actors in different firms are trying to convince other firms to go along with their conception of the market" (Fligstein 1996:663). Especially in times of crisis, Fligstein argues, the institutional conditions that were supposed to guarantee stability to firms' interactions, are put into question in a way that parallels social movements' questioning of mainstream thinking or regulation. Both firms defying established market hierarchies as well as social movements contesting mainstream thinking, question the legitimacy of institutional patterns guaranteeing current hierarchies. As Hellmann (2007) adds, what makes niche competitors or challengers successful is their efficient framing. They need to stay flexible and adapt argumentation strategies to the current public problems. In addition to institutional resources, consequently, the right timing is as important as the right argument. This is especially important for organizations whose main purpose it is to contest prevailing institutional frameworks via well-targeted and specific problem framing, i.e. lobbies. In the European automotive sector, environmental groups have been playing this role, as Chapter 4 will show. In sum, challengers can perform the following roles in institutional settings: impose new problems, suggest a

---

[26] Hellmann (2007) confirms that economic sociology has not explored this hypothesis. But it has inspired the sociology of marketing and consumption (Cochoy 1999). Marketing is the construction of meaning of products for consumers or to "mobilize" consumers to shift from passive status of disinterest to active status of willingness to buy. As a consequence, firms, for example car producers marketing "green" cars, would need to mobilize a considerable amount of 'framing' through marketing activities in order to change current perceptions of automobility.

different way to perceive an existing problem or adapt to different prevailing problems.

There are more parallels between social movements and institutionalized economic or political spaces such as the European automotive sector: both contexts are shaped by hierarchies. The fact that the concept of framing is used to describe a social movement's activity means that it is applied in a social space in which power relations are not equal. Benford and Snow emphasize that framing becomes an instrument to oppose existing power relations. This view meets Fligstein's assumption that social spaces such as markets or industries, in which interaction creates meaning, are built and maintained on previously established hierarchies. However, empirical analysis suggests that the degree of actors' 'interpretative autonomy' depends on the specific historical and economic context in each industry or market. In the automotive industry, the 2008 economic crisis, for example, changed the perception of environmental problems due to their possible economic consequences.

First assumptions for a framework of path change can be built on these concepts on interpretive action and its impact on institutional configurations. To understand how these work on the micro-level, we can formulate conditions for the rupture of existing paths, and how ideas can eventually change their configuration and create new institutional orders.

- Alternative frames discredit a given semantic legitimacy and suggest a new narrative. Groups promoting collective frames aim at changing market interactions by changing the way these are justified (semantic change).

- Collective frames contain expectations of the market's future: new actors, new negotiation arenas, extend existing networks, in sum: new patterns of governance (structural change).

The introduction chapter has shown that the current path of European automotive sector upholds dominant narratives in each domain:

- Technology: How the internal combustion engine needs to improve continuously

- Politics: How national car manufacturers and employment need to be protected in their global core markets in Europe, US and Japan

- Market: There is universal demand for individual car ownership and use

Semantic coherence seems to persist within the entire field, i.e. among the three institutional domains of the industry. In order to transform these stabilized structures, new narratives in each of these domains have to be shared, and supported. A further assumption to be explored empirically is thus if a new path emerges in each of these domains or only if all three domains change coherently (pace of change).

A model explaining collectivization of frames needs to take into account both discussed approaches: On the micro-level, the interactionist concept of framing; on the macro-level, the idea of collectively shared patterns of legitimacy that reproduce market hierarchies. Both theories however, lack an intermediary concept that would translate agreed frames into collectively accepted norms and, consequently, ways of organizing exchange, political negotiation and support or demand for a specific offer on the market. The following sub-chapter suggests an intermediary concept that acts on semantic and organizational structures in parallel: policy instruments.

2.3. Policy instruments as collective problem solving

A theory of policy instruments provides the missing link between collective framing on the micro-level and the legitimacy of hierarchies in sectors, markets or policy fields. Instruments are carriers of (new) ideas. If put forward by challengers, they can contribute to path creation.

French constructivist political sociologists suggest a theory of 'instrumentation' (Lascoumes/Le Galès 2012). As part of a sociology of public action, they describe the process of creation and implementation of policy instruments. This process provides the building block complementing the analytical framework developed so far: Instruments are considered practices that translate actors' shared interpretations or evaluations of their perceived reality, discussed via communicative interaction on the micro-level into action. They are a means of objectifying shared meanings, or institutionalization in Zucker's sense. As agreed measures taken by groups of (interested) actors that transpose a shared idea into an agreed future way of doing, or favouring one problem solution against the other, instruments are first and foremost an objectified evaluation of a present state of affairs, of a market, an industry, or simply a shared problem. Instruments are therefore

- a means to collectivize shared meanings in order convince more and other actors, e.g. public authorities, competitors or consumers,
- a means to objectify shared meanings by prescribing objectives to market actors, for example meeting new environmental standards. The implementation of instruments can produce new organizational structures based on shared meanings.

33

As a means of objectification of shared understandings, instruments are not stable: they evolve over time and produce institutional effects through implementation. Le Galès and Lascoumes consider instruments shared narratives that keep unfolding effects in the course of being applied. Instruments may transcend initial intentions or effects actors ascribed to them, and thus create market interaction such as competition in a different way than originally planned. The transformative power of policy instruments, as Le Galès and Lascoumes (2007) find, lies in the way instruments are enacted[27]. Standards for vehicle emissions for example, are enacted by firms, controlled by authorities and corrected, softened or restricted by interest groups. This actors' work determines on a day-to-day basis the actual impact of the prescribed problem solutions called a policy instrument. In their constructivist understanding of policy fields or sectors, the authors do not presuppose a causal relationship between instruments and institutional change; rather, instruments are partly autonomous actors themselves. "Instruments at work are not neutral devices: they produce specific effects, independently of the objective pursued (the aims ascribed to them), which structure public policy according to their own logic" (Le Galès/Lascoumes 2007: 1).

As a functional part of path creation, instruments guarantee the transfer of shared narratives into institutional structures. Instruments carry (out) visions of how public life and interaction should be organized in the domain that they address. These visions contain an evaluation of the current state of the art of an issue or a problem: They contain an evaluation of a market's state of being and thus confirm or question an existing legitimacy pattern. Instruments enact frames or rational fictions, i.e. imagined better future states of the present market, industry or policy field. In Beckert's sense, they represent a specific form of micro-foundation in markets. But beyond the fact that it rationalizes a way

---

[27] In this sense, instruments are not only transformative, but *performative*. Once implemented, they *enact* the value judgement they contain. The concept of performativity has been elaborated by a school of constructivist sociologists interested in how instruments and other devices shape reality. An instruments' performativity differs from its 'impact' in that its effects can be different from, even contradictory to, what has been intended originally. Independently of the goal actors intended to reach by implementing an instrument, the implementation of instruments has performative effects on the institutional structure. This is because the very categories of legitimacy it appeals to may be formed only with its implementation. Performative instruments *shape* social reality: With reference to Foucault's account of how different political rationalities have shaped government, the diffusion of power and social judgement overtime, Desrosières (2000) has described how the way social statistics are created, shapes new categories of problems perceptions and governance. In economic sociology, MacKenzie and Millo (2003) show that the way calculation and visualization devices work at a stock exchange, condition how financial markets work and business can be done within them. Instruments and devices shape the very character of what is possible on global financial markets.

of influencing the present according to the actor's evaluations, Lascoumes and Galès suggest that it acts out these evaluations, due to their performative character. As a specific kind of collective framing, every policy instrument contains a value judgement on how the sector should look, on how power of incumbent firms be justified (legitimacy), by which qualities (environmental, economic etc.), about how the relationship between demand and supply should be structured. This ranks from environmental standards (what is "sustainable transport" and how should vehicles contribute to it) to seemingly technical issues such as car type approval that defines a product's use and life cycle. To define what is a small or a medium car, or to determine through test cycles how much gasoline it uses per kilometer is more than stating facts. It is *producing their very meaning* through the definition of indicators and the ways to measure them. Instruments produce attributes that determine products' market value, actors' strategies and observers' categories of evaluating these. On the macro-level, they provide a micro-foundation for path creation.

Instruments' performative effects explain path creation because they reach beyond implementation of (already existing) shared meanings. The instrumentation of specific measures has macro-level consequences of a different kind. Analysing instrumentation "involves not only understanding the reasons that encourage the retention of one instrument rather than another, but also envisage the effects produced by these choices" (Le Galès/Lascoumes 2007: 4). Contrasting the utilitarian definition of instruments as purposeful means to reach ends, their implementation can be defined as "the set of problems posed by the choice and use of instruments (techniques, methods of operations, devices) that allow government policy to be made material and operational" (Le Galès/Lascoumes 2007: 4).[28] Consequently, by studying the suggested solutions we can see which problems firms' strategies and policy instruments provide an answer to.[29] Typical situations are conflicts, in which sectoral actors debate how instruments are created and enacted. Conflicts are based on issues actors consider to be problematic, for example environmental performance, unfair competition or the integration of radical innovations such as the electric car into the existing automotive market. Conflicts on instruments or strategies and their impacts thus become apparent if they challenge the existing control conceptions of firms. Studying the emergence of instruments across conflicts can

---

[28] This definition indeed reminds us of the garbage can model of how organizations produce rationality (Cohen/March/Olson 1972).

[29] Firms' (product) strategies can be considered an equivalent of public authorities' instruments on markets. In business strategies, companies articulate their evaluations of a market's present state, and announce how they seek to adapt organizational structures according to an expected future state of the market (Beckert 2013).

thus unveil where path change is likely to come about. Methodologically, this implies a research design that takes into account sequences of conflicts and their impacts on the sectoral trajectory (elaborated below in Chapter 3).

Based on the outlined theoretical framework, this study will analyse the emergence, stability and change of European government by asking how shared narratives and critical instruments can open up locked-in institutional trajectories. The research task is to investigate conflicts on the micro-level, the framing policy problems and suggested solutions, in order to identify governing and market practices that disrupt given patterns of legitimacy. The question to answer in order to qualify institutional configurations as new institutional paths is the following: Do these three dimensions of a sector build a new coherent configuration which reflects an imagined future – a new narrative that could underline a new institutional order? The next chapter (Chapter 3) presents how this research is designed and specifies how the theoretical framework applies to the case study.

3. Research Design and Methods

"Qualitative researchers are in some ways [...] criminal detectives: they solve puzzles and explain particular outcomes by drawing on detailed fact gathering, experience working with similar cases, and knowledge of general causal principles."
(Mahoney/Goertz 2006: 241)

The task of Chapter 3 is to translate the theoretical research question – how can we study path creation? – into a methods toolkit to answer it (empirically). A study's research design determines its scope and structure. This chapter first summarizes the explanation model, justifying why an explorative research design based on qualitative case study was the most appropriate choice. It then details methods of data collection (expert interviews listed in Annex B, document analysis and participant observation) before briefly discussing possible biases through fieldwork effects. This chapter shortly assesses the range and quality of data collected and reflects the data collection process.

3.1. The explanation model

The explanation model puts the theoretical concept on path creation (Chapter 2) into the empirical context of this study. Following the literature, the objects of study are historical sequences that structure an institutional path. These follow each other and change in moments of conflicts or crises. In these moments new paths can be created. The history of environmental conflicts in the automobile industry begins in a moment of economic transformation: the integration into the common market and the harmonization of emission norms in the 1990s.

The empirical field of empirical analysis, an industrial sector, needs to be defined. Literature often does not make a difference between industries and markets as empirical fields, partly because the English term industry covers both. But this difference is crucial. Markets can be understood in the narrow sense as mechanisms of demand and supply. The main actors involved are firms. In his theory of markets as networks, White (2005) develops a model of semantic interaction in a network of companies that mutually observe each other and build their market positions.[30] An industrial sector, on the other hand, is a broader institutional structure which involves not only firms and consumers, but also public authorities and interest groups. It covers the fields of demand, supply and regulation. Fligstein's theory of markets applies, following my definition, to industrial sectors. He argues that the state as a regulatory context, plays a crucial role in maintaining conceptions of control through adapted politics. "The state must ratify, help to create, or at the very least, not oppose a conception of control" (Fligstein 1996: 658)[31]. In processes of path change, governments, or in the case of the European sector the European institutions, can thus develop autonomous dynamics and push developments that go against current dominant interests and legitimate narratives.

As specified in Chapter 1, industrial sectors comprise three domains of activity, in which different types of actors interact, solve potential conflicts and appeal to shared narratives:

- the supply domain, in which new technologies, products and pricing strategies determine new offers

- the regulative domain, where policy instruments build solutions of conflicts between public authorities of all decision making levels and firms or other actors (or interest groups)

- the domain of demand and use patterns, in which classical market interaction of buying and selling dominates, however, shaped by expectations and regulative context known to all actors.

Industrial sectors are not only organizational networks of firms, interest groups, consumers and authorities, but also *semantic* networks. This makes them an arena for the interactions at micro-level which can produce path-changing narratives.[32] Sectors are networks in which (economically and politically) interested reflective actors observe each other. They communicate their strategies and instruments concerning i.e. technological or related political issues, and con-

---

[30] "Markets are self-reproducing social structures among specific cliques and other actors who evolve roles from observations of each others' behavior. [...] the key fact is that producers watch each other within a market." (White 2005[1981]: 518).

[31] As Fligstein sets out, rules of competition and property law are the main levers through which the government contains market action, and thus competition between incumbent firms. "Property rights, governance structures and rules of exchange are arenas in which modern states establish rules for economic actors. States provide stable and reliable conditions, under which firms organize, compete, cooperate and exchange. The enforcement of the laws affects what conceptions of control can produce stable markets." (Fligstein 1996: 657).

[32] Literature refers to this type of semantic interaction as 'political work' (Jullien/Smith 2008) or 'institutional work' (Lawrence/Suddaby 2006).

stantly evaluate each other's positions (see also White 2005). Through this constant interaction, a social structure is maintained and legitimated, in which some firms are dominant and others are dominated. Incumbents act in close reference to the sector's prevailing pattern of legitimacy (conception of control), ensuring control of competitors. Challengers critically address and attempt to change this mechanism. Extending on Fligstein's description of the 'architecture of markets', in the definition of industrial sectors suggested here, not only firms can be incumbents or challengers, but also interest groups (such as the car makers' representation) or political authorities that take positions on certain issues.

The above definition of the sector determines the types of interaction that can be directly observed (or reconstructed) on the micro-level. Depending on the nature and character of conflicts, the semantic and organizational interaction to be observed takes place in different arenas. These can range from informal meetings between different interest groups to formalized stakeholder hearings organized by different parts of the European Commission. It can be local project meetings in cities where electric car demonstrations are taking place.

The units of analysis, consequently, are located on the micro-level of observation across the three domains of a sector. They contain the factors explaining how alternative narratives emerge in markets, i.e.

- Supply: companies' technological and product strategies
- Regulation: policy instruments: regulation and investment
- Demand: consumers' mobility patterns and consumption

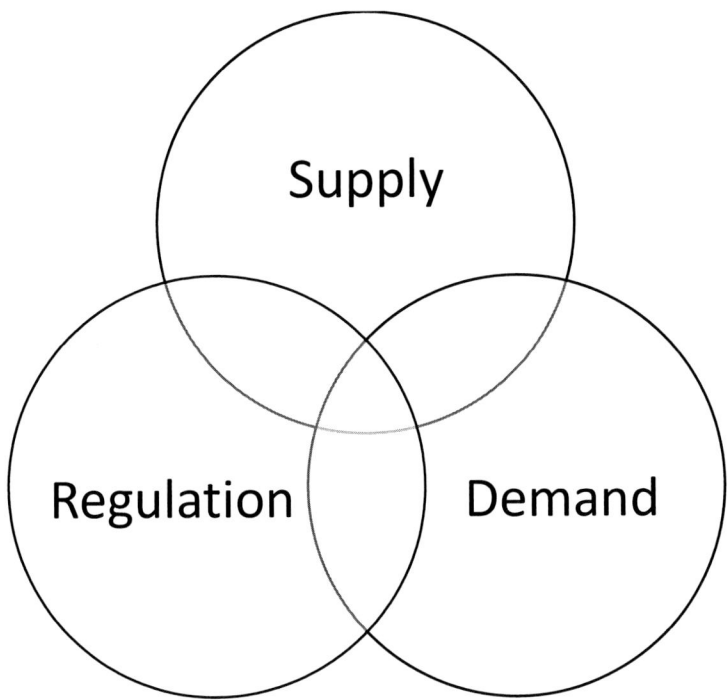

Figure 1: units of analysis. Source: own compilation

My analysis seeks to reconstitute historically the arenas of conflict, actors who participated, arguments that were exchanged, and interpret these conflicts in a larger context: In what way does this conflict threaten the dominance of certain actors, and suggest a different hierarchy in the industry? Based on which arguments do challengers act; and does this represent a coherent narrative that could provoke path change? The study paid specific attention to positions and arguments communicated (through publications or informal communication) among the identified actors on the micro-level. Research question and interests therefore strongly suggest adopting a 'qualitative' research design.

A 'qualitative' research design

The research question 'how do institutional paths emerge?' already implies a specific understanding of causation, and thus of the way causes can be legitimately explained: it focuses on the effects of variables, i.e. explaining factors of influence that have led to an outcome. Compared to quantitative research, "[a] core goal of qualitative research is the explanation of outcomes in individual cases" (Goertz/Mahoney 2006: 230), rather than correlations between different, often many, cases.[33] This understanding of causation is common to historical approaches (cf. Goertz/Mahoney 2006: 232), which identify individual causes of specific situations in prior (sequences of) events. Tracing the recent history of the automobile path, the analysis pursues a historical explanation approach identifying sequences of events. Based on a preliminary document analysis (described in 3.2.), events were reconstructed retrospectively during the research process. For example, the recent conflict among car makers on the electric vehicle and their possible market impacts in 2008 disclosed that the regulative preconditions of the importance of EVs for the CO_2 performance of car makers were rooted in the 2008 legislation, the history of which had started with the car makers' voluntary agreement in 1998. As a result, an additional historical sequence was identified which possibly explained the sectors' institutional transformation and extended the list of factors potentially causing the outcome.

The study's aim - to identify conditions of path creation in order to better anticipate future developments - is characteristic of a qualitative research design, typically seeking to "identify combinations of variables of jointly necessary and sufficient causes" (Goertz/Mahoney 2006: 232). One cause might be neither necessary nor sufficient, but needs to be grouped with others to meet one or the other condition. "[...] it is one cause within a combination of causes that are jointly sufficient for an outcome. Thus, with this approach, scholars seek to identify combinations of variable values that are sufficient for outcomes of interest." (Goertz/Mahoney 2006: 232). Resuming the findings of the empirical analysis of conflicts in the car industry's historical paths (by sequences), Chapter 6 identifies conditions of path creation. My research thus focuses on the impact of combinations of variables to explain a single outcome. This implies certain weaknesses and strengths.

An often cited weakness of qualitative research designs is their limited generalizability. As Goertz and Mahoney (2006) put it, "In qualitative research, it is

---

[33] This study draws on Goertz' and Mahoney's "tale of two cultures" (2006) in social scientific research to explain the chosen research design. The prevailing terminology of "quantitative and qualitative" research is indeed not well suited to describe the differences between two research postures. Rather, "better labels for describing the two kinds of research analyzed here would be statistics versus logic, effect estimation versus outcome explanation, or population-oriented versus case-oriented approaches" (Goertz/ Mahoney 2006: 245f). However, this chapter will stick to the terms as they are by far the most used and relate to an intuitive understanding of a research posture and corresponding methods.

common for investigators to define the scope of their theories narrowly such that inferences are generalizable to only a limited range of cases.," (237) because "causal generalizations in qualitative work are more fragile than those in large-N statistical analyses" (238). The focus of the qualitative study of a few cases is, at the same time a strength, if one considers that the criteria for validity of results of qualitative research are necessarily different from those of quantitative research. They introduce at the same time the strengths and difficulties of a qualitative research process. Strübing's (2004) discussion of validity criteria based on Corbin and Strauss's (1990) grounded theory is helpful here. This qualitative research method builds theory from initial (common sense) concepts by reiterative data collection and conceptual interpretation.

Reliability, designating in quantitative research the possibility to obtain the same results when repeating measurement, can be translated into a re-iterative process of interpreting data with the same concept and thus excluding false interpretations. Guided by the question of market dominance through the reproduction of rules (Fligstein 2001), this analysis aligned environmental conflicts in the sector since 1990. This re-iterative process of contextualizing events as solutions to conflicts produced the assumption that the voluntary agreements (1998) and the discussions of an obligatory standard (2008) as well as those of supercredits for EVs (2013) could threaten the car manufacturers' dominance.

Representativity as a second criterion does not refer to samples of populations as in quantitative research, but to a concept's capacity to be applicable to a large variety of data in different contexts – for example to path creation in different countries, levels of decision making or industrial sectors, across different periods of time. Here, generalized results of qualitative case comparison can be extended to others based on similar derived comparisons and generate further insights into path creation in general.

The third criterion, *internal and external validity of a study*, refers to a lack of contradictions in the same study as well as its adequate description of social reality (Legewie 2006: no page indicated). Qualitative research responds to this criterion by ensuring the internal and external validity of the study by detailed documentation and extensive data collection. Having been repeatedly interpreted in an iterative process of applying concepts (internal validity), the more detailed a case or object is researched, the more its interpretation is valid in different contexts (external validity). This assumption funds the method of case study research, a very common qualitative research design[34]. Based on these

---

[34] Institutionalist research has a tradition of working with qualitative case studies. The theoretical framework described in Chapter 2, as well as the discussion on institutional change in literature

criteria, the next section will detail why a case study is the appropriate design for my research question.

The case study method

The logic (and idea of validity) behind this popular way to qualitatively collect data is simple: by describing cases and gaining detailed knowledge on usually few exemplary objects of a larger, more general or more abstract entity, the mechanisms of the larger entity (to be explained) can be explored representatively. Formally speaking, constructing a case is to construct a valid representative research object, because it is one (exemplary) case of a larger entity of others (other industries for example). From this point of view it is not surprising that "Qualitative researchers usually start their research by selecting cases where the outcome of interest occurs (these cases are often called 'positive' cases)" (Goertz/Mahoney 2006: 239). In contrast to testing a given hypothesis on a selection of cases in a quantitative logic, which usually implies a rather large n and few variables to find similarities and differences, case study research designs aim to explore rather open research questions in order to generate hypotheses. This means, it is more advisable to look at fewer cases but more variables in order to explore in depth the functioning of each case.

The single-case research can be considered a sub-variant of qualitative few-n case study research designs. It is appropriate in fields on which the research can exert little control on his or her case (Yin 2009). The automotive industry's recent path change implies research on an *ongoing transition*. In contrast to a purely historical account, this analysis has less control over the case. Actors' behaviour or events can change the part of social reality studied. Single case studies are especially adapted to illustrating a process of a historical transition from one institutional hierarchy to a possibly future one. In this design, validity is produced through the detailed manner by which the one single case is looked at (cf. Legewie 2009 and Yin 2009). The logic here is that one single case represents a number of similar cases (i.e. similar European industrial sectors), if

---

underlying it, draws on various volumes assembling and comparing case studies on countries' socio-economic models or nation states' democracy configurations (Thelen/Streeck 2005, Mahoney and Thelen 2010). Comparative research on industries, their European governance as well as their trajectories, has also been built on points in common across case studies: Either comparing different sectors across specific policies (Jürgens/Sablowski 2008), or across countries (Lung/Amable 2008), or both, from the viewpoint of supra-national policy-imperative (Jullien/Smith 2014). In each research design, the 'case' contains a historical sequence in a sector and the market's interaction with politics on a given question.

not for industrial sectors in general. For a number of reasons, the automotive sector can be representative for a study on path change in industrial sectors.

- All industrial sectors consist of hierarchical relations between firms, are influenced by demand dynamics and political regulations. The degree to which they do, differs. Conflicts in each sector differ empirically, but the ways conflicts are solved can have, in all sectors, consequences on their institutional structure.

- In all sectors (touched by the economic crisis in 2008), the question whether change is policy-driven or market-driven is key to understanding its future trajectories and eventually develop policies.

- Industries known for their path dependency such as energy, steel, machine tools, manufacturing are an especially interesting object when researching conditions of path change.

Choosing environmental politics as the conflictive field that could cause these dynamics has further empirical reasons (Chapter 1) but also reasons related to the theoretical model:

In many sectors, European environmental politics are an inter-sectoral field of conflict, and are especially salient for transport(-related) industry (cars, aerospace, fuels) and other large manufacturing sectors (chemistry) or industries that deal with primary resources.

Environmental politics were born as a field of conflict parallel to other procedural changes in European sectoral governance in the early 2000s: The open Method of Coordination, voluntary agreements and other horizontal approaches to governance were often linked with regulation in the field of environment, fostered by the CO_2 debates since the 1990s (Dezalay 2007, Jullien/Smith 2014). An objective of the case study is therefore to link the field of environmental policy to more general changes in sectoral policy and the Lisbon Process.

Another reason for a single long-term case study is the (historical) time period covered in the analysis. The longer the time period covered, the more potential sequences and conflicts can be revealed for study. A single case study is especially apt at covering larger historical trajectories. This is consistent with historical institutionalisms' pre-assumptions of path continuity that necessarily requires research over time in order to emerge as a long-term pattern. Any study that aims to contribute to the debate on institutional change needs to consider a sufficiently large period in time in order to identify historical causes of change. Jullien and Smith's collective case studies on the European Government of Industries (2014) comprise a historical account of each industry's trajectory across roughly four decades, and ends with the economic crisis in 2008. This issue-focused single case study enlarges this researched historical path with a contemporary account of recent post-crisis change through environmental conflicts, building on first hypotheses on environmental policy-induced change in the car sector through the debate on electric cars (Carter et al. 2014). This study continued to investigate questions and related hypotheses: Why did the electric car debate unfold in 2008? Why did the European Commission regulate emissions in 2008 with specific standards? How are new mobility patterns linked to innovations in alternative powertrains? Extending on-going work by an in-depth case study, a qualitative research design was an obvious choice.

The research process

Empirical research was conducted throughout and between different periods of fieldwork from early 2012 to early 2014. In an explorative process, these periods were reiterative and interlinked, to broaden understanding of different (sequences of) conflicts which would reveal the concepts by which best to explain their outcomes. Especially in qualitative work, any structure given to the research process thus necessarily emerges during and after the actual fieldwork.

The main steps were:

- Identification of conflicts: the electric car and the CO_2 emission debate
- Identification and mapping of actors and their positions in the conflicts
- Reconstruction of an institutional trajectory through three sequences

Main conflict sequences were:

A) 1998-2008 the debate on CO_2 emission regulation

B) 2008-2011 the debate on the electric car

C) from 2011 onwards: experimentation through publicly financed programmes and market niches

(A) CO_2 Regulation → (B) EV regulation → (C) EV experimentation

The following assumptions were built on how 21st century automobility as a conception of control could have changed.

(A) The emission regulation policy instruments created environmental consciousness as a shared narrative in the sector.

(B) This gave credit to public and private investments in electric cars, and public demonstrators / market niches for their shared use.

(C) By creating a market, this could change the regime of automobility and discredit the basis of car makers' dominance.

The following sub chapters detail how data was gathered and verified by controlling with actors' view of events in each sequence.

3.2. Methods of data collection and analysis

The specific understanding of validity in qualitative case study method determines the ways evidence is selected and weighted. "Qualitative researchers are in some ways analogous to criminal detectives: they solve puzzles and explain particular outcomes by drawing on detailed fact gathering, experience working with similar cases, and knowledge of general causal principles." (Goertz/Mahoney 2006: 241). Qualitative research implies the difficulty of identifying and interpreting evidence, being guided by gathered information in the research process, without imposing one's preliminary interpretations of the right outcome, or a tempting all-around-explanation of the way things really happened. Recognizing evidence as such, or not, and evaluating its relevance in order to conclude with an overall coherent interpretation requires an open mind for creative solutions and the courage for trial and error. "From the stand-point of this detective method [...] not all pieces of evidence count equally for building an explanation. Rather, certain observations may be smoking guns that contribute substantially to a qualitative researcher's view that a theory is valid. By the same token, much like a detective whose initial hunch about a murder suspect can be undermined by a single new piece of evidence (e.g., an air-tight alibi), a new fact can lead qualitative researchers to conclude that a given theory is not correct even though a considerable amount of evidence suggests that it is." (Goertz/Mahoney 2006: 241). The researcher needs to constantly reflect her or his own presuppositions. The researcher asks: "Given my prior theoretical beliefs, how much does this observation affect these beliefs? When testing some theories, a single piece of data can radically affect posterior beliefs" (Goertz/Mahoney 2006: 241).

By combining different methods of data collection the analysis aimed to study the case in the most complete way. As Platt puts it, case study research is "a strategy to be preferred when circumstances and research problems are appropriate rather than an ideological commitment to be followed whatever the circumstances" (Platt 1992: 46, cited from Yin 2009: 17). Appropriate methods for the historical reconstruction of events in order to fully grasp the institutional trajectory were document analysis and participant observation (Yin 2009:8). The following subsections discuss how each method was applied.

Expert interviews

First, in an explorative or descriptive interest, "facts, problems, decision-making structures and networks" (Welch et al. 2002: 613.) were reconstructed. This includes determining the role the actor played in a decision-making process, understanding the position he or she took as a representative of his/her organization. The second objective was to determine how actors' knowledge on conflicts and each other's positions emerges and what this changed in the process – can it develop policy-shaping power? What kind of knowledge is produced over the environmental conflicts, by whom, and how is it used to shape the course of events, for example to create policy instruments, shape alliances etc.? In conceptual terms: How can it reproduce and discredit legitimate positions of others in the sectoral field?

The term expert interview refers to the fact that interviewed actors dispose of specific types of knowledge that help to answer the research question. This knowledge is not necessarily consciously present. Actors can be distinguished by types of knowledge they act upon (Littig 2008).[35]

- Technical: specialized knowledge, administrative competences
- Process-related: interactions, decision-making, organizational configurations
- Interpretative-evaluative: everyday knowledge on processes and how other (sectoral) actors perceive facts and interpret events

Disposing of all these levels of knowledge to different degrees, experts are interviewed as a valuable and unique source of knowledge. "Experts are informants who dispose of knowledge to which the researcher cannot have access otherwise." (Littig 2008: 3). According to different types of knowledge, Bogner and Menz (2005: S.36ff) distinguish three different types of expert interviews.

---

[35] These categories are sociological distinctions and may not be consciously enacted by actors in their field of action. But they help the sociological observer to understand and interpret the actions of an observed and interviewed expert.

- The 'explorative' expert interview, conducted in a field of research hardly explored.

- The 'systematizing' expert interview, aiming at the reconstruction of 'objective' knowledge (or 'technical knowledge') in a specific field, for example to reconstruct a sequence of events and causes of developments as seen by a specific group of actors.

- The theory-generating expert interview, aiming not only at the expert's explicit knowledge but at their implicit procedural and interpretive knowledge acquired through professional practice.

Different types of knowledge were in the focus of the 42 expert interviews held in total for this study (Annex B), accordingly, different types of expert interviews were held at early, mid-term and advanced points in time.

A first wave of (explorative) interviews was conducted to learn about actors' technical knowledge, based on the most recent conflict in the car industry, the debate on the electric car. Problems, stakeholders, interests and the impact of the conflict were studied from a precise point in time, and a precise political instrument: the European Union's programmes on the electric car, based on the pre-crisis *European Green Cars Initiative* and the post-crisis *European Strategy on Clean and Energy Efficient Vehicles* (2012). Based on initial interviews with staff on working level within the European Commission allowed the identification of the first conflicts and links between environmental policy and innovation policy as automotive industry support, and lay the ground for the events reconstructed in Chapters 4 and 5. The technical knowledge collected in these interviews helped to systematize events, as many of the interviewed staff are at the same time technical experts and policy makers.

Interviews at the political level, on which responsible staff decide on political strategies of the European Commission's different departments aimed at procedural knowledge, were needed to construct a coherent sequence of events during and after the crisis in 2008/2009. These interviews generated an assumption of how the sequence of events could have looked like, and to which degree public authorities or companies played an active role in shaping institutional trajectories that resulted from it. An example is an interview at DG Enterprise & Industry (Interview 9).

"No, when the crisis starts in mid-2008, we start to see that there is a problem in the US markets that is impacting certain European markets. The Commission's first reaction is to support growth in order to prevent this problem. So there is an action plan foreseeing a "green cars" part. But this is only the first strategy which is limited, in the "green cars" part you will see that simply ex-

isting research instruments were mobilized to develop green cars. It's a first try. This is done in 2008. Ok. In November, December, we understand that the situation is getting worse. [...] So in January 2009, we realize that the green car measures are not sufficient [...]."

Interviews showed at which point the conflict on the electric car in 2008 was linked to the financial crisis and the question of how public authorities anticipate and try to shape future institutional trajectories. Two of the interviewed actors (Interview 25 and Interview 19) explicitly assumed that European regions, metropolitan regions as well as large automotive production sites, would play an important role in the future as levels of decision-making. They finance and carry out experimentations with alternative powertrains in public/private fleets, they are suppliers of infrastructure and policy-makers in decisions where innovative R&D and production will be located. The findings opened up another field of inquiry. They led to a second wave of explorative interviews conducted in spring 2013 in Paris and Berlin to identify local political conflicts and institutional configuration in an emerging market of electric mobility, as a consequence of previously researched national (Hildermeier/Villareal 2011) and European (Chapter 4) innovation investment strategies. Both cities already displayed innovative projects, though very different in institutional nature (Hildermeier/Villareal 2014). The same type of explorative, and then systematizing interview, helped to understand additional local conflicts, and the links between conflicts and national innovation policy strategies such as the French 'Plan Véhicule Electrique' or the German 'Regierungsprogramm Elektromobilität'. Reconstituted in Chapter 5.2. the conflicts on emerging niches of e-mobility allowed me to estimate risks and opportunities of these developments in creating a new institutional path in the sector. In the second wave of interviews addressed the *procedural knowledge* commercial actors as well as public administration staff. This helped to contrast different points of view on the same story. An example is a critical standpoint of Berlin's Senate representative.

"This is absurd! Realities and facts emerge through market forces, vanity, who has the largest fleet, who is the first, who is most prominent etc. All these non-sustainable and short-term strategies will have to be corrected, charging stations will have to be rebuilt. This is frustrating and expensive. It would be better to cooperate from the beginning." (Interview 41)

The third type of interview, gathering interpretive knowledge, came into focus at a later stage in research when the discussions on CO_2 emission regulation for passenger cars between 1998 and 2008 were the sequence of events preceding and conditioning the electric car debate. Interpretive interviews correct and amend the researcher's interpretation of events by contrasting it with key actors' views. Interview partners were accessible through media attention during an on-going debate on CO_2 regulations for vehicles. Germany, and the German car industry, had lobbied for less strict standards, a much opposed viewpoint from other industrial countries on the European level, parts of the European Commission and environmental interest groups. Interest groups such as car manufacturers, environmental and consumer associations and also Commission staff were eager to speak about their view of events. The interpretive interview, aiming to reconstruct experts' implicit knowledge about a process or their procedural interpretation of events (which justifies their role as experts in the sector) is the most difficult type of interview to conduct. Therefore, the narrative interview type was chosen instead of the usual semi-structured interviews.

Bogner and Menz stress that the reason why interpretive and evaluative knowledge of the expert is relevant to social scientific research is that it can structure the expert's practice – and thus be potentially structuring on power relations in the expert's field, determining the scope of action of his/her interlocutors. "The expert's knowledge, how he orients his actions and what is relevant for him/her allow him to become hegemonic in practice in a specific functional context. This means, the expert disposes of options to impose his orientations. As the knowledge affects practice, it structures the conditions and contexts for other actors." (Bogner/Menz 2005: 46, cited in Littig 2008: 4). It is through this type of knowledge that actors can, if they want, transform an institutional setting through discrediting its basis of legitimacy. Interpretive knowledge includes the role of the actors' own organization in influencing a decision-making process. The interviewed policy officer at the European Consumer Organization reflects this.

"We are lobbyists ourselves! We observe very closely, and we strongly criticized what has happened since June. People working on the topic in Brussels know our position. I think it is very valuable that there are several organizations that watch closely what is happening." (Interview 26)

A member of an environmental organization reflected on the impact of their strategies:

"I mean in the beginning when we didn't have the information, obviously not. But as soon as we could get hold of that information and these words could come out, it became one of the best lobbying-tools that we had, because nobody else had that information, nobody else was undertaking the analysis." (Interview 24)

Collecting and interpreting interview data are two different though strongly inter-related stages of empirical research. In a hermeneutical research process, this analysis combined the exploration of a field and the building of assumptions with the verification of preliminary conclusions. Consequently, through-out the research process, the purpose of data gathering switched from explora-tory to descriptive to explanatory. Interviews accompanied the research process over almost one and a half years.

In addition to the 42 expert interviews, which took place in a more or less for-mal setting framed by the roles of researcher and expert, informal talks were a valuable source of information during the research process.

The reconstitution of the building of narratives on the micro-level through in-terviews enabled the role of an environmental stakeholder to be placed in the conflict negotiations with others since the mid-2000s. The history of emission regulation as a power struggle between a dominant car industry and weak na-tional and European government, however, begins in the late 1990s. The pri-mordial aim on the macro-theoretical level was to reconstruct how emission regulation has contributed – if not constituted – an institutional path, i.e. insti-tutionalized hierarchies. The research was therefore extended by *document analysis* in order to grasp the historical context, and communication among actors by written and published positions.

Document analysis

Beyond gathering factual information on the 'what' and 'how', document anal-ysis also enables actors' positions and comments on a problem to be collected, either explicitly or between the lines. It is therefore as much a tool of data col-lection as a tool for testing ad-hoc hypotheses (from expert interviews or previ-ous document study). Objectives were to understand dimensions of environ-mental conflicts, map networks of participating actors and grasp the dynamics of the debate: Who has which competences to organize interaction and to influ-ence the constitution of public narratives, which solutions are discussed, which arguments are accepted while others are seen as innovative? Analytical ques-tions therefore had some points in common with methods of *content analysis*[36], looking at facts that were transmitted in communication (what), actors (who) and recipients (whom). According to the concepts of framing, questions for analysis were: Who considers which issue as a problem? Who takes part in which meeting with which intention? Which organizations make similar argu-

---

[36] Document analysis needs to be distinguished from content analysis (Mayring 1990) which can be applied to documents and transcribed (expert) interviews. Taking the text as a medium of objectified communication, this method seeks to systematically code terms and subjects of a text in order to grasp its underlying pattern of meaning, investigating first and foremost the text as the object of research representative of social reality looked at.

ments (or use similar vocabulary)? Content analysis asks which role the communicated message plays for the recipient.[37] As the effect is difficult to measure without additional sources, a question to analyse position papers, press statements, policy papers and reports was: What is the intended effect of the communication? The above research questions helped to qualify documents as sources. After a first reading to grasp date, time, speaker, the communicative situation and arguments presented, often in the disguise of facts, documents were analysed reiteratively in order to seize framing actions. How did the argument and the place and time of speaking relate to the organizations' political work? This, of course, exceeds text analysis limits and relates to interpretation and contextualization, aiming at making explicit procedural knowledge.

The same analysis revealed positions and strategies in a more institutionalized structure of stakeholder hearings, where organizations can publish a more or less detailed written statement in advance, archived on a Commission DG's website, and are then invited to defend these statements publicly during a hearing. Documented stakeholder hearings on CO_2 emission standards were a valuable source. They partly replace field observation in those arenas that were not open to the public or accessible as part of the fieldwork. Another valuable source of documentation is institutionalized arenas of negotiations such as CARS21. This exercise, inaugurated by the European Commission in 2004, serves as a professional arena where sector-related policy issues are discussed in working groups, and reports and documents are publicly available. Most of the debates on working group level, however, are dedicated to technical questions. This arena and similar others were at the same time sources of documentation and objects of research as networks and spaces of European automotive governance. The history of the CARS 21 policy arena which emerged as a space for promoters or the car industry's existing conception of control will be illustrated in the case study. The different DGs of the Commission are, at the same time, administrators and interested actors in these arenas. They are responsible for providing and assembling knowledge and evidence on specific problems, a role in which the difference between information and framing is not clearly drawn.

General and specialized media played an important role for document analysis, both as archives, documenting events and conflicts, as well as arenas of ongoing conflicts. They also are used as communication channels by interested stakeholders to launch debates. When starting to analyse the dimensions of the

---

[37] Different types of sources disclose different types of knowledge. While reports often disclose mostly factual knowledge, these and shorter "fact sheets" as well as "Questions and Answers" are never neutral but always disclosed as part of the actor's market or political position.

conflict on electric cars in mid-2011, media attention was at its recent peak, before falling in 2013 (evidence from Germany).

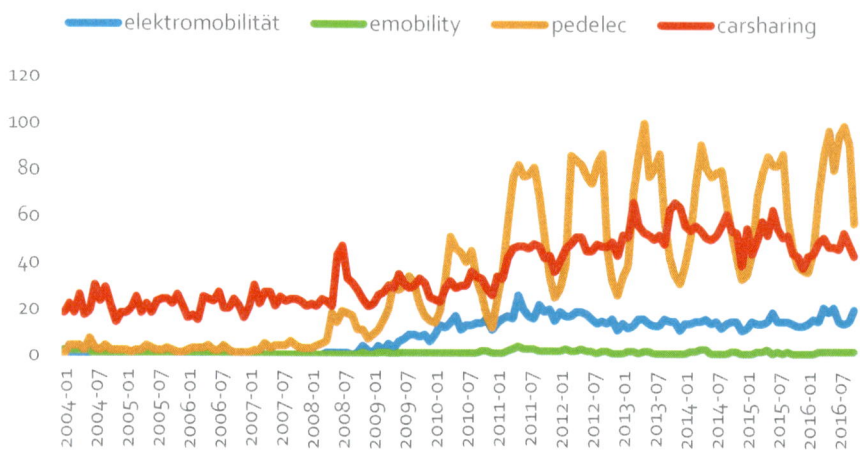

Figure 2: Web search statistics by keywords.[38]

Particularly due to the stark contrast to a non-existing market and products, announcements of strategic investments by firms and governments were visible in the media. The media, as a discursive arena, certainly played a role of multiplicator or "performer", in the sense that it drew public attention to a possible future reality, and therefore contributed to fostering the collectivization of shared narratives.

Participant observation

Participant observation was used at an advanced level of empirical research *after* having reconstructed the historical sequences and possible conflictive path changes through document analysis and interviews. It was mainly conducted at meetings, expert conferences, and a research stay at an environmental organization in Brussels.

---

[38] Reproduced from Google Trends:
https://www.google.de/trends/explore?date=all&geo=DE&q=elektromobilit%C3%A4t,emobility
,pedelec,carsharing&hl=de, published in http://blog.e-stations.de/2013/google-trends-
auswertung-zur-elektromobilitaet/

Participant observation can be defined as "the process of learning through exposure to or involvement in the day-to-day or routine activities of participants in the researcher setting" (Schensul, Schensul and Lecompte, 1999: 91, cited in Kawulich 2005:2). The term 'exposure' describes the situation whereby the researcher immerses him/herself in the surroundings of the field or organization he investigates. Being exposed to the field implies that the researcher consciously does not try to control activities by preceding interpretation or guidelines for action. In contrast to the stable and fixed setting of expert interviews, he or she has "an open, non-judgemental attitude, being interested in learning more about others, being aware of the propensity for feeling culture shock and for making mistakes, the majority of which can be overcome, being a careful observer and a good listener, and being open to the unexpected in what is learned" (Dewalt/Dewalt, 1998, cited in Kawulich 2005: 3). In order to guarantee this openness, participant observation comprises more than observation in the strict sense of looking at what is going on. It requires the observer to interact as one of them while at the same time being able to take up distance and write up field notes, and, eventually, an interpretation referred to as ethnography.

Participant observation, more than expert interviews, allows an organization to be looked at from the inside. It allows "researchers to check definitions of terms that participants use in interviews, observe events that informants may be unable or unwilling to share when doing so would be impolitic, impolite, or insensitive [...]" (Kawulich 2005:4). As a complementary method of data collection, this can increase the validity of interpretations[39]. Before engaging in participant observation, the organization was identified as a key actor in the emergence of CO_2 emission regulation, additional participant observation allowed the reconstruction of this historical sequence of conflicts to be extended, making industrial and environmental policy's imperatives meet and test working hypotheses. As far as types of knowledge are concerned, participant observation is better able to grasp procedural and interpretive knowledge in comments and unspoken knowledge of participants than expert interviews do.

3.3. Fieldwork effects

---

[39] As Kawulich summarizes (2005:4, citing from DeWalt/DeWalt (2002)), "observations may help the researcher have a better understanding of the context and phenomenon under study. Validity is stronger with the use of additional strategies used with observation, such as interviewing, document analysis, or surveys, questionnaires, or other more quantitative methods. Participant observation can be used to help answer descriptive research questions, to build theory, or to generate or test hypotheses." (also confirmed in Yin 2009).

The way in which research is conducted and the social, physical and geographical surroundings in which it is carried out has a particular influence on the qualitative methods of data collection. Across the described methods of data collection, the method of fieldwork determined access to data. As far as expert interviews are concerned, methods research confirms that the interview situation always has an impact on the outcome: "Whether investigators wish it or not, interviewing is a social relationship and the interviewer is part of the relationship. The interviewee's inarticulate and unexamined conception of the audience guides and determines what he says" (Dexter 1969: 115). This applies to the same degree to participant observation, if the researcher is an active part of the setting she or he observes. As different methods of investigation suggest, the researcher switches roles between being the 'layman' (in 'expert' interviews) or the expert (conducting participant observation). The researcher's own level of expertise can be, but is not automatically, a useful tool to raise the quality of interviews. Throughout the whole period of field work, the researcher will reflect her or his own level of expertise. This reflection is the basis of any expert interview. It can be used variably depending on the type of interview and the type of knowledge aimed at.

Team interview

Team interviews were highly beneficial. About half of the expert interviews at the beginning and half-way through the research process were conducted in a (bi-national) team of researchers. In some cases, the combination of language options and nationalities helped to gain access to interview partners. Access to actors in the automotive industry generally is very difficult. Being part of an international network of automotive researchers raised our legitimacy as researchers especially in dealing with automotive manufacturers. We could therefore use existing contacts to approach sectoral representatives.

This chapter detailed how the empirical study was designed and conducted. It concentrated on the micro-foundations of path change: organizational and semantic interaction of different types of actors in the sector. The following two chapters present and interpret the empirical findings. They reconstitute the emergence of new shared framings and narratives, and their potential to transform the present automobile configuration. Data collection methods chosen for each chapter vary depending on the time period the studied subjects cover: Chapter 4 details the preconditions of a collective action framework contesting given hierarchies, on the micro-level. Covering a long period of time, it is essentially based on document analysis of online archives and draws occasionally on interviews. Chapter 5, reconstructing the sequences of path creation during the crisis, reconstitutes recent events, mainly through explorative interviews to understand the competing problem framings and their impact.

4. Roots of change: European environmental politics

Chapter 4 as the first of two empirical chapters explores the question if and to what extent environmental conflict in the car industry challenged the institutional pillars of 20th century automobility. The goal is to understand how the conflict has transformed the organizational and semantic structures of the sector's institutional configuration. Although air pollution from emittants such as Nox and Particulate Matter (PM) are equally hazardous and have been discussed since the uptake of diesel technology[40], the debate on vehicles' CO_2 emissions and their climate impact in particular, and environmental and mobility innovations that followed, presents a case in point for challenges to the legitimacy of the sector's 20th century institutional configuration. The first section (4.1.) reconstitutes institutional micro-level interactions between automotive industry, environmental interest groups and regulative authorities that changed expectations towards environmental performance of vehicles and car makers. Chapter 4.2 illustrates why and how emerging CO_2 regulation produced alternative 'collective frames' on the macro-level, contesting car makers' dominance as economic and political decision-makers in the sector, affecting technological and product strategies. It is shown that, as a consequence, policy instruments created new organizational patterns in the entire industry and diffused narratives contesting the prevailing conception of control.

4.1. Emission legislation – Europeanization of the automotive sector

The history of environmental conflict in the car industry and the roots of path change are linked to the European Single Market established with the fall of custom barriers between European countries in 1993. In the beginning of the 1990s, firms of all sectors intensified their commercial and political interaction across national borders, extended their organizational structures including those for conflict negotiation on the emerging European level of decision-making (Stone Sweet et al. 2001). The determining role, in terms of emission regulation, that car makers would play in the following years on EU level is closely linked to the fact that they benefited from the Common Market to strengthen their common interest representation. The car makers' lobby had already existed before (as CCMC, Comité des Constructeurs Automobiles du Marché Commun). This group had represented mostly the national champions, i.e. the

---

[40] The EU Commission introduced standards on other air polluting gases such as NOx, CO and particles in 1988 (Euronorm 1) that have been updated with stricter emission limits since.

largest French, Italian and German manufacturers[41], in the European policy process, and had served as an arena to coordinate international market strategies and protect the domestic markets since the 1970s.[42] In the relatively small circle of leading firms, decisions were taken on unanimity; every car maker thus had a veto power. In 1990/1991, the members dissolved CCMC and re-founded ACEA, representing all car makers present on European markets, including US Subsidiaries Opel (Vauxhall in GB) and Ford[43]. From then on decisions were taken based on majority vote[44]. Through its successful reform, car makers set the internal preconditions for their influential position until today.

The organization professionalized rapidly as a lobby with a high degree of expertise in market observation. From the few reliable sources on the internal functioning of ACEA (as archives are not open to the public), it can be considered that the lobby established working structures with about 18 permanent staff at its foundation (Pardi 2011: 515), compared to none at CCMC. As the association of the largest automotive firms, whose technical and economic choices affect all dependent suppliers in the value chain, their decisions indirectly affect the approximately 12 million employees (as of 2014). Based on

---

[41] Germany: BMW, Mercedes-Benz, VW, France: Renault, PSA, Italy: Fiat, UK: Rover. Not included were American subsidiaries established quasi-independently in the German market, Ford and Opel; nor Swedish car makers SAAB and Volvo.

[42] For example on the question of how to deal with Japanese competition through a quota of local production in the EU, in which the head of PSA, Jacques Calvet, was strongly opposed to the opening suggested by his colleagues of the leading CCME members, Raymond Lévy (Renault), Carl Hahn (VW), Umberto Agnelli (Fiat) and Eberhard von Kuehnheim (BMW) (Pardi 2011: 513ff).

[43] BMW AG, Daimler-Benz AG, Fiat Auto S.p.A., Ford of Europe Inc, General Motors Europe AG, F. Porsche AG, PSA Peugeot Citroën, Renault SA, Rover and Volkswagen AG, Saab and Volvo. (Reconstructed from T&E 2000, Lenschow/Rottmann 2005)

[44] The internal conflicts the car makers had to solve in order to reform the structures of their interest representations are an early indication of their ability to reach compromise, despite strategic disagreement and competition. The CEOs of VW, BMW and Fiat were in favour of opening the political representation of car makers to the Swedish Saab, and German US subsidiaries Ford and Opel, which had de facto become German companies in the 1980s (Pardi 2011: 214). French car maker PSA opposed, fearing combined influence of German firms in the organization, at the time the European Commissioner for Industry was the German liberal Martin Bangemann. In order to realize this common position against PSA's veto, on the 27 November 1990, all company CEOs left the CCMC in order to de facto dissolve it and recreate ACEA (Association des Constructeurs Européens d'Automobiles) as the car makers' lobby with changed internal statutes. At the price of being obliged to find internal compromise, this allowed car makers to be operational in European politics, for example on the question of emission reduction. Being operational was, in fact, one of the main political targets of this radical reorganization. The journalist Gandillot observes that, as a consequence of this internal struggle, car makers "vont [...] changer les statuts et la composition du CCMC afin d'en faire un véritable outil de combat", (Gandillot 1992: 83, cited in Pardi 2011:513).

this argument, the standpoints of car manufacturers against further emission regulation carried strong economic weight in discussions on how to reduce CO_2 emission on cars.

The heterogeneous members of the European car maker lobby competed in very different market segments, from heavy, polluting premium cars to small and energy-efficient compact cars. Every car maker emitted a different average score of CO_2, depending on model range and market segments covered. Overall, car makers' products emitted ca. 188 g CO_2/km on average in 1990 (ACEA 2005). From the very beginning of the debate on CO_2 emission reductions, the lobby took a position against obligatory reductions. Car makers considered CO_2 limits too costly with severe impact on product strategy and thus creating competition between market players.

In the early 1990s, national governments in the EU's Council could not find a compromise on CO_2 limits (EEC 91/441: 2). The idea of including CO_2 emissions into an annual circulation tax, suggested by an expert group in the European Council was rejected in a Council meeting on 9 December 1992 (Keay-Bright 2000: 18). During discussions, the main difficulty was that tax harmonization at European level requires unanimous consent in the Council, and member states disagreed on ceding tax sovereignty to the EU level. Fiscal regulation on environmental and transport issues was clearly rejected by the UK and Ireland that did not want to concede this competence to the EU Commission (Quandt 2010:8). In addition, some governments represented in the Council intended to protect their national industries. In 1992, the expert group in charge of finding appropriate solutions[45] examined, but dropped the option of an additional tax weighted by CO_2-emissions on car sales as for example implemented in Austria (Com final 1995/689:9). The Commission thus could not take a decision within the deadline that it has been given itself by end of 1992. The first attempts of public authorities in the early 1990s to impose CO_2 limits had failed.

The conflict gained complexity as the European Commission was internally divided on the topic. Having failed with initial proposals, the Commission did not succeed in suggesting a coherent alternative to the problem. Cini (1996) explains these internal differences with the co-existence of incompatible administrative cultures that relate to different ideologies on the role of environmental regulation in the emerging single market, industrial compliance and climate change more generally. Cini's institutionalist perspective on the sociol-

---

[45] Motor Vehicle Emissions Group (MVEG) constituted by Directorate General [DG] Enterprise&Industry (previously called DGIII) and reported to the two involved DGs, Environment and Enterprise&Industry.

ogy of decision-making process brings to the fore the connection between the semantic and structural level of political conflicts within European institutions. She defines the European Commission with reference to March and Olson as "a dynamic, living, changing set of 'arenas for contending social forces... collections of standard operating procedures and structures that define and defend values, norms, interests, identities and beliefs' (March/Olson 1989:17)" (Cini 1996:5). Cini's observation suggests that the emission regulation conflict reveals a larger underlying struggle between ideas on economic policies, which explains why the conflict has been ongoing until the time of writing – beyond the introduction of sanctioned CO_2 limits in 2008. The short introduction also shows how early attempts to solve the emission conflict produced instruments that redefined the relationship of car makers and public authorities, and thus a condition of stability of the existing automobility path.

Competing ideas on EU economic policy (1990s)

The EU authorities' attempts to reduce CO_2 emissions by law was embedded in a broader conflict on two ideological positions: the question whether a state-led top-down approach would make the car industry reduce its emission in the long-term, or if a cooperative, horizontal approach respecting economic interests would be more efficient, divided the European Commission. The emission question became subject of an ideological struggle between defenders of a Keynesian and liberal economic policy in general, and automotive policy in particular, within the European institutions. This struggle over principles on the appropriate way to regulate CO_2 involved two Directorate-Generals from the European Commission, DG Enterprise & Industry, representing industrial interests, and DG Environment, advocating for environmental interests including other transport actors and consumers. The instruments each DG suggested as solutions will reappear in the latter course of the conflict: they form the roots of possible alternative paths. The DG Environment's marginalized position partly explains why a consumer- and behaviour-oriented transport policy on emission reduction, that finally would question the automobile path, had not been considered a solution until the 2008 crisis.

With its foundation in the late 1960s, the DG Environment had become the voice of ecologists as a separate organizational entity in the European Commission. Equipped with comparatively few staff (60-80 staff since in 1989, Cini 1996), it has had comparatively little impact among the General-Directorates in the Commission.[46] On CO_2 emission regulation, DG Environment favoured a formalistic standard-setting approach such as CO_2 taxes or sanctions on emission limits, in the beginning of the 1990s as well as during the later negotiations. However, DG Environment, at least where official policy discourse was concerned, did not withhold the increasing liberalization that diffused within the Commission leading to the Lisbon Agenda in 2000. The 5th Environmental Action programme (EAP, a document renewed with each legislative period explaining the normative foundation of European environmental policy) prepared the ground by introducing the principle of shared responsibility among industry and public administration; while the following 6th EAP explicitly endorsed voluntary agreements as a solution to impose environmental constraints among heavy-emitting industries. While this might explain why the more liberal view defended by DG Enterprise & Industry (see below) was adopted by the Commission, although reservations and resistance among DG Environment staff may have remained. An interviewed staff member agreed that the final introduction of CO_2 standards in the car industry was a victory against industry (Interview 10). This internal divergence in the context of the EU Commission's overall movement of liberalization was finally partly addressed through an organizational shift: by the creation of the new DG Clima, called 'Climate Action', in 2010 which was assigned the administration of CO_2 questions and tasked with pragmatic environmental policy in the sense of sustainable development, reconciling growth and climate change policy.

DG Enterprise & Industry, on the other hand, favoured market-based instruments to encourage industries to commit to common policy goals such as emission reduction. These goals were formulated in line with an industrial policy for the sector with the overall objective to maintain its global competitiveness. Labelled with terms such as 'horizontal governance' or 'sustainable governance', the EU Commission officially encouraged the co-creation of legislation in a dialogue with all concerned parties (stakeholders). In the contrast to DG Environment's interventionist ideas of setting binding emission standards, DG Enterprise & Industry embraced the idea of *voluntary agreements*. This mode of soft regulation, in which public administration cooperatively negotiates common standards with representative firms of an industrial sector, had become increasingly popular across the European institutions in the early 1990s

---

[46] As Cini (1996) points out, staff consisted mostly of environmentalist and thus politically active national experts, and less by career European officials who can be considered more neutral by professional socialization. "The situation was not always easy for the DG XI staff. The Environment Commissioner was often in a minority position in the College of Commissioners, particularly where environmental measures were concerned that could impact Europe's competitiveness" (Cini 1996: 468).

(Lenschow/Rottman 2005). In a White Paper on sustainable governance from 2001, formulating principles of good governance in the European economy, the Commission explicitly encourages voluntary agreements, i.e. the self-obligation by companies to reach environmental objectives, as a means to re-place former formalistic approaches to produce European harmonized regula-tion. It stresses that especially the "social partners should be further encouraged to use the powers given under the Treaty to conclude voluntary agreements" (European Commission 2001: 12). DG Enterprise & Industry benefitted from this argumentative template to argue why the European Commission should encourage voluntary agreements on emission reduction in industries with strong interest representation such as the car industry (Lenschow/Rottmann 2005). On this basis, the further analysis of the emission regulation conflict at the micro level reveals that voluntary agreements accorded, at least in short terms, significant decision-making power to industrial partners.

The 1998 voluntary agreement on CO_2 reduction: industry in control

Little data is available that would allow us to reconstruct in detail the negotia-tions between the two DGs and the ACEA during the 1990s on how and to what extent CO_2 emissions from cars should be regulated.[47] This is due to the lack of transparency in the decision-making process itself: It was, by and large, an informal bilateral negotiation procedure between ACEA and the Commis-sion. The lack of documentation unveils a significant transparency deficit of early European sectoral environmental policy. In addition to case studies on voluntary agreements from European governance research (Lenschow/Rottmann 2005; Quandt 2010), the main source for this historical reconstruction is Keay-Bright's (2000) detailed report on the emergence of the solution that both sides finally agreed upon, the 1998 voluntary agreement on CO_2 limits on passenger cars.

Negotiations started in 1995 when the Commission accepted ACEA's proposi-tion of regulating emissions by voluntary agreements. They ended in 1998 when a common limit of an overall CO_2 average across all fleets of all car makers of 140 gram CO_2/km was agreed 10 years later. This result copies, not unintentionally, the solution that the German Government had introduced in agreement with the German Manufacturers Association VDA in 1995 (VDA 1998). The same manufacturers, mainly German premium car makers Daimler and BMW (with former Swedish car maker, Volvo), producers of the largest

---

[47] The European Commission's online archives only go back as far as the beginning of the 1990s.

and most CO_2-intensive cars, are susceptible of having imposed their national position against any emission regulation on European level using ACEA's majority vote system.

Taking a closer look at the negotiations at the micro-level of interaction confirms this assumption. The individuals involved were convinced that European politics on industries had to be based on market-industries and to be discussed with stakeholders: they considered car makers as the legitimate voice of the car industry. Following Quandt's analysis (2010: 7), the two policy officers in charge of negotiations on the EU Commission's side were two former diplomats who valorised and were personally convinced by the advantage of a soft law approach in industrial environmental regulation. They favoured a voluntary option because of its informal character and the strong integration of stakeholders. The liberal economic policy discourse was underlined by DG Enterprise's organizational dominance.

After the EU Commission had generally accepted the idea to allow voluntary agreements as an option among others to reduce CO_2 emissions in the car sector, DG Enterprise & Industry assigned the task to negotiate the agreement's conditions to its expert group (Motor Vehicle Emissions Group) from 1995 onwards. It was to be the first voluntary agreement in the sector on European level, and the process proved difficult as it was likely to set a precedent for future conflicts. The group comprised professionals of the automotive industry in member states that were invited by the DG Enterprise & Industry as experts to evaluate policy options. The actual negotiations were conducted by only four individuals: two Ford engineers named by ACEA, and two policy officers (administrative personnel), most probably one for DG Enterprise & Industry; one for DG Environment. DG Enterprise & Industry thus cumulated its direct influence on negotiations and hosted not only the expert group dealing with the issue but also the administrative staff in direct negotiations. The few case studies that are available on the decision process suggest that the selection and role of administrative personnel had an important impact on its outcome: The unequal distribution of technical expertise shaped the final agreement's conditions along car makers' requirements.

Between 1996 and 1997, the two policy officers and two engineers representing ACEA met once a month. Keay-Bright emphasizes that there was a strong asymmetry of information between negotiation partners when it came to estimating cost and technical feasibility of the suggested CO_2 limits. The Commission officers do not seem to have received much support during negotiations. "ACEA admitted that the Commission desk officers would have benefited from technical support. At the same time the two Commission desk officers did not

63

receive much in the way of higher-level political support and were very much left to their own devices [...]. In addition, the voluntary agreement had to compete for priority with the air quality directives that were high on the Commission's agenda during this time [..]. Due to time and financial constraints, DG 11[48] believes the Commission could not have conducted its own technical and economic analyses, but moreover believes that attempting to establish consensus between differing technical analyses of the Commission and industry would be near impossible and likely to result in deadlock [...]. The Commission also viewed that it would have been difficult to ensure the independence of such technical studies as it is the automobile industry that possesses the technical knowledge [...]." (Keay-Bright 2000:22)

All factors, the ideological setting in which negotiations were led, the framing of a voluntary agreement as the most efficient solution, and DG Enterprise's dominance in organizing the knowledge resources involved, impacted the final result of negotiations. The European Parliament, Council and the Commission had initially agreed to demand an objective of 120g CO_2 per Kilometre by 2005, at the latest by 2008. But ACEA suggested 167g CO_2/km in 2005, which was considered insufficient by the Commission in return. Only in 1998, "when the Commission made clear that it was going to take the legislative route unless ACEA would accept a 25% reduction of emissions which meant a value of 140g CO_2/km, ACEA accepted in order to prevent uniform, legal standards" (Lenschow/Rottman 2005). Because standards, that would be imposed and controlled by the Commission, were a much worse option for car makers, they accepted the final compromise. The EU Commission finally recommended in February 1999, that "The members of the European Automobile Manufacturers Association (ACEA) should, mainly by technological developments and market changes linked to these developments, collectively achieve a CO_2 emission target of 140 g/km CO_2 [...]", (Commission of the European Communities (1999 :1).

The macro-perspective on this conflict reveals why its institutional impact should not be underestimated: the debate on the mode of regulation of CO_2 limits can be considered a debate on the sector's generative rules – the way future rules would be made. The 1998 voluntary agreement fostered not only collective investments in emission reduction. Moreover it justified a new mode of sectoral governance. From 1999 onwards, car makers' would be able to decide on their own, guided only by a collectively agreed target, *how and to what*

---

[48] Before changing to names and acronyms, the Commission's Directorate-Generals were referred to by numbers, not areas of responsibility. DG XI was DG Environment.

degree they would achieve the agreed CO_2 reductions. Automotive companies were thus still in control of their emission reduction efforts. Therefore, the CO_2 question, seemed initially to have a stabilizing impact that environmental policy should have on the sectors' institutional configuration as a whole, and thus an important institutional pillar of automobility: car makers' control of sectoral governance. In summary, the institutional impact of the agreement can be characterized as follows:

- Stabilization of hierarchies: Car makers managed to keep the power to spell out environmental politics in a language and as a domain under firm control: as a matter of technical emission reduction. A *voluntary* agreement, by definition, excluded the EU Commission from *defining how* emission reduction should be reached. All car makers can thus control emission targets: by agreeing on individual targets by which each company should contribute to the overall target. Beyond negotiation with fellow competitors, firms can control and plan the progress by including emission targets into their strategic planning and product politics. Chapter 4.2. shows that each firm decided a way to commercialize innovations (mainly in combustion and alternative engine technology) according to their product range and market position. Emission reduction had thus successfully defined as an industrial issue to be defined by dominant firms in the sector.

- A restricted network of actors and exclusion of civil society stakeholders emerges. The agreement was negotiated exclusively between industry and the European Commission. As illustrated in the reconstruction of the decision-making process, other (possibly critical) civil society representatives such as environmental NGOs and consumer/driver representations were excluded. Ironically, this outcome was justified by a horizontal mode of governance that initially wanted to reinforce the voice of stakeholders such as civil society. Instead, the car makers had appeared as dominant stakeholders during the negotiations.

- Simplified problem framing: The framing of an emission problem as one of technical emission reduction omits solutions from other domains for example *the consumer*, and possible of changes in demand or car use that could reduce vehicle emissions. As a consequence, CO_2 emission reduction remains a purely technical question to be solved by those that produce and sell the technology. The Commission defined that ACEA should achieve the CO_2 reduction goal "mainly by technological developments and market changes linked to these developments" (EU Commission 1999b:2).

- Technicization of discourse: the language in which actors framed the problem of emission reduction for the European car sector appears reductionist. Emission reduction is determined as a technical measure of *grams of* CO_2 *per driven kilometre*. This measure is an average defined for each car model when tested on a standardized European test cycle before released for sale. Because car makers pay private testing laboratories (i.e. TÜV) to determine each model's average test cycle emissions[49], they can indirectly still keep control over this procedure and produce lower numbers than the vehicle would produce on the road in real world conditions. With the voluntary agreement and reduction targets on average emissions, the political relevance of this measure has increased significantly and opened up channels of influence for testing institutions.

- Collectivization of a dominant narrative: through the instrument of voluntary agreement, the new mode of governance was justified by public authorities on a general level: The EU Commission itself claimed a procedural shift from government (understood as a bureaucratic, over-formalized and centralized rule of public institutions, as incorporated in DG Environment's legal emission sanctions approach) to a new form of de-centralized, inclusive open and variable approach of governance; in which the EU seeks adequate instruments for problems by including stakeholders. Summarized in analytical terms, the voluntary approach as an instruments and a technical problem frame thus promised to become an instrument to secure the status quo, integrating emission reduction into existing narratives and organizational hierarchies.

On the background of the car industry's hierarchical structure, the history of the 1998 voluntary agreement's emergence suggests its stabilizing institutional impacts: The organizational and semantic structures put in place by the instrument do not challenge, but confirm the sector's generative rules. A frame had been agreed upon to solve the conflict on CO_2 emissions without threatening the sector's existing conception of control. However, tracing its history into the

---

[49] The former and outdated European NEDC test cycle, basis of the CO_2 regulation until 2017, was set up in 1970 and vehicles' real world emissions were on average 40% higher on the road that in the test. Even by introducing the renewed and more representative test cycle WLTP, problematic practices of cheating test cycles cannot fully be resolved. Real driving emissions can still be expected to be up to 25% higher than the measured ones, with a growing trend (ICCT 2015).

first years of application reveals the opposite, and thus unforeseen, effect. The fact that car manufacturers did not keep to their own promised targets created space for action for those critical observers that had not been heard before 1998. Their strategies allowed an alternative narrative to gain support. This contestation, it is argued, set the first conditions of a process of path change.

A contested victory: emerging environmental criticism

The history of emission regulation could simply be considered a classic conflict of interests. One could interpret the EU Parliament's acceptance of car makers' voluntary agreement to reduce emissions in 1999 as a surrender to the industry's interests and according soft modes of regulation. One could further interpret this example as a victory of neo-liberal ideas within the EU Commission of what industrial policy should look like, protecting competitiveness and turning environmental regulation into support for economic emission-efficient technologies. However, embedding my analysis of the decision-making process in its historical, social conditions and semantic context reveals a more complex picture. This section will show that the details of the voluntary agreement's mechanism and its conditions of compliance themselves caused its failure 10 years later. This initial paradoxical result can be explained by looking at policy instruments as (performative) means of organizing interaction (Lascoumes/Le Galès 2007). The fact that the agreement did not produce the expected results will also lead to a more general loss of belief in voluntary solutions (and in horizontal coordination with industry and in self-controlled progress). The voluntary agreement is at the beginning of a series of institutional developments that could dissolve and redefine the structural conditions of car makers' economic, political and semantic dominance in the sector. Once companies' voluntary efforts are discredited, it will pave the way for a new wave of public investments in alternative, especially electric engine technology as the main focus of European automotive industrial policy and a new narrative of the consumers' voice as the critical and 'market-making' factor (Chapter 5).

In order to understand how the voluntary agreement could initiate its own failure, we first need to look back at the legislative context in the early 2000s. The seeming European shift towards neo-liberal and horizontal legislation was strongly opposed by diverging interests within the Commission. By accepting the voluntary agreement, the Commission accepted the legitimacy of the industry's problem framing, addressing environmental problems in a purely technical fashion. However, this acceptance was the smallest common denominator both sides could agree on. Those in the European Commission committed to reducing environmental impacts through regulation and emission targets would have preferred a more ambitious commitment by public authorities. Although powerless in practice, their opposition had given birth to an ambitious framing of the problem as part of a planned and larger environmental policy strategy. As a result, the document in which it accepted the idea of a voluntary agreement (European Commission 1995) recalls that there were alternative solutions that the EU Commission could not impose, and that it would continue to seek to impose them at the next opportunity. These semantic alternatives formulate the roots of an alternative conception of automobility: "[...] CO_2 emissions from road transport can only be reduced by a package of measures. In principle, these can aim at reducing the use of motor vehicles, influencing driving behaviour (e.g. speed) and achieving a higher vehicle fuel efficiency by a combination of technical and non-technical measures." (European Commission 1995: 3). The document accordingly defines three pillars by which emission reduction had to be achieved, including non-technical factors such as the harmonized labelling of emission standards of all cars on sale across Europe[50] and resuming the idea of fiscal incentives the EU had discussed in the early 1990s.

The document reaffirmed the Commission's right and the intention to regulate CO_2 emissions at a later point in time, with setting the target of 120 g per km – i.e. by 20 grams more ambitious that the industry's final target - by 2012. Once published in the form of a Commission proposal, therefore, it could serve as a reference for future negotiations.

In the early 2000s, parts of the Commission made another unfruitful attempt to impose CO_2 taxation.[51] DGs Environment and DG Taxud (responsible for har-

---

[50] This translates a quest that the European consumer organizations, including the European Consumer representation BEUC, have pursued for a long time, up to the present without success (Interview 26).

[51] This initiative has not been finalized. Fiscal measures being the far more sensitive issue, a first communication to Parliament and Council was published in September 2002 in which the Commission, based on the preparation work of the expert group, called for harmonizing existing passenger car-related tax systems under CO_2-related criteria (European Commission 2002). The Commission justifies the fact that vehicle taxation was to be related to CO2 reduction criteria, being an "important complementary instrument to support the realization of the EU-target of 120g CO2/km for new cars by 2008-2010, and to contribute to the accomplishment of the EU engagements under the Kyoto Protocol." (European Commission 2002:18). The aim was to abolish differences between vehicle taxation in member states and, based on an annual circulation tax depending on cars' average emissions, to introduce the emission targets via tax policy. In an effort to convince relevant committees in fellow European institutions, the Commissions stresses that the tax harmonization efforts to simplify the trade and use of cars in the single market, with its combined environmental effects, would be profitable for administrations, car makers and citizens (European Commission 2002: 3). Of more importance to member states was the fact that this communication implied that vehicle taxing was to be managed under community legisla-

monizing taxes) installed an *Expert Group on Fiscal Framework Measures* and a sub-group of this committee as the *Group on Fiscal Framework Measures to Reduce CO_2 Emissions from New Passenger Cars* in 2000 with the objective of elaborating new options to reduce CO_2 through car-related fiscal measures. Both gathered external expertise, engaging a number of observers of the on-going conflict: research institutes evaluated options and experts from the industry itself evaluated the feasibility of the proposed measures. "Advice was sought, where necessary, in contacts with experts from other Commission Departments, the car industry and car consumer associations, as well as from the Member States applying taxes similar to those envisaged in the proposal" the Commission justifies in a (later revised) proposal for a CO_2 reduction directive to Parliament and Council (European Commission 2005:4). In all, European institutions consulted over 2 years until the proposal failed in November 2003 (European Commission 2005:3). Even if unsuccessful, through long consultation processes behind the scenes, a broader range of potential stakeholders and informed observers were already following the debate. An important institutional effect of this renewed legislative initiative was thus the creation of a network of actors on the question of environmental legislation in road transport.

The devil in the detail: impact of policy instruments

What seemed to be a victory of the stronger interest group in the short term, turned out to be the beginning of a shift of decision-making power towards public administration as co-regulating actor. This is due to the implementation of a specific control instrument of the agreement. Accepting the voluntary targets to reduce car emissions, the European Parliament [EP] criticized the fact that the agreement did not allow any public observation and evaluation of firms' annual progress. To compensate for this lack of transparency, the EP voted for an annual monitoring mechanism in form of progress reports from ACEA to the Commission in 2000 (Monitoring Decision, 1753/2000/EC). The instrument allowed observers, and other previously excluded stakeholders such as drivers/consumers and environmental critics to follow and judge firms' performance. In parallel to the DG's legislative efforts described above, the monitoring thus created a critical public for alternative forms of emission regulation.

---

tion in the long run. Although the Commission cautiously writes, "the Commission, based on these principles and in the light of the results of the consultation process, could submit proposals for Community legislation…" (22), as in 1992, it did not succeed in diluting the governments' doubts.

It gradually discredited the previous bilateral agreement as car makers did not reduce emissions quickly enough. As a result, an alternative narrative on transparency and public control of companies gained momentum.

The condition at which ACEA, in turn, agreed to the reporting was that the data on car makers' progress remained aggregated. In order to protect the sensitive information on car makers' competitiveness, no conclusions on firms' individual efforts and distances to the target could be drawn publicly. This condition reveals the strategic importance CO_2 regulation had for companies. In addition, car makers could benefit from the fact that for a comparative measurement on European level, no emission reduction data had been generated so far. Car manufacturers themselves were the only actors that could disclose information on how their fleet average CO_2 emissions had changed on a year to year basis. Both parties agreed that until the EU set up an independent monitoring system (by 2003), ACEA would disclose data purchased from a French automobile observatory agency (AAA). This agency is referred to in the first monitoring report as an "independent organization under public mandate, whose business it is to develop and sell data to clients" (European Commission 2000:9). However, the AAA liaised closely with the association of French car makers and it is not impossible that ACEA could have control on sensitive data via the French car makers association.

Consequently, in the short term, the European Parliament's claim for transparency had little effect in practice due to lack of independent means to control companies' action via independent data. In the medium-term, however, the instrument prepared important transformative impact on the sector's governance structure because the data base became a source of independent expertise. In 2003, as anticipated, the Commission had put into place an independent monitoring procedure, carried out by the European Environmental Agency (EEA). National car registration agencies reported emission data on every car model sold and thus registered per year directly to the EEA, without car makers' validation. The EEA could establish a detailed and rich data base evaluating the companies' progress. Five years after the long and hard negotiations on the agreement's conditions, data on progress was independently seized and publicly available. CO_2 reduction by car makers had now been made measurable and comparable on a European level.

Once a regular reporting practice was established, the 'distance from target' measures allowed critics to interfere as soon as they could prove that car makers' efforts were insufficient. However, the monitoring progress did not provide full transparency on firms' environmental performance as data was still published only aggregated for all car makers and not made available to a non-

expert public outside the European institutions. The environmental organization Transport & Environment, a European federation of national environmental associations campaigning for cleaner transport, had been critically observing
the car makers' agreement since the early 2000s (Transport & Environment
2000). The title of its first report importantly set the line of argument that critics would follow for the next eight years, implicating that it would not only be
an environmental, but also a moral problem if the industry did not keep its
promise as a stakeholder in European politics. "Will the European Motor Industry be able to honour its commitment to the European Union?" This promise, it seems to say, was also one to Europe's citizens and car users alike. The
problem framing will extend into a shared narrative of critics of the voluntary
agreement.

In 2005, the environmental group launched a communication campaign on the
car makers' lack of environmental accountability; stating the important data
and transparency gaps: *It is currently possible to find out the emissions of
individual car models, but there is no publicly available information linking
these figures to sales by company. In other words it is not possible to see how
an individual manufacturer is doing at cutting overall emissions of its new car
fleet.*" (Transport & Environment 2005a: 9). The environmental NGO investigated the EEA's monitoring reports. It obtained, through a request on access to
these documents, data on the performance of individual car makers'. Based on
this exclusive access, Transport&Environment was able to start building additional expertise in favour of a restrictive legislative solution on CO_2 emissions
such as the DG Environment had been demanding since the early 1990s. This
way it could build pressure on ACEA in the years that followed. The developing critical narrative itself, however, was not sufficient to discredit car makers.
It had to be enacted by organized structures of interest representation, paired
with access to essential negotiation arenas of sectoral policy making. One reason why T&E could undermine car maker's control conception was that it
worked with the same 'technical' discourse and tools based on scientific evidence.

Cars and CO_2 reports: an alternative problem framing emerges

In 2005, based on the obtained data, Transport & Environment published a first
detailed report assessing the potential of car makers to achieve the set emission
limits. The report, titled "Reducing CO_2 Emissions from New Cars. A progress
report on the car industry's voluntary agreement and an assessment of potential
policy instruments" (T&E 2005b), concluded that emission reduction was first

and foremost a political problem. *"From a technological point of view the manufacturing industry should have no difficulties producing cars which on average emit 140g CO_2 per km in 2008 and 120g in 2012. However, under current rules, manufacturers, wholesalers and car dealers have no incentive to sell fuel-efficient cars."* (T&E 2005b:17). In line with the DG Environment's approach, the NGO argued for stronger fiscal incentives for car makers, either in the form of a tradable emission scheme or a CO_2-specified sales and registration tax for new cars. T&E's goal was to prove, against car makers' claims, that the EU's more ambitious limit of 120g CO_2/km by 2012 was feasible. The group gained credibility by using the European Environmental Agency's independent data base. T&E started to gather detailed (technical) knowledge on alternative engine technologies that were currently discussed in the industry (see 4.2): "A number of recent independent technological studies all indicate that the 120g/km target can be met with widely available existing technology. A number of improvements offer the chance to reduce fuel consumption, including advanced lightweight materials, advanced drivetrains, stop/start engines, regenerative braking, hybrid drivetrains with smaller petrol and diesel engines. So technologically it is possible. But technological progress comes at a price, which someone has to pay." (T&E 2005a: 10).

T&E attracted public attention because they met two semantic conditions of the dominant automobile narrative. First, they acquired technical knowledge which so far was the dominant language in the discursive space they were acting in. Second, proving car makers' own emission projections to be wrong and insufficiently ambitious showed that other actors, not just car makers themselves, could anticipate future market strategies, and challenge their ability to shape the future based on their assumptions and strategies. The NGO succeeded in building a specific type of expertise with which they started to promote an alternative framing of the emission problem.

Box A : The construction of technical expertise

Relying on recent independent expertise helped the small organization to construct scientific credibility. T&E seems to have relied first and foremost on a recently published impact assessment published in 2004, by request from DG Environment (IEEP/TNO/CAIR 2005). Subcontracting impact assessments to applied research institutes, at an agreed point in time, for example at the midterm of the voluntary agreement, is a usual procedure in the Commission. This opens up a channel of influence on the Commission's own evaluation of its policies and subsequent action. Up to this day, the control over the choice of scientific subcontractors remains an open question. Especially concerning impact assessments, which are meant to evaluate a policy's impact as objectively as possible, there is a blurred and delicate line between expertise and political opinion-shaping that remains subject to interpretation.

The construction of evidence in order to evaluate policies is therefore subject to important choices. The first refers to the organization carrying out the evaluation. The impact assessment in question was written by consultants, think tanks and research institutes such as the Institute for European Environmental Policy (IEEP), TNO Netherlands, and the Centre for Automotive Industry Research (CAIR, UK).

The second challenge is how to build evidence itself. In the report, scientific proof is constructed through detailed scenario-building techniques, based on baseline assumptions of technology, legal and market development. As in many scenario-building techniques, these assumptions reflect convictions and close-to-reality prognoses by researchers. In this case, these baseline assumptions were discussed and adapted with the DG commissioning the research: "The work has benefited from regular dialogue between the partners and with the Commission services, where assumptions, analysis coverage, method and working results were regularly discussed." (IEEP/TNO/CAIR 2005: 1). The study estimated that CO_2 limits were realistic: car makers were capable of reaching stricter 120g emission limits by optimizing existing technology and investing in most sustainable alternative technology such as hybrid motors and biofuels under certain conditions. The report accordingly judges that emission reduction costs are less than stated by the car industry, an argument the environmental lobby reiterates in its own language: "*Inevitably, a central argument repeatedly used to argue against the 120 g/km target is that the technology would be too expensive. But it isn't! According to recent independent studies, reducing average CO_2 emissions to 120g/km can be done at a very reasonable cost (corresponding to as low as 1-2% of the price of a new car). For example, the 2005 IEEP report for the European Commission said the costs would be €577 per car, on average. The report also says that figure is likely to be an overestimation.*" (T&E 2005c:11)

The evidence was then shared with other stakeholders. The NGO organized a conference[52], bringing car industry representatives together with environmental

---

[52] Held on the 20th of January in Brussels, the conference entitled: "Clean Cars 2010. A discussion on European environmental policy for the passenger car".

associations. While in the light of the further events this seems rather unusual, each actors' thinking at the time can be explained: the small organisation needed to confirm its (critical) knowledge with those accused, by learning and judging at what point the car makers were actually successful in emission reduction. ACEA, on the contrary, had changed its discursive strategy into what was discussed as the integrated approach (4.2.): As soon as car makers realized they would not be able to reach the limits only by emission reduction technologies, they opened a dialogue with all interested parties to discuss which other measures could contribute to the objective, thus making use of the EU Commission's initial idea to reduce emissions by more than technological measures.

This short period of dialogue, however, does not seem to have worked on organizational level. Shortly after this conference, T&E changed strategy and directly accused the car makers of unfair influence on the EU Commission. *"Unlike at national level where extensive bureaucracies exist, officials of the EU's institutions work with very little specialist support. It is therefore crucial to the functioning of the EU that Commission officials and MEPs can rely on expert input from outside sources. Thus it is entirely natural that the Commission relies on input from the European automotive industry (among others) in drawing up its emissions parameters for new cars. But the relationship between the car makers and the EU has become distorted and manipulative. The car industry has dragged its feet at every stage of the CO_2 emissions process, and on this and other issues has constantly exaggerated the difficulty and cost of making technologically feasible improvements."* (T&E 2005a:13) This confrontation opened the way for the environmental group to accuse firms of intransparency and unfair play.

In the following years, T&E thus aimed at exposing car makers' emission reductions in order to evaluate if they were reaching their own targets. While the reports in 2005 and 2006 are based on aggregated data for car makers (European, Japanese and Korean firms) and split retrospectively by country and discuss efficiency measures in general, the CO_2 reports had an increasingly larger impact from 2007 onwards. Approaching the final evaluation year of 2008 (for the respective years 2006 and 2007), the NGO could show that the industry probably would not reach its targets, and point out individual emission reduction performances as the reason for this failure. With access to individual moni-

http://www.transportenvironment.org/events/20012005-clean-cars-2010-brussels, accessed 28.7.2014.

toring data, the organization could show in 2007 that 11 out of 13 producers were far behind the CO_2 limits[53].

Manufacturer Group	Sales 2006 (in 1,000)	Average Co2 emissions (g/km)		
		2005	2006	%
Toyota	848	161	153	-5.0
Honda	249	160	154	-3.9
PSA Peugeot Citroen	1929	146	142	-2.7
BMW	761	188	184	-2.5
Mazda	242	177	173	-2.0
Nissan	534	171	168	-1.6
Hyundai	308	168	167	-0.8
Renault	1275	148	147	-0.8
Fiat	1088	145	144	-0.5
Ford	1571	163	162	-0.5
General Motors	1500	157	157	-0.3
Volkswagen	2940	165	166	0.9
Suzuki	229	164	166	1.8
DaimlerChrysler	876	182	188	2.8

Figure 3: reproduced from T&E 2007: 7

Technical Expertise had thus become political capital for the organization. "These reports were a major lobbying tool", a Transport&Environment member commented retrospectively (Interview 24). They disclosed information on competitiveness on the problem of emission reduction, at a critical point in time (2006, two years from the end of the agreement). The report allowed all readers to compare companies and evaluate their progress. The "Cars and CO_2" reports had created an audience, and a larger public. Political observers in Brussels, research institutions, and stakeholders from other industries could use

---

[53] The differences in CO_2 neatly reflect the technological choices and market segment positions of car producers. They range from French and Italian from small and medium cars to upper segment and heavy cars by German producers.

this information to build pressure. Potential and current customers could access information on products that had not been disclosed by car makers themselves.

Against the rising pressure, ACEA reacted immediately by building on their relations to DG Enterprise & Industry. From the evidence that Greenpeace collected in a detailed report (Greenpeace 2008), ACEA intended to postpone any CO_2 legislation as far as possible. In May 2006, Sergio Marchionne, CEO of Fiat, was elected president of the ACEA. He immediately tried to cut the pressure on European institutions trying to anticipate a new legislative proposal by the Commission. He wrote to Verheugen that "it is improper to propose legislation on CO_2 emissions at this time" (cited in Greenpeace 2008:4). The letter was addressed in copy to EU Environment Commissioner Stavros Dimas as well as Austrian Ministers that held the EU presidency at the time, and French and German Ministers. The choice of the addressees shows ACEA's communication to its network of sectoral actors. The letter can be interpreted as a warning for Dimas not to re-initiate a CO_2 regulation proposal, and informs the relevant national governments of the largest markets Germany and France of their intention to prevent this.

By 2007, CO_2 emission reductions had become subject of a fierce confrontation between public authorities, green groups and the car makers and supportive parts of the Commission on the other hand. At the same time, a new problem framing had emerged among promoters of a strict and public emission law: that of calling on the responsibility of car makers to stick to commonly agreed targets in a transparent way.

Introduction of CO_2 Emission Standards 2008/9

The availability of data as well as the narrative on transparency and responsibility had had visible effects on decision-making structures in the sector. Transparent progress comparison in terms of emission reduction and political pressure allowed the Commission to act quickly as soon as the voluntary agreement had ended. Since 2007, the design of future regulation was discussed in stakeholder meetings (European Commission 2007a), in which the car industry agreed with a 120g target with implementation from 2015 onwards. Contrarily to previous negotiations, consultations now took place among a broader network of organizations, accompanied by considerable media attention.

By the end of the 2007, the network of stakeholders in the negotiations on the future regulation had expanded. The reports of stakeholder hearings also show that the interest conflict had become more complex. Taking a more moderate position, CLEPA, the suppliers' association, pointed out that long-term emission targets were needed and stricter targets were feasible. ACEA, still defending a flexible and market-based solution instead of emission standards, adapted its position to a now existing majority of actors claiming stricter rules. Greenpeace International (Greenpeace 2008), German environmental group BUND (2007) and other observers actively took part in the debate, launching similar pieces of expertise and raising pressure on strict emission limits. T&E was officially participating in the Commission's formal consultations on a legal proposal. The European consumer association BEUC promoted stricter regulations in order to achieve fuel economy for consumers. A network of further allies, such as IEEP, DG Environment, Greenpeace echoed the critics' call for transparency and helped to build pressure on car makers. T&E assumed the role of a multiplying body polemicizing critical judgments on environmental performance of car makers. They succeeded in spreading the shared view that "the voluntary agreement has failed" (Transport&Environment 2005a: 8-11). In 2007, "the failure was undeniable" (Quandt 2010: 9) and expected by all observers.

Indeed, approaching 2008, car makers' investments in alternative powertrains (see Chapter 4.2.) had not paid off in time. Firms reached 153.6 grams CO_2/km on average instead of 140g and thus missed the limits by a considerable 13.6 grams. Efforts to reduce emissions took effect too late in order to sufficiently lower the overall emissions.

Year	CO_2/km	Annual Change
2000	172.2	n/a
2001	169.7	1.45
2002	167.2	1.47
2003	165.5	1.02
2004	163.4	1.27
2005	162.4	0.61
2006	161.3	0.68
2007	158.7	1.61
2008	153.6	3.21
2009	145.7	5.14
2010	140.3	3.71

Table 1: EU car makers' annual emission scores 2000-2013
(Source: adapted from European Commission (2012): Impact Assessment of CO_2 and Cars Regulation 2009, p. 13.)

In a concentrated lobbying effort against the planned regulation, ACEA intended to benefit from the Commission's internal divide, and directly confronted Environment Commissioner Dimas. On January 17, 2007, ACEA (president Gottschalk) wrote to industry Commissioner Verheugen thanking him for his "clear statement on the relevance of the competition policy on the upcoming decisions – especially for German producers" (letter from Gottschalk to Verheugen, 17.1.2007, cited in Greenpeace 2008: 10). The letter confirmed the high the expectations ACEA had on its alliance to the German Commissioner, not least to respect the VDA's interests and German premium car makers' difficulties to meet low emission targets. On January 27, 2007, Marchionne wrote another letter to Commission President Barroso: "I cannot stress sufficiently how serious the implications of such a policy would be for the competitiveness of the European car industry and employment." Marchionne threatened with economic and social consequences he characterized as "detrimental to the welfare of Europe as a whole".

But reports on failing commitments and consumers' disadvantages had stimulated a semantic shift in the meantime, and car makers' economic arguments were viewed in a different light. The Environment Commissioner argued that industry was obliged to keep its promises. In June 2006[54] the European Council had confirmed that "in line with the EU strategy on CO_2 emissions from light duty vehicles, the average new car fleet should achieve emissions of 140g CO_2/km (2008/09) and 120g CO_2/km (2012)" (Renewed EU Sustainable Development Strategy, Council of the European Union, 8.6.2006). By October 2006, the news about DG Environment's efforts to propose a new piece of legislation on CO_2 by 2008 (the end of the voluntary accords) had spread widely. On several occasions Environment Commissioner Dimas announced that he had "lost patience with car makers" and "faith" in the agreement (European Council news, 31.10.2006)[55]. Dimas calls on his colleagues to support binding legislation, aiming at a collective approach for a limit of 120g CO_2/km. On the occasion of a speech in Parliament on October 25 in Strasbourg, the Commissioner announced that "this year, the Commission will review the possibilities for further reductions of carbon dioxide emissions from cars after 2008-2009,

[54] The sources on detailed negotiations in the following paragraphs are taken from Greenpeace 2008.
[55] http://www.eceee.org/all-news/news/news_2006/2006_10_31_c, 12.8.2013

with a view to meeting the Community target of 120g of carbon dioxide per kilometre by 2012. That will, of course, require legislation"[56].

ACEA reacted publicly through press reports and denied that it had failed to meet the emission target. No direct communication through letters is documented, which suggests that direct communication channels were much less established with the DG Environment than with DG Enterprise & Industry. ACEA "noted with surprise press reports alleging that you stated to the media that ACEA would not meet its Commitment on CO_2 emissions from cars and that DG Environment therefore supported replacing the Commitment with legislation" (cited in Greenpeace 2008: 8)[57]. However, by the end of 2006, these efforts to win time were not credible anymore. They rather showed at which point the lobby was convinced of being able to shape an institutional path of which they no longer controlled the narrative nor the organizational structure.

The first official proposal for the first ever legislation on CO_2 emissions by new cars in the sector, suggested by the Commission on 7th February 2007 (European Commission 2007b), set into motion a large debate on the form of fiscal sanctions. The proposal did not come as a surprise for any of the actors involved in the topic since the early 2000s. In the text, the Commission adopts its initial framing, and presents the regulation as the final realization of the third pillar of the "CO_2 Strategy" announced in 1995, and as thus a necessary action regarding stricter climate goals, parallel progress on energy and climate policy and the support for alternatives to petrol-run forms of car use. Alternative technologies seem to have gained credibility in the eyes of European public administration, justifying the CO_2 regulation as a means to prepare their market. The European Commission also seems to build on the argument of instrumental obligation, referring to a preceding policy instrument as justification for the following steps: "As the voluntary agreement did not succeed, the Commission considers it necessary to resort to a legislative approach and underlines that in addition to the proposed legislation urgent action should also be taken by the public authorities to keep the emission reductions on track, also towards 2008/2009, for instance through fiscal incentives and green public procurement." (EU Commission 2007b: 6).

---

[56] Intervention of Stavros Dimas in European Parliament, Wednesday, 25 October 2006 – Strasbourg, http://www.europarl.europa.eu/sides/getDoc.do?pubRef=-//EP//TEXT+CRE+20061025+ITEM-015+DOC+XML+V0//EN&language=EN, accessed 12.8.13

[57] Greenpeace cites an unpublished source. "Hodac, I. 2006. Documents in respect of meetings with any representative of certain organizations and companies, at which CO2 emissions are discussed. Letter to Stavros Dimas, 6th November 2006."

In the public debate that followed in 2008, the new problem framing by environmentalists and the Commission had translated into new decision-making procedures. They were more transparent and more cooperative, as participation opportunities had broadened. There now was a public agenda organizing the definition of the legislation's details in stakeholder hearings. The fact it was public, and no longer behind the scenes (1998/9) or at least semi-public (CARS 21 in 2005) ascribed some democratic legitimacy to its outcome. The Commission explicitly opened the debate: "This Communication provides the basis for exchanges with other European Institutions and all interested parties on implementing a next stage in the Community strategy to reduce CO_2 emissions and improve fuel efficiency from light-duty vehicles with a view to reaching the EU objective of 120 g CO_2/km by 2012. On the basis of the conclusions drawn from these discussions, the Commission will propose if possible in 2007 and at the latest by mid-2008 a legislative framework to the Council and European Parliament in order to reach this objective." (European Commission 2007b: 8). Making the conflict *public* was a means of institutionalization of the emission-reduction problem. The stakeholder consultation process between March and July 2007 received 28 contributions by individual citizens, 41 from registered interest groups and 2478 petitions with signatures from 11 countries, revealing the high public interest in this debate.

The technical options discussed as the basis of the new regulation to come emphasize that alternative engine technologies were anticipated as innovations. Positions oscillated between two main options of formulating an emission standard: 120g by 2012 and 130g by 2015. A large part of the discussions focused on a difference of 10-20 gram of average annual emissions and the year of introduction. In order to reach the 120g target, for example, the Commission suggested that in the case of cars only 130g could be reached, and an additional 10g reduction through additional measures such as using biofuels or efficiency measures such as reducing tire resistance, better and lighter air conditioning systems and others. These efficiency measures were the preferred way to reach CO_2 reductions without questioning core technologies and thereby market strategies, segment positioning and thus the foundations of the European car market. Alternative powertrain options such as hybrid and electric also found emphasis in the regulation, though only in theory: Passenger cars emitting less than 50 g CO_2/km could be calculated with the factor of 3.5 on the total emission average until 2015. This strong incentive to build electric cars however, was not yet relevant, as there were no vehicles to meet these criteria on the market. (This principle named "supercredits" would be reintroduced by car makers themselves in 2013 when the regulation for 2020 was discussed and electric cars had been produced).

Overall, the legislation created some incentives for car makers to look into alternative powertrains through encouraging firms' investments in emission efficient technologies. But to a large extent the range of discussed solutions remained focused on improving the efficiency of internal combustion engines rather than promoting alternative solutions for cleaner mobility. By 2009, the Commission imposed a formal and legislative approach in form of a weighted CO_2 tax (443/2009), a step that is considered "a victory" by a DG policy officer (Interview DG Environment, 2011). Having transformed the governance structures from voluntary to regulatory, the EU Commission built on its scope of action: "This legislation is the cornerstone of the EU's strategy to improve the fuel economy of new cars sold on the European market" as the DG Clima states.[58]

Conclusion 4.1. Elements of a new institutional path

In summary, the political struggle on the first legislative action on CO_2 emissions in the sector's history created (loose) elements of a different future path.

First, it institutionalized a new problem framing of emission reductions. The expertise brought forward in the name of stricter environment and transport regulation created a new discursive frame of reference amongst the network of decision makers: With the EU Parliament, T&E, Greenpeace and others claiming transparency, they invoked civic arguments. "Consumers have the right to know how much every individual car brand is doing to cut emissions." (T&E 2005a:8). They referred to the general right to information to get access to data, claiming this right in their statements accusing ACEA's data protection measures. But, what is more, they linked this argumentation strategy to a technical knowledge, to the IEEP/TNO/CAIR report proving the lower cost of emission reduction, to the still prevailing industrial convention. In addition, they also used market arguments. Continuing the argument cited above, they added: "This would also provide an incentive for manufacturers to cut emissions and capitalise on their environmental performance." (T&E 2005a:8). The fact that they implement arguments from different ways to interpret the problem, as a technical problem of innovation, a political problem of transparency, or a democratic problem of fair interest representation, helped to broaden the problem framing to an emerging network of actors that could adopt it as a shared narrative. Without the building of networks, the alternative problem framing could not have been conveyed. The narrative and its promoters' active

---

[58] Homepage DG Clima: http://ec.europa.eu/clima/policies/transport/vehicles/cars/index_en.htm.

participation in the debate had co-promoted a shift in public opinion, and successfully discredited the industry's strategy of voluntary self-regulation.

Second, it discredited voluntary solutions as part of the EU's sectoral governance. The voluntary de facto standard of 1998 had turned into an obligatory de-jure standard in 2008.

- As initiated by the EU Commission as early as 1995, a CO_2 standard was agreed upon to be implemented in 2012.

- Due to the intense debate with public attention, the network of actors involved had significantly grown.

- Car manufacturers lost credibility as decision-makers, but not as providers of emission-efficiency and therefore as legitimate actors to solve the problem.

Instead, cooperative decision-making procedures were institutionalized. ACEA, stakeholders and the Commission set emission standards with a limited validity. The process produced and stabilized a change in the mode of governance by which these standards were negotiated, channelling lobbying interests through a formalization of negotiation procedures.

This chapter's analysis of micro-level interaction between different interested parties showed a broader critical public was emerging that judged companies' efforts in emission reduction as unsatisfactory. Transport&Environment's reports, and other stakeholders' criticism produced a new publicly shared set of references by which firms were now being judged. The emerging critical public opinion produced the preconditions for an emerging new collective problem framing.

This framing, however, did not question that the agreed standards ascribed the legitimacy to define emission-problems to car makes. Importantly, setting these standards as an instrument reducing emissions closed down further options of future legislation for the near future, by excluding or postponing further additional measures targeting consumption or transport policy. The way to solve the emission reduction problem, it seems, was defined as being a technological one only.

The longer-term institutional consequences, the full impact of emission regulation and possible changes in the automotive path cannot be understood without the context of technological development during the 2000s, during which the European car industry reacted to increasing global competition on greening cars. The following subchapter describes the market dynamics that started to question the car makers' autonomy and dominance from a technological perspective. Competition in alternative powertrain technology challenged the petrol-based combustion engine as the core of global automobile culture – and OEMs' semantic and structural dominance. The combination of regulative pressure (as shown in this subchapter, 4.1.) and investment in emission-saving innovations (the next subchapter, 4.2.) created the necessary conditions in which the financial and structural crisis of the sector allowed alternative narratives to become public.

83

4.2. Eco-innovations and industrial policy: charging the car market's architecture

"Because of its limited usability, electric cars will remain a niche application."
(Volkswagen 2000: 18)

"Volkswagen will be the first car maker to offer every customer an affordable electric car" (Volkswagen 2010: 50)[59]

The shift in Volkswagen's position towards electric cars is representative for a significant semantic shift, transforming the European automotive sector's configuration in terms of technologies and products on offer. Under the impression of the political developments described in the preceding chapter, European automotive firms developed economic and technological strategies to respond to increasingly strict emission regulation. These strategies can be regarded as performative instruments, analogical to policy instruments as defined earlier: companies' technology investments and product strategies set market goals, and by doing so, anticipated and shaped future developments at the same time. As part of the emission conflict, understanding firms' strategies helps to seize their reaction to increasing environmental pressure. While alternatives to the combustion engine had always existed (cf. Chapter 1), the internal combustion engine vehicle's (ICEV) dominance as the mass technology had not been politically questioned before. In connection with political pressure to reduce emissions, cleaner alternatives to the combustion engine showed a new large-scale rupture potential of the automobile path in the late 2000s. Based on public support for the development of fuel cell technology, however, and later plug-in battery technology (with both options a car drives electrically without local emissions), the electric car emerged as a realistic alternative to the combustion engine car in company strategies and policy makers' reflections. In the context of the economic crisis beginning in 2008, the electric car was going to play a central role in questioning car makers' dominance and the hegemony of conventional automobility in European society (Chapter 5). The conditions of its institutionalization, however, were set before, through organizational and semantic integration of emission efficient technology into car markers' strategies, as shown in the following sections.

---

[59] Empirical data collection for this study was finalised in early 2015, later events could not be included in detail. In 2016, after the 'Dieselgate' emission scandal, Volkswagen reinforced its strategy and aimed at selling one third of its vehicles as pure electric battery cars by 2025, http://www.volkswagenag.com/content/vwcorp/info_center/en/news/2016/06/2025.html.

Organisationally, the ground for the electric car's market introduction was prepared through adapting financial resources, Research & Development (R&D)
investments or collective interaction with competitors, for example building
technology networks. Automotive firms, car makers and first tier suppliers
engaged in an increasing number of cooperations with public or private research institutes, industrial partners from other sectors such as telecommunica-
tions, battery and energy production and distribution. Institutionalization of
alternative drivetrains continued as firms had to legitimize these strategic
choices. In order to justify these investments they needed to semantically valorise emission reduction. One narrative strategy to do so was to embed the question of technological emission reduction in a discourse on sustainable development.

Competing alternative technology paths

If technology has been a key pillar supporting the automobility path's stability,
this is due to the hegemony of car makers as dominant firms in the sector's
hierarchy of economic relations. As system integrators, i.e. those firms that
integrate a complex technological system and assembling a product from self-
produced and supplied parts, car makers have been dominating the industry's
complex value chain. The technical term for car makers, Original Equipment
Manufacturer (OEMs), designates this central position in the sector, which
translates into a key role in defining future market developments. Innovations
in engine technology therefore have historically been and still are at the heart
of most automotive firms' competition strategy.[60] Continuous R&D activity is
considered a principal source of innovation and knowledge – and competition,
in particular between engineering departments for bringing future technologies
to market. Historically, this on-going competition for powertrain innovation
created different technology paths that car makers follow through a series of
investments. By the 2000s, two alternative technology paths had emerged as
relevant: fuel cell powertrains, and battery-driven engines (Aigle et al. 2008).[61]

---

[60] Especially in companies such as BMW (originally named Bavarian Engine Producers, Bayer-
ische Motorenwerke) that historically have evolved as engine producers, the organizational
identity and overall market strategy is strongly linked to powertrain development.
[61] A third variant, hydrogen engines, was developed among others by BMW (Aigle et al. 2008).
Hydrogen engines are directly fuelled by combustion by hydrogen, emitting water, while the
related fuel cell engine feeds energy into an electric engine. This alternative, however, has so far
remained marginal and will not be looked at in detail in this study.

Box B: alternative powertrain technologies

Fuel cells produce electric energy from hydrogen and oxygen, emitting water, thus no local pollutants. Electric energy is stored in a battery, which runs an electric motor. The main problems are expensive storage and supply infrastructure for hydrogen, as well as cost and emissions from hydrogen production. Daimler and Toyota are two leading companies in fuel cell technology development. Daimler developed its first fuel cell transporter in 1994. Having invested over 1 billion Euro in fuel cell R&D since then, the firm also disposes of the largest global fleet of test cars (passenger cars and buses); and produced small series of Mercedes B Class and the transporter Vito E-cell. The car maker has initiated an industrial network to promote fuel cell technology (H2 Mobility, September 2009), in which energy providers and car makers collaborate to build a sufficiently dense supply infrastructure for hydrogen filling stations (see below). The timing is not a coincidence: In September 2009, after European CO_2 emission standards were laid down, this represents a further step towards the commercialization of alternative powertrain technologies.

In contrast to a fuel cell car, *a battery car* runs with an electric engine alimented by a battery. For a purely battery-driven electric car (BEV) the electric energy, however, needs to be charged externally by a plug or by induction technology (wireless charging). At the current stage of development, BEVs have a range autonomy of about 150 km on one battery charge, depending on power-consuming equipment such as air conditioning. When battery prices started to fall globally by the end of the 2000s, and battery technology matured, this alternative was considered a market option by European car makers. In the late 2000s, mainly Asian car makers such as Nissan brought BEVs to market, as the electronics and battery industry is mainly located in Asia. As a consequence, European OEMs and industrial policy makers invested relatively late, fearing a loss of ICEV market shares due to this innovation. Battery prices will continue to fall[62], but electric vehicles often stay more expensive than a comparable combustion equivalent and have not yet become price competitive, even though they are cheaper to use.

---

[62] Since 2008, battery costs were cut by a factor four and battery energy density had a fivefold increase, and studies predict that the cost of batteries will continue to decrease significantly over the next decade,
(http://www.iea.org/publications/freepublications/publication/Global_EV_Outlook_2016.pdf).
According to the IEA's global EV outlook, PHEV battery cost estimates fell from about USD 1 000/kWh in 2008 to USD 268/kWh in 2015, which represents a 73% reduction in seven years. The US Department of Energy considers that cost-competitiveness of PHEV batteries relative to conventional batteries will be achieved at USD 125/kWh by 2022 in the United States.

Parallel to investments in alternative powertrains, car makers also invested in a large variety of technologies to reduce emissions from ICEV cars: start-stop mechanisms, light construction with light materials such as carbon fibre, the reduction of tire resistance etc. These measures are generally referred to as efficiency measures. To market these, many car makers brand greener variants of existing car models with special eco-labels.[63]

The figure below shows that emission reduction policy on European level had an impact on car makers' technology strategies. They accelerated spreading efficiency technologies across their vehicle range since the early 2000s, when first imposed targets by the voluntary agreement. In the following years, this unleashed unprecedented investment dynamics among firms to bringing these formerly 'niche' technologies to market. As emissions could not be reduced fast enough, the closer the 2008 target got, the greater these investments became. For German car makers, Bratzel (2010: 77) observes that in the second half of the 2000s "German car makers all moved their innovation focus dramatically towards optimizing conventional powertrain technology, but also developed alternative powertrain options. In 2005, Daimler and BMW only invested 19% in innovating in powertrain, afterwards, this figure doubled."

By the end of the 2000s, two developments converged: Competition on greening of the product range, both promoting more efficient combustion engine technologies *and* the development of alternative technologies and the application of stricter CO_2 regulation. This can be seen a *co-evolution* process of regulation and technology in the European car sector, thus of two key institutional pillars of the 20th century automobile configuration. But the debate still remained technology-focused. (Apart from considerations of consumers' willing-

---

[63] Among European car makers, BMW was the first company to react to innovation pressure by inventing an efficiency-label. It set out a product policy aimed at reducing emissions of all models in all segments through implementing efficiency measures from 2005 onwards. This strategic reorientation was framed by the term of 'sustainability' (see below) that postulated a profitable synergy between development costs and emission targets. By advocating that 'greening' was possible in the current model range of premium combustion engine cars, the company aimed to secure traditional engine technology knowhow, production and R&D structures, and thus profitability of their technological path in the context of increasingly strict emission regulation. This solution was especially convenient for premium car makers: they could optimize fuel consumption while improving performance and improving their green image. Efficiency-labels such as BMW's 'Efficient Dynamics' became a popular marketing solution (BRASS 2010: 30). All other European car makers followed with similar brands: eco² (Renault), BlueMotion (VW) etc. Branded as commercialized, eco-efficient cars created new arguments with which car makers could justify increasing investments into greening technologies to stakeholders, experts and media observers, customers as well as the general public.

ness to buy efficiency-labelled premium cars, the third pillar, the consumer, so far had not been considered.) The following sections explain organizational and semantic impacts of competition on greening cars.

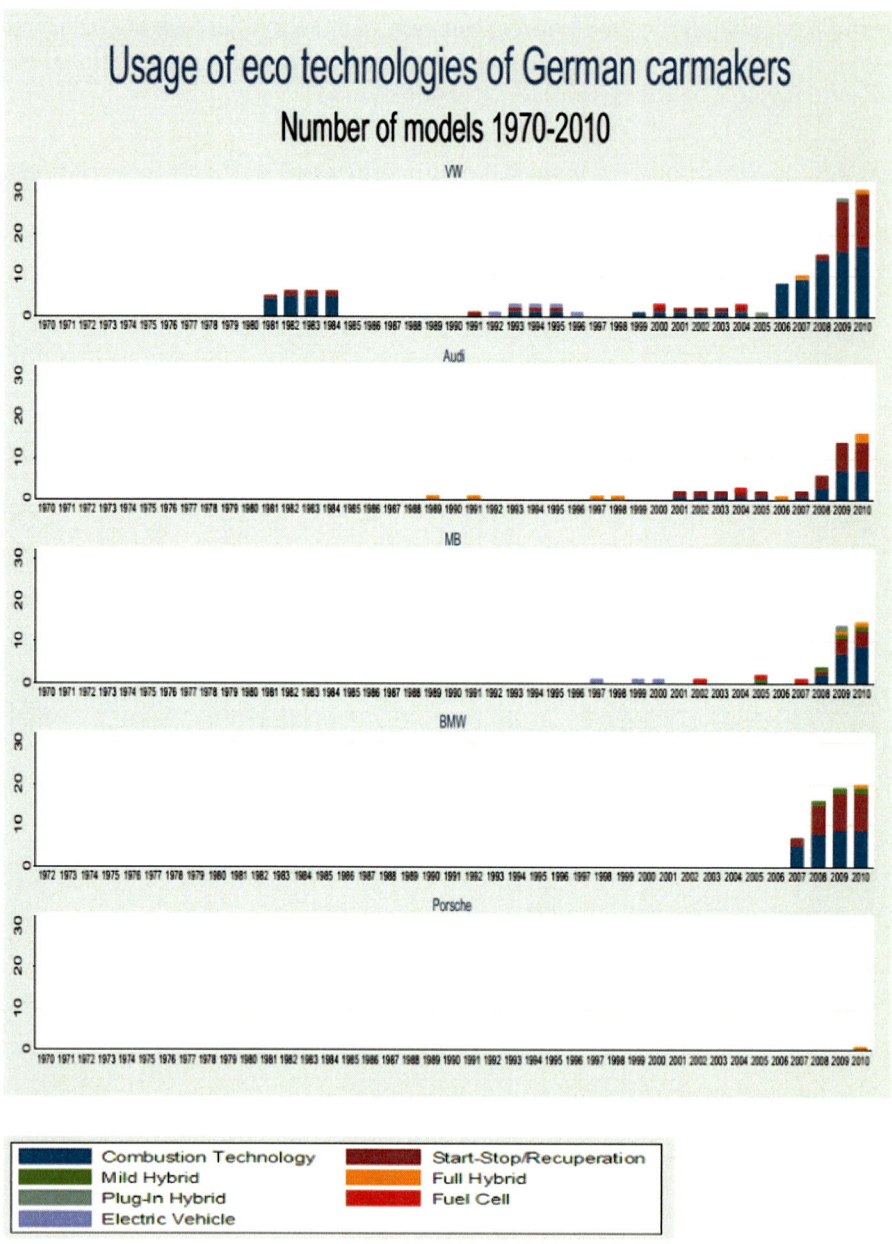

Figure 4: Alternative technologies of German car makers since 1970 (prototypes and small series). (Source: Jürgens et al. 2010: 235)

Organizational shift: alternative technology networks

Through financial investments in Research and Development, in combination with investing in political lobbying resources, alternative powertrain technologies became part of the sector's semantic and organizational structures. Early political support for hydrogen/fuel cell technology had already helped alternative powertrain options to gain credibility among political actors of the sector.

Hydrogen and fuel cell technology as an alternative engine technology was especially valorised in the early 2000s (Marz/Galic 2010, 2012). Taking public investments as an indicator, Marz and Galic (2010) show for Germany that funding hydrogen and fuel cell Research&Development [R&D] projects has been growing significantly. After a first increase in support in the 1990 (phases 2 and 3), support doubled in the 2000s (phase 4) and rose exponentially in the second half of the 2000s (phase 5).

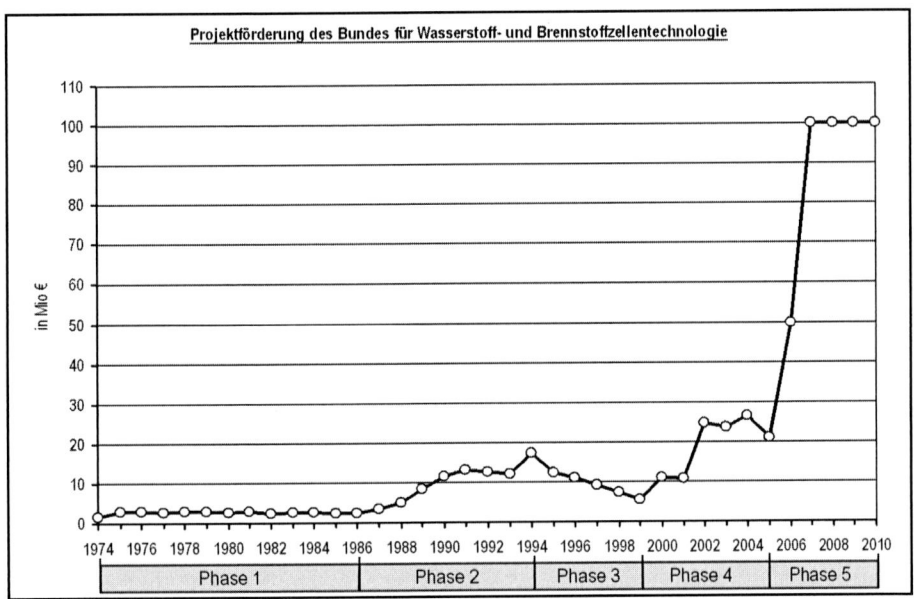

Figure 5: Public funding of R&D of hydrogen and fuel cell technology in Germany in million Euro (Source: Marz/Galic 2010: 26)

Figure 5 further illustrates the potential impact of public innovation funding on the marketization of alternative technologies and thus, organizational change.

We can read the depicted funding peaks as a curve that ascribes value (through granting R&D projects) to the technology as an alternative to combustion-engines. The higher the funding, the more expected social and economic benefits of the innovation could be justified, the more credible and necessary actors judged alternative hydrogen and fuel cell technology. Linking this development to the history of emission regulation, the curve confirms the structural coherence or co-evolution between the sector's political and economic developments.

The first peak around 1994 corresponds to the beginning of the environmental policy debate at European level and the first examination of fiscal limits. The car market underwent a significant sales crisis during those years; the need for alternatives to the dominant model was rising. The same pattern is repeated in the early 2000s (phase 4), when fuel cell technology funding increased again. Efforts into meeting the voluntary targets of 2008 had begun. Industry gathered in technology promotion networks to raise public funding, these associations further increased public authorities awareness of R&D needs, which in turn secured further funding. Public innovation funding is also intrinsically linked to companies' own R&D investments, as the state usually only co-finances projects by a maximum of 50% of the overall investment budget. The European emission limits are likely to have played a role in investment choices and raised the share of overall R&D resources allocated to alternative powertrain development, explaining the exponential rise of innovation funding in phase 5. With upcoming fixed emission limits through the voluntary agreement, compnies and the state invested even higher shares of R&D in fuel cell development. The exponential rise of funding since the mid-2000s, at the mid-term time of the voluntary agreement when the gap to target became public, forced firms to increase investments.

The assumed direct link between political pressure through regulation and company strategy has not been discussed by literature, which focusses either on market, or on policy developments, but rarely on both. More research needs to be done to further prove it.[64] It can be explained by a process of organizational adaptation of the car sector's innovation policy structures in the mid-2000s on the national and European level: Increasing need for emission-efficient technologies created a process of network building, advocacy for funding and public debate on this topic. Consequently car makers' technology strategies need to be considered also as political investments. Research in science and technology studies as well as cultural studies of technology have considered niches of al-

---

[64] There is, however, further evidence for Germany: in 2001, the NIP started a larger investment into fuel cell research, very soon after the agreement of emission limits in 1999.

ternative technologies as a structure consisting of networks of actors and coherent narrative that seek to create value of these marginalized technologies in
the broader public (Marz/Galic 2010). In this perspective it is not surprising
that these more or less formalized networks function similarly to political interest groups. They unite professionals and firms in a primarily technical interest
to promote R&D in a specific technology, in particular through large innovation funds such as European Research Framework Programmes, and are often
industrial, or public-private.

Germany's public-private strategy to lower emission through fuel cell technology is an example of a technology advocacy network. It is no coincidence that
in May 1998, when the emission reduction agreement had taken shape, the
coporations ARAL, BMW, Daimler, MAN, RWE, Shell and VW founded a
network on a "transport economical energy strategy" (*Verkehrswirtschaftliche
Energiestrategie* - VES) jointly with the German Transport Ministry (later
joined by Ford, GM/Opel, Total and Vattenfall). This association is unique in
its trans-sectoral character: "An association of representatives of government,
the car industry, mineral oil companies and energy providers unique in Europe"
(VES 2007: 5) VES' initial priority objective, to lead global competition in
alternative energy technologies for road transport was revised after a few years
of operation in the early 2000s). Instead, companies focused on the reduction of
emissions and oil dependency (Marz/Galic 2010:32). The rising pressure of
European emission regulation in those years appears to have caused this organisational reorientation.

The VES network aimed at social and political recognition for fuel cell technology at national and European level. The main goal was to initiate demonstration projects on the European level, so as to create legitimacy for this alternative through illustrating its practical feasibility and create positive public
awareness. The network's second aim was to promote technical standards to
facilitate its introduction in European road traffic. These activities created a
growing international expert network of automotive engineers, politicians, and
promotion organizations. Expert networks allow participants to create additional fora to exchange and promote ideas beyond the strategic limits of the company.[65] However, even with increasing support, the hydrogen and fuel cell
lobby did not fully succeed in discrediting important obstacles perceived by
industry and public authorities. One reason that fuel cell technology remains
marginal today is that cell cars need hydrogen supply, which requires a costly
infrastructure over the entire European market. Hydrogen production, and stor-

---

[65] The German dominance in these networks is largely explained by the fact that German car
makers, Daimler and BMW, MAN, invested most in fuel cell technology.

age, is equally costly. However, the niche can be expected to grow in the future, as for example Toyota continues investments in fuel cell technology (automotive news 2014).

Emerging technology networks produced organizational structures for future path change. In Germany, the National Organization for Hydrogen and Fuel Cell Technology (NOW), was founded in 2008, to coordinate the national innovation programme on hydrogen and fuel cell technology. This organization will build the future governance structure of electric vehicle support politics (Chapter 5) ascribing social and economic value to alternative propulsion technologies (Marz/Galic 2010). The European equivalent, the Fuel Cell and Hydrogen Joint Technology Initiative (FCHJTI) was also founded in 2008. When the FCHJTI was founded, a major step towards the institutionalization of support for fuel cell technology was achieved (Interview 13). To the extent that public innovation politics contributed financial resources to the development of these technologies; and emission reduction efforts were critically followed by the public, fuel cell electric cars gained credibility as future replacements of the combustion engine.

In the late 2000s, parallel to the increasingly broadly organized innovation funding of fuel cells, the battery-electric car gained support as a second alternative powertrain technology. Initially, this alternative had remained in the margin of car makers' and political attention, as Volkswagen's estimate from 2000 shows. But with cheaper batteries and electricity, battery cars turned out to be manageable in terms of infrastructure, as they can be charged anywhere, even at household sockets or at public charging stations. These are cheaper than hydrogen stations. The association AVERE (Association des Véhicules Electriques Routiers Européens - European Association for Electric Road Vehicles) was among the first to promote its advantages.[66] Compared to the relatively well organized networks advocating the fuel cell, the BEV lobby had fewer financial and personal resources at its disposal. Nevertheless, since 2008 battery car technology has received more and more political attention, and subsequently funding, by public authorities. It seems that in 2008, despite the fact that fuel cell funding was still very high, public attention shifted to a problem-solution-framing that embraced the battery electric car as the solution for the many of the entire industry's problems, for example overcapacities in Europe

---

[66] Founded in 1978; the association was active in the 2000s on a European scale. It relies mostly on secondary data and external expertise and promotes advantages of BEVs at different discussion fora of automotive policy. However, in the late 2000s, the association has been more prominent in France as a 5 staff observatory where it could concentrate knowledge and create events after 2009. On the European level, other sectoral associations such as those of battery producers or electricity providers participated more actively in the debate (5.2.)

and comparatively cheap batteries from Asia. The co-evolution of "problem/solution framing" (Marz/Galic 2010) between public authorities and companies in regards to specific technology options is also confirmed for the battery electric car since the 1970s (Callon 1979).

The following section argues that on the background of increasing organizational integration of alternative engine technology, the collective semantic adaptation of the (battery) electric car solution prepared its path-breaking impact during and after the 2008 economic crisis. From the mid-2000s onwards, firms sought to valorise their R&D efforts and thus openly debated the role technological strategies should play in emission reduction in particular, and industrial policy in general. The concept of sustainable development served as an argumentative template to spread an image of greening and companies' environmental responsibility. Linking investments into alternative powertrains to companies' contribution to sustainable development created semantic preconditions for the collectivize diffusion of a new common problem framing on green alternative drivetrains, accompanying the organizational shift.

Semantic shift: sustainability reporting

Since the late 1990s car makers had used the term 'sustainable development' linking their strategic decisions, for example R&D investments in alternative powertrain strategies, to wider ecological, economic and social benefits. The main medium of this public framing exercise justifying new investment strategies were companies' so-called *sustainability reports*, published regularly in addition to the obligatory annual report, addressing shareholders and stakeholders likewise. These reports are a useful source revealing firms' argumentative strategies, in fact, they document a considerable semantic shift. Emission-efficient conventional and alternative powertrain technologies were no longer presented as an additional environmental cost a company had to face but as an economically promising investment in the future. A good case in point are Volkswagen reports: While Volkswagen considers environment protection still a costly trade-off in 1995: ("environmental protection is costly", Volkswagen 1995: 41), eight years later, the company claimed synergies between ecological and social goals in order to meet economic targets: "We are convinced that long-term economic success is only achievable by integrating social and ecologic aspects into company policy."[67] (Volkswagen 2003: 8).

As a communication instrument for companies, sustainability reports represent the spirit of voluntary agreements in the sense that they represent corporate instruments to tackle emission reductions – based on their problem framing. They were created as a means of publishing results from firms' commitment to conduct voluntary eco-auditing schemes such as the European Eco Management and Audit Scheme (EMAS). Open for participation since 1995, EMAS allowed companies to develop strategic objectives to meet sustainability goals (economic, ecological and social targets) and gain consent to these by public authorities.[68] Companies soon entered into competition for environmental certificates, with sustainability reports as a marketing tool to provide visibility for their voluntary efforts to increase their sustainability. But although environmental management systems have become an integral part of environmental strategy on company level[69], literature emphasizes that in this voluntary scheme, company compliance means they were entitled to co-produce their results and therefore (mis-)use a public control mechanism, maintaining control over greening their image (Reverdy 2005). In this sense, sustainability reports also reflect how car makers had adapted and made use of a dominant neo-liberal shift from environmental government to sustainable governance that had emerged with the Lisbon Agenda on EU level.

As a widely diffused marketing tool, SD reports had increased public attention to car makers' environmental policy by the mid-2000s. The reports were therefore used as a basis for "dialoguing with [partners and] challengers" as VW puts it (Volkswagen 2003:6), for example to communicate with critical observers such as environmental groups. Based on global guidelines for sustainable development and transparency, for example the Global Reporting Initiative developed in 2000 with the United Nations Environment Program, they provide an additional tool to comparatively judge companies' market behaviour in environmental terms: Did they invest sufficiently in emission-efficient technologies? A critical public of experts, including consumer organizations, started to observe and compare car makers' performances based on similar sustainability rankings (IÖW/Future 2009; Merten 2009). These rankings by external expert observers provided a public and scientific legitimation of corporate strategic

---

[68] Reporting EMAS results, in 1995 Volkswagen published a report on "VW's environmental policy", the first of a series of reports that would later transform into broader 'sustainability reports'. Among German car makers, compliance to environmental standards however differed: VW appears to be a forerunner by applying eco-audits to its German sites from 1995, BMW and Daimler were forced to follow by the early 2000s

[69] In 1996, the international ISO 14001 standard for environment management was drawn up, and was integrated into the revised EMAS II (2001) and EMAS III (2009) eco-audit schemes by the European Commission.

investments. As a communication tool, multiple ranking and reporting practices diffused a narrative on sustainability as a part of overall company competitiveness. During the 2000s, the umbrella term of sustainable development was increasingly stretched to justify R&D investments and economic profitability, countering its initial idea of long-term resource efficiency ad absurdum. Firms had succeeded in turning sustainable development into a profit strategy. Its use corresponds to the increasingly neo-liberal use that European politics made of it in the debate on emission reduction (Dezalay 2007). Car makers' use of the concept confirms Carter at al.'s (2014) finding that it has "increasingly been subordinated to the norm of competitiveness as enshrined in 'the Lisbon Strategy' of 2000" (Carter el al. 2014: 167).

The semantic shift of companies endorsing sustainability provided a medium for car makers to anticipate European environmental regulation. When competition on commercialization of alternative technologies had become explicit by 2007 (see below), reports included increasingly long and detailed sections on how each car maker had invested in emission-efficient, hybrid or electric cars. This justified car makers' efforts to their shareholders and other stakeholders. Publicly reporting the willingness to invest in alternative technologies through sustainability reporting helped stabilize, at least in the short term, the car makers' control of the discourse. OEMs focused on technology as a controllable variable to reach required emission reductions.

But the semantic shift to sustainability provided an opportunity for alternative narratives on mobility to emerge. Consumers were more explicitly addressed through extensive reporting. Firms put forward the environmental benefits of green cars and green mobility as fitting consumers' purchase and driving attitudes. Presenting their products as coherent with these criteria, a new discourse emerged in which the consumer/driver is ascribed a more active role than in the classic supply-oriented automobility path. Volkswagen in particular had been communicating on the topic of sustainable mobility since 1998. It presented current trends in shared on-demand bus services and shared car fleets, which remained, however, at the experimental stage in the 1990s (Volkswagen 1999:88). Ten years late, this argument was indeed pioneering a larger trend and institutional shift in the sector (see Chapter 5). One reason why the company developed an additional narrative, that of shared mobility, may be the strong influence of progressive workers' unions on the company's strategic development.

New narratives develop: Shared and sustainable mobility

"The dominant position of the automobile today needs to be rethought to make it part of an integrated approach to the traffic and transport system...This objective requires a change in our thinking and cooperation on the part of all stakeholders involved: automotive manufacturers, car drivers, politicians, urban and traffic planners, the trade unions, environmental groups and automobile associations.(...) We need an integrated approach that puts the complex interrelations and interactions of environmental, transport, industrial and employment policies into one strategic perspective." (Peters 2007: 15)

This 2007 vision by the head of the most influential German Workers' Union IG Metall is surprisingly progressive for two reasons. First, it outlines a transport system in which the car's status as the predominant means of transport is replaced by it being part of the larger transport system. Second, it suggests a new hierarchy for the sector's governance: align the objectives of different stakeholders in coherent guidelines by which the industry should be developed. Emission reduction is presented here as an industrial policy of which every actor would benefit. Peters articulates the need for a restructuring of the combustion-based automobility path and the way it is governed.

This radical view shows that during the 2000s, car makers' investments and the emergence of a discursive space on integrated ecological and economic investments had created room for *different visions of automobility as a whole*. As employees of large car makers and suppliers, workers' unions benefit at the same time from the success of the combustion engine car, securing jobs, and from their employers' investments into innovations, which result in value creation and the building of new competences. They are therefore critical observers of the car makers' politics but also interested in a sectoral policy securing their strong role in the industry.

The European Commission had contributed to institutionalise this space of discussion in which unions could put forward such ideas. In 2007, sectoral actors were developing a coherent vision of the industry's future, at the initiative of the European Commission. In order to create a forum of coordination, and to incite firms to overcome national competitive thinking to the benefit of a harmonized European market, the leaving Enterprise & Industry Commissioner Verheugen initiated the "industrial restructuring forum" in 2007. Next to industrial supply chain associations and firms, the EU Commission (DGs Employment, Enterprise & Industry, Regional Policy) and the European Investment Bank, automotive cluster regions (Piemont, Slovenia), trade unions at national and European level, the French labour minister and applied research institutes were present. The high and diverse participation confirms an interest in cooperative industrial politics, addressing mainly the urgent problems of relocation and cost pressure on European production.

But also other stakeholders started to formulate ideas on how increasingly researched alternative engine technologies could contribute to reduce emissions. During the negotiations on the CO_2 limits in 2007, which were to replace the voluntary agreement by car makers, one among 50 registered stakeholders that advocated the electric car as a means to significantly reduce emissions of cars: AVERE, the Paris-based 'European association for battery, hybrid and fuel cell electric vehicles' drew "the European Authorities' attention to the fact that battery and hybrid electric vehicles are available solutions that offer immediate benefits for energy economy and CO_2 emission reduction." (AVERE 2007:1). In its communication, the association of firms from different sectors that are interested in the promotion of this technological niche, asked the European Commission to support research, development and demonstration programmes of e-car batteries, and study the potential of integrating e-cars as an emission-free car in urban transport systems.

By 2007, the narrative diffusion of different technological solutions to the emission reduction problem (through reporting and marketing) was no longer a discursive control tool of car makers. A more open debate inspired a wider range of stakeholders such as environmental groups and trade unions to express other ideas on the role of the car and its use, starting to question the dominant alternative path, semantically as well as organisationally. Although these discussions remained marginal at the time, they contributed to the fact that car markers found themselves in an ambiguous position. On the one hand, increasing R&D investments allowed them to officially embrace arguments for the greening of car traffic in general, and thus valorise their R&D efforts and political commitments. On the other hand, they feared losing autonomy over defining technology strategies which so far had been publicly accepted as the best solution to tackle environmental problems. This hegemony, supported through technology advocacy networks, had guaranteed firms a market for their innovations and was now losing exclusive influence over the allocation of R&D resources.

On the backdrop of increasing pressure on emission-reduction, competitive risks for each car maker to find technological answers and given the remaining structural overcapacities on the European market, the entire automotive industry engaged in talks with the European Commission to identify ways of supporting its competitiveness. The CARS 21 talks of 2005/2006 were an institutionalized stakeholder forum and as such a novelty in the sector in that it allowed an inclusive strategic coordination on formally bilateral industrial poli-cy-making. The fact that environmental policy and CO_2 limits were on the agenda, allowed formerly excluded stakeholders to become part of the extend-ed network of decision-makers in the EU automotive sector.

Towards a more diverse and balanced EU industrial policy?

The so-called CARS 21 process, seeking to install a 'Competitive Automotive Regulation System for the 21st century' emerged as an arena used by industrial actors to determine future legislation - and avoid too much of it. Dominated by car makers who defined terms and contents of talks, they were necessarily re-stricted to a perspective of industrial policy and competitiveness. Yet, this pub-lic-private coordination exercise produced further deviations of the formerly hierarchical power structure in the sector, mainly on an organizational level. First, due to its official character, the arena was open to critical stakeholders who made use of this opportunity. Second, car maker lobby ACEA had changed discursive strategy. Instead of claiming a unique framing of the emis-sion problem as technical and thus subject to product politics, they had realized with the approaching limits that they would benefit from sharing the burden, promoting what they referred to as the "integrated approach".

The forum allowed an official stage to be established upon which future envi-ronmental struggles could be fought - and critics such as environmental NGOs became visible as actors of general industrial policy making. However, this was clearly not the intention at the beginning of the talks. With the goal to raise competitiveness in a harmonized European car market, CARS 21 was the first policy arena dedicated explicitly to industrial policy making at European level. In January 2005, the High Level Group[70] CARS 21 was set up, in a bilateral manner under the main initiative of Verheugen and then ACEA President Bernd Pischetsrieder, ACEA president in 2004/2005 and CEO of VW from 2002 to 2006.[71] The effort to create democratic legitimacy through a public

---

[70] High-Level Groups comprise experts and stakeholders and are constituted by the European Commission. They are assigned a specific task, often to work out detailed legislation options from different represented viewpoints, for a limited period of time. High-Level Groups comprise administrative technical working groups but also representatives of political decision-makers, and are set up for various policy fields. In the European decision-making process, they allow compromise on legislation to be established beforehand, and are thus an instrument of coopera-tive policy-making.

[71] As the press release announcing the first meeting on 11 April 2005 details, "The group's ob-jective is to generate recommendations to improve the worldwide competitiveness of the Europe-

character remained rather symbolical. The group was reported to consist of "prominent representatives of the EU car sector, member states, the European Parliament, trade unions, NGO, users and the Commission" (Cars 21: 2005). On closer inspection, participation was clearly not that balanced[72].

But even if the analysis of the events shows that ACEA and the DG Enterprise had pre-defined the arena in terms of scope, focus, participation and outcomes along their *terms of play*, the fact that these were officially set, created the de facto right for other stakeholders to claim access. Critical stakeholders could legitimately claim access to the decision-making process. The European consumer organization BEUC, representing consumers in all sectors including drivers and car buyers, criticized the constitution and terms of discussion. "We would like to reiterate that consumers are not represented in this group. We already expressed at several occasions our concerns regarding the establishment, composition and method of working of the group itself." (Degallaix 2007:2). Transport&Environment, jointly with the European Transport and Safety Council[73], characterized the bias as a major obstacle for progressive environmental politics in the sector: "We're concerned that safety and the environment will not be at the top of this group's priority list unless groups such as ours who represent experts as well as all road users are present" said ETSC director Jörg Beckmann. Jos Dings, T&E director commented, "We are also surprised to see that neither the transport or environment committees of the Parliament (responsible for safety and emissions legislation respectively) are

---

an automotive industry. It shall make recommendations for the short, medium and the long term public policy and regulatory framework for the European automotive industry that enhances global competitiveness and employment while sustaining further progress in safety and environmental performance at a price affordable to the consumer." (Cars 21 2005:1).

[72] With seven representatives of individual car makers' and their lobby, the suppliers' association and the petrol industry, 3 commissioners, 2 European Parliament deputies and 5 ministers from member states, voices critical to competitiveness-enhancing legislation were represented quite poorly: The director of the environmental Think Tank IEEP was supposed to generally represent environmental organizations. Consumers were represented by the FIA, the Fédération Internationale de l'Automobile, a drivers' association promoting "the rights of motoring organizations and motor car users throughout the world via campaigns and activities that defend their interests" (FIA 2014). It represents national drivers associations such as ADAC in Germany which is the largest member. FIA can be considered to be the more conservative consumer representation, while Europe's general consumers' association BEUC, was not invited to the consultations. Finally, the European Trade Unions Federation was invited to represent industry's employees' interests. Note that Transport&Environment, who started to publish emission reports at the time, were not included either.

[73] ETSC (European Transport Safety Council) is an independent think tank specializing in promoting road safety. Located in Brussels, the organization is financed by the European Commission and various firms from different affected sectors.

represented on the group. If the Commission is serious about 'clean' and 'safe' then we look forward to being invited to participate when CARS-21 meet for the first time in March." (T&E/ETSC 2005).

Critics link the lack of transparency in the talks to the weak results in terms of environmental policy. As Greenpeace sums up: "The objective of CARS 21 was to avoid emission legislation" (Interview 27). This judgement does not seem exaggerated. Document analysis reveals that CO_2 regulation was dealt with in very vague terms, which suggests that participants could not find a compromise.[74] According to the available documents of the meetings, the discussions on the emissions strategy consisted in a joint evaluation of the current regulatory situation – the voluntary agreement in force and the EU's attempts to replace it by fiscal legislation – and the formulation of a common strategy on how to deal with the topic in the following years. Most representatives of the car industry successfully agreed on the integrated approach: mobilize not only technology-based measures to reduce CO_2 emissions from cars, but also add infrastructure efficiency and driving behaviour. "Specifically for the CO_2 emissions and the road safety sections, the discussions *were structured on the basis of an integrated approach* [emphasis J.H.], in which a number of actions aimed at reaching the policy goals and coming from vehicle technology, infrastructure and the driver were identified and assessed. The conclusions reached in these two areas reflect the approach followed." (European Commission 2006: 69). For a short period, the term was picked up by most of the organizations that discussed CO_2 regulations and industrial policy in general, but not all of them agreed on its content. While workers' unions' chairpersons had suggested a new vision of transport policy and the car (see above), car makers seem to have had a vision of burden-sharing in mind as far as the cost of the upcoming emission regulation was concerned.

---

[74] Environmental policy was one out of four topics in total that were covering the most important issues of collective industrial policy at the time: "Better Regulation" (which could be qualified as harmonization efforts in line with industry goals), "Competitiveness", "Environment" and "Road Safety". The pillar on "Environment" dealt with "pollutant emissions (for light and heavy duty vehicles, respectively), CO_2 emissions (follow-up to the Community strategy on CO_2 emissions from passenger cars, as well as alternative fuels and public procurement), mobile air conditioning systems and end-of-life vehicles directive." (European Commission 2006: 69). These issues were all answers to current regulative approaches by the European Commission.

Box C: Attempts at adverse problem-framing: the 'integrated approach' and why it failed

Fearing sanctions on emission limits, car makers intended to spread the idea of an integrated approach among networks of stakeholders. This idea allowed the CO_2 question as well as other issues such as road safety to be re-framed without publicly admitting the failure of the voluntary agreement. In a well-researched report on the ACEA's role in environmental conflict from 2004/5 onwards, Greenpeace (2008) has identified this as a 'hegemonic strategy' to delay urgently needed efforts to reduce emissions.[75] The political context confirms that this effort of framing was indeed a promising way to regain lost definitional power on the topic of emission reduction: In 2004 the voluntary agreement came under the Commission's scrutiny when an impact assessment was conducted (DLR 2004). Already at that time, ACEA had spread the message in the press that in order to efficiently reduce CO_2 emissions, the EU should consider "a broader range of factors when setting emissions targets from 2008"[76]. This standpoint indicates a sharp contrast to 1998, when the same firms tried to prevent public interference in emission regulation by all means. On the backdrop of the EU Commission's multiple initiatives to realize CO_2 reduction by other means (labelling, tax harmonization, ...) six years later, and realizing that meeting the targets would not be realistic, ACEA members called for dividing the emission sharing burden on many shoulders. This shift indeed reveals the lobby's new strategy to remain in control of ways of decision-making in the sector and to secure its dominant position. By trying to forge a new collectively accepted narrative, they hoped to shape the distribution of roles after 2008, beyond the end of the voluntary agreement. Their efforts fell on fruitful ground as the DG Enterprise & Industry Commissioner, the German Günter Verheugen, was known to be favourable to the car industry's cause, promoting a liberal economic policy and the important revenue- and employment-securing function of the car industry. The strategic intentions behind this term are revealed by a letter by ACEA president Marchionne to Commission President Barroso: "Unfortunately, we note today that certain services of the

---

[75] Even if some of its claims are overstated due to its interested role as an active opponent, in favour of stricter climate goals, the report is a valuable source of information, transparent in its research and sources as well as in its messages. Much of this chapter's information on lobbying by nature difficult to access activities is drawn from this report (Greenpeace 2008) as a secondary source.

[76] Off target: the UK must double the pace of its annual emissions reductions to meet targets. In: The engineer, 2.4.2004, by David Fowler, in: http://www.highbeam.com/doc/1G1-116068422.html, cited in Greenpeace 2008:9.

Commission do not respect the *Integrated Approach* [emphasis J.H.]..." (On January 27, 2007, cited in Greenpeace 2008: 10).

But concerning emission reduction regulation, car makers did not succeed in shaping the future regulation through an adverse framing. It did indeed allow industry to secure autonomy in the sense that it remained a dominantly techno-logical approach. But how parts of the burden were to be distributed among other stakeholders remained unclear. In contrast to the technological, engine- and fuel-related measures to reduce CO_2, no agreement could be reached on the additional non-technological measures that were discussed: "What concerns those pillars, which have thus far been left out of the quantified integrated ap-proach (i.e. eco-driving, infrastructure, traffic management), it should be inves-tigated whether and how it is possible to measure their contribution in the fu-ture." (European Commission 2008: v). Vague results do not surprise: those stakeholders that would have detailed non-technological-' aspects were not officially part of the debate.

The need to coordinate strategic orientations with public authorities was taken further in the industry. CARS 21 was not the only arena of sectoral decision-making that was created on the European level. In mid 2005, when car makers where pursuing the development of alternative technologies, there was a need to attract generous financial support for on-going investments in alternative and efficient engine technologies. The car industry, therefore driven by the large suppliers, simultaneously created its own lobby organization ERTRAC. First-tier suppliers are those companies in the automotive value chain that produce most of the innovations and of the actual added-value. They are therefore most dependent on engine innovations. ERTRAC was founded in 2004, as an answer to the OEM-dominated official consultations, mainly by suppliers to coordinate research and public support demand on the European level.

The organizational and semantic rearrangement of sectoral policy had an im-pact that car makers had not anticipated: Because no consensus on non-technological measures of emission reduction such as consumer information and CO_2 taxes could be reached[77], this alternative had now become an official alternative and helped a marginalized narrative to obtain a more important role in the discussion. For the first time, the need for a long-term vision in which

---

[77] "Stakeholders agree that the integrated approach is most effective when a strong demand-side framework complements measures taken on the supply side and therefore recognize that taxation policy has an important role to play with regard to consumers." (CARS 21 mid-term review 2008:v)

cars are part of a larger transport policy problem, was articulated. As a result of the new common problem-framing as integrative, ACEA lost some problem-definition capacity.

Towards 2007, the strategic shift of car manufacturers towards alternative technologies, and the previously discussed narrative on sustainability converged into a common effort to redefine the governance of the industry itself. The emerging network of political and economic actors defining terms of industrial governance, including environmental policy, illustrates that an important conception of control and reproduction mechanism of the automobile path had transformed: Instead of deciding through hegemony, car makers seek co-ordination with public authorities. In coherence with the new framing of sectoral governance as an integrated approach, the emerging network of actors is an important pre-condition for a new institutional path to emerge.

Market diffusion: global green car competition in 2007

"We want to become the world's most environmentally friendly car maker"
(Volkswagen 2009: 9)

The joint dynamics of CO_2 regulation, investments in alternative engine technologies and coordinated sectoral policy for Europe had placed emission reduction at the heart of car makers' competitive strategy and competitiveness in the late 2000s. The financial and marketing investments of car manufacturers resulted in rising competition on greening the car fleet in the second half of the 2000s. As figure 4 shows, in a long-term comparison, many more models are equipped with alternative or conventional efficiency technology; and efficiency technologies diffused into available models.[78] European competition on the single market was significantly accelerated as Japanese Toyota, the world's largest car maker and fierce competitor of Volkswagen for this position, had reached a surprise success in Japan and European markets with the hybrid car 'Prius'.

---

[78] For example, VW's share of models equipped with start-stop-fuel-saving-mechanisms are almost 50% of the whole fleet. The introductory quote shows that the firm makes environmental targets an important development objective.

Box D: The surprise success of the Prius

The first hybrid car in series had transformed quickly from an outsider to a bestseller: the first generation of Toyota's Prius went on sale in Japan in 1997 and was globally sold 123000 times. The car emitted by then 114g CO_2/km. By end of June 2013, global sales reached 3 million units in total, the current model emitting only 89g CO_2/km[79]. The surprise success of the Prius in Europe raised awareness among European car makers to the fact that low emission cars had become a competitiveness factor worldwide, and that they would lose domestic market shares if they did not offer similar products.

Japanese competition had been a point of conflict and a significant feature of foreign trade policy since the early 1990s and the very reason of ACEA's refoundation. By 2008, it was not only Toyota's investment strategy as the world's largest car maker which threatened European competitors, but also the fact that battery prices fell significantly by the late 2000s. Japanese car maker Nissan, as well as Chinese firms such as BYD explored the market for battery electric cars.

Realizing that Japanese and even Chinese car makers had built a competitive advantage should alternative technologies become the technological foundation of mass market one day, European car makers reacted with fierce competition. This situation showed some similarities to that of the early 1990s when European car makers feared Asian competition. The need to build sufficient R&D and production capacities to offer hybrid and later pure electric cars at competitive prices had been reactivated as a guiding idea in arguing for an even more strongly coordinated industrial policy among European authorities (Chapter 5).

Forced into market competition on a not yet matured technology, each European car maker faced different trade-offs on how to integrate alternative powertrain options into their product and future market strategies. Volume producers such as VW, French car makers Renault and PSA and Italian Fiat were less concerned, as they were strongly represented in small and medium segments. German premium car makers were specifically affected, as it is more costly to reduce emissions of heavy cars (heavy engines with heavy comfort equipment) that consume much fuel. The way especially BMW and Daimler will solve the difficult trade-off between the pressure to produce low emission cars on the one

[79] Source: http://www.toyota.de/news/details-2013-57.json

hand, and conserve their brand image as premium car makers[80] and meet related consumer demand patterns will determine an important market change, setting market conditions for the electric car in 2009: they foster technological conditions such as lightweight construction, and, by means of compensating CO_2 emissions of upper-range cars, developed the emission-efficient mini cars in the lower market segments.

The developments summarized in the following, illustrate deviations from the classic conception of automobility of 2007/2008:

- New segments emerged: A strategy of premium car makers to lower average CO_2 emissions across the entire fleet was to diversify their product range by investing in new car segments (Blöcker/Hildermeier forthcoming). Both Daimler and BMW run a twofold strategy in order to meet new regulation and consumer demands at the same time. The low emission mini cars Smart and Mini are vehicles that can compensate for heavier and emission-intensive vehicles as the CO_2 average emission is calculated over the entire range of products. As small, light cars for urban use, these models can be easily electrified. Smart is available as an electric version and thus counted as a zero-emission car for EU emission limits. The mini car segment was to set the structural conditions for the development of new mobility concepts a few years later (Chapter 5).

- New materials are used: In order to nevertheless meet new ecological demands, car makers increasingly use light materials such as carbon fibre. An example are BMW's investments in producing electric carbon fibre cars i3 and i8, which are the first passenger cars in which the passenger cabin will be entirely built of carbon fibre. For premium car makers, however, this poses a challenge to traditional ways of design as heavy steel constructions are still associated with safety. Environmental associations criticize that materials reducing weight not necessarily reduce emissions – especially when the material itself requires a lot of energy to be produced such as aluminium. The same is true for

---

[80] Premium car makers are expected to deliver quality products. The brand image remains especially bound to heavy luxury materials such as leather, increasing a car's weight. They also need to meet highest safety standards which require more equipment. The role of premium car makers is an important one, shaping the European market economically and politically: value-added per sold unit is higher than that of a volume car. Premium car makers chose to follow political developments without compromising their profitable business model. They tried to preserve the value and the diffusion of the combustion engine as a key part of what defines a premium car.

the production of hydrogen for fuel cells or lithium-ion batteries where naturally scarce rare earth is used.

- Firms build new know-how and extend R&D relations: These innovations require an increasing number of R&D collaborations beyond traditional sectoral borders (Chapter 5). The fact that OEMs invested in these R&D collaborations and produced new development 'in house', instead of having them built externally by suppliers, shows that firms consider them of great strategic importance. This confirms the traditional role of premium car makers as drivers for innovations in the value chain.

- New marketing concepts are tested: To secure brand values, premium car makers start marketing green luxury vehicles. The label was supposed to facilitate consumers' acceptance of converted premium car models into green premium cars (such as BMW7er and the X6 as mild and full hybrids). However, premium car makers struggle to accept this term.

Conclusion 4.2. Cooperative sectoral governance

Chapter 4.2. showed how a collective problem framing on CO_2 emission regulation had developed into a broader and shared narrative anchored in the governance structures of the entire sector. Although the CO_2 emission standards in 2009 officially rather narrowly defined the solution to emission reduction as technological alternatives to be defined by car-makes, two developments helped alternative and broader concepts of sustainable mobility emerge. First, the instrument of voluntary reduction was discredited by 2007 through the advocacy work of a coalition of critical civil society representatives. Second, emission reduction efforts affected car makers' product policies and market strategies. Anticipating a change in regulation in 2008, firms and public authorities collaborated. As a consequence, new governance structures emerged which placed the question of emission reduction and support for technological innovations to achieve it at the heart of emerging European automotive policy. The way firms, authorities and interest groups formalized and increased their coordination allowed a new shared narrative to gain legitimacy: that emission reduction is part of a company's economic performance, and that this performance needs to be achieved in public-private coordination. One pillar of the 20th century automobility configuration, governance, had changed.

This growing inclusiveness towards stakeholders and formalizing of an agenda-setting process through CARS 21 and stakeholder hearings on the European level, however, had not opened up the range of solutions, i.e. instruments discussed to encounter the emission problem itself. The 2009 CO_2 regulation had produced a slightly more balanced structure of interest representation, accompanied by a narrative that had changed from pure (technological) expertise to arguments of public responsibility, transparency and institutional obligation. However, the debate remained now channelled in a formal decision-making process and in the technical language of grams of CO_2 per driven kilometre. The alternative frame involving consumer information, driving behaviour and other non-technological measures that had shortly appeared during the CARS 21 discussions had not been translated into policy. Because the debate on emission reduction had remained focused on technologies to reduce CO_2 from cars, i.e. the adaption of the current and future products to the agreed limits, the final solution was purely defined as a matter of vehicle supply. Even if the combustion engine is de facto questioned as the heart of the historical automobile path, the question of how people would use (electric) cars was largely ignored during the 2000s. The shared narrative's focus on changing the supply instead of demand explains why the debate on electric cars and shared mobility took so many observers and firms themselves by surprise.

Conclusion 4.: Convergence of technological and political dynamics

Chapter 4 asked if and to what extent conflict over CO_2 emissions challenged the pillars of 20th century automobility. Many institutional preconditions of this path were challenged, but not disrupted, until 2008. The analysis shows that the combination of regulative pressure (4.1.) and investment in emission-saving innovations (4.2.) create the necessary conditions in which the financial and structural crisis of the sector *allows alternative narratives to become public.* The increasingly realistic alternative of the electric car challenges the petrol-based combustion engine as the core technology of global automobility culture. Chapter 4 revealed that until 2008, new narratives could institutionalize only partly. In terms of governance, a partial democratization of decision-making structures did not aid the problem understanding of actors beyond pure technological options of emission reduction. In terms of technologies, the focusing on the development of alternative technologies had *not* (yet) compromised the car makers' dominant market position in Europe. Facing Asian competition, companies had prepared conventional and electric car technologies to reduce emissions. But as these innovations were thought to diffuse only through new car *sales*, the underlying assumption of automobility through ownership was not questioned.

Nevertheless, several developments converged into a new institutional constellation that would unleash path change, as the next chapter will show: Investments in low-emission technologies, stricter emission regulation coincided with a severe sales crisis in Europe in the second half of the year 2008. The crisis overlapped with on-going efforts to innovate the sector to encounter stagnating sales, growing competition from Asia and overcapacities in European production sites. The 2008 crisis emerged soon into a 'crisis of legitimacy' in which the role of the consumer, the car, and the technologies offered, were undergoing profound reflection, including by industry itself. Innovation support, mainly public budgets, would play a main role. This chapter has shown the preconditions of changing the organizational and semantic foundations of the sectoral hierarchy, and mechanisms by which traditional automobility was already being questioned before 2008. It is on the fertile ground of a sales crisis that the electric car will fall, as a disruptive solution for all environmental and economic problems (Chapter 5).

5. Towards a new path of shared electric (auto-)mobility

"Coherence at EU level is vital – a situation where (for example) one Member State opted exclusively for electric cars and another only for biofuels would destroy the concept of free travel across Europe." -
EU White Paper for Transport (European Commission 2011:5)

The emerging economic crisis in the second half of 2008 put the stability of Europe's automotive sector to the test. Until then, car makers' semantic hegemony, national governments' support for combustion engine car sales and drivers' unquestioned demand for new automobiles had weakened through increasing awareness that the car industry had to solve the environmental problems caused by its products. The preceding chapter showed how European governments emerged with increasingly ambitious environmental standards for the industry and more collaboration between the public and private sector and civil society. In the course of a severe sales crisis in the 3rd and 4th quarter of 2008, car makers' dominance, formerly guaranteeing the control over solutions to these problems, was further questioned: the European automotive industry was no longer considered able to face global competition and thus securing employment and wealth in Europe. Much of the concern of governments and market observers was about companies' lack of innovativeness. The electric car, an innovation pushed into global markets by Japanese and then Chinese car makers, had by 2009 become a symbol of a new path that could help the European industry to reform, a challenge to which car makers and suppliers had to find a common response. In 2008, European firms had prudently met environmental requirements through improving conventional technology. The cleaner but more expensive and innovative solution, alternative powertrains such as electric vehicles, was left in a development stage (Chapter 4). Surprised by the success of the first hybrid car, the Toyota Prius, companies had not anticipated the sudden price fall of electric vehicle batteries in Asia, which Chinese, Japanese and Korean firms used quickly to build a competitive advantage against European and US-American competitors. Leapfrogging towards building the electric vehicle from scratch, EV makers such as the Chinese BYD (Build Your Dreams, a battery production company) or US-American Tesla Motors, successfully circumvented the existing know-how and technology path on building the combustion engine (Wang/Kimble 2013). Meanwhile, the US and European economic crisis accelerated the destabilization of the sectors' former institutional order and allowed technological, but also behavioural alternatives to 20th century automobility to diffuse more quickly into the market and politics. With increasing investments into electro-mobility, a European government of sustainable transport emerges.

Chapter 5 identifies the changes that created European government structures in the field of sustainable transport through policy instruments that support innovation (5.1.) and company competition regarding the electric car (5.2.). With their increasing success, the collective narrative of 20th century automobility starts to dissolve, and new ideas of emission-efficient car use gain momentum, especially in urban areas. Formerly marginal actors in the industry such as regions and cities, as well as challengers on the market have increasingly drawn the attention to electric cars as an ecologic and behavioural innovation, as it allows shared, short-distance and low-emission vehicle use. A new conception of control emerges. The user, so far an *invisible third party* and largely ignored in market projections, is becoming the decisive actor that will determine the new path(s) of 21st century (auto-)mobility and, beyond automotive issues, will constitute the generative rules of how sustainable transport as a whole will be governed in Europe in the future.

5.1.: Signs of path rupture: European green car politics during and after the crisis

The institutional transformation of the car sector in 2009 cannot be attributed to market factors, nor to external events such as a uniform economic crisis. Rather than from a demand-pull, it resulted primarily from a push through new emission regulation, requiring car makers and the entire industry to make investments into low-carbon technologies. More precisely, it results from a series of collective interpretation processes that public authorities and firms materialized through support instruments such as financial support and loans linked to specific innovation strategies. In particular the 2009 CO_2 standards for vehicles were also an instrument to push electric vehicle sales and are widely recognized as a key driver in today's EV sales. At the same time, more European research funding was bundled to develop electric cars as a long-underestimated technological alternative. In the course of the start of the economic crisis in 2008, an emerging electric car market was increasingly framed as the essential part of a vision of a new profitable European automotive sector. This placed the electric vehicle at the heart of a new collective narrative in a fairly short period of time. Specific problem framing and instrumentation processes on European level explain this shift.

Actors in the field of European research policy were the first to frame electric cars as the new need for automotive innovation in Europe and to suggest specific policy instruments to support their development. At the time when most car makers still considered the electric car at pre-competitive stage, competition on finding alternatives to the combustion engine increased and car makers and large automotive suppliers accumulated development resources and built joined interest platforms such as the Fuel Cell and Hydrogen Joint Undertaking (FCHJTU) and the European Road Transport Research Advisory Council (ER-TRAC) to influence future research priorities jointly on European level. Reacting to these interest manifestations, the European Commission's Directorate General Research&Innovation (R&I) had initiated the first large public-private partnership (PPP)[81] on battery electric cars. The European Green Cars Initiative (EGCI) aimed at uniting on-going R&D work on electric cars by firms from different sectors under various aspects, such as materials, energy and environment. This joint call had a structuring impact on bringing the electric car closer to market by concentrating resources to this aim on European level, as a leading policy officer explains: *"Basically we had, by chance, but [...] also by looking at the development, already thought of making a whole call on electric vehicles in 2008"* (Interview 13). *"Maybe certain things would have happened anyway, but by putting all this together, [...] we could do bigger calls and fund more things in a concentrated way"*. With the explicit aim to launch a collective European dynamic of research and development on battery electric cars, the authors of the strategy defined electric engine research, battery development and electrification of freight transport as areas in which collaborative R&D projects of firms were intended to be funded by an overall 500 million Euro until 2014.

Defining research needs and financing battery car development are a process of collective problematisation - the way in which research topics are defined (batteries, electric engines, electrification of freight) addresses previously identified needs and strategies of firms in the sector, which then develop common development objectives for the sector, based on a shared understanding of which technologies should be supported. *"This is a cycle: we start with writing the topics, the content, in consultation with stakeholders, then we have evaluation [...] and then the negotiation and the contracts [...]"*. *(Interview 13)*. The instrument established alternative powertrain technologies – especially the electric vehicle – as a first institutional answer to a new problem definition. The main justification of this support instrument, as its authors explain, was to reduce emissions. The initiators of the programme shared the assumption that *"[...] If you look at the environmental situation, the air quality issue, it's clear*

---

[81] Following a cooperative approach in R&D, public-private partnerships enroll firms and public authorities in the development of specific products, applications, market segments or innovations. The EU Commission uses this tool to develop some economic sectors and build competitiveness through innovation capacity.

that [...] there will not be a solution coming from conventional cars" *(Interview 13).*

Justifying R&D investments helped the electric car narrative to leave its niche and to gain broader support within different but linked spaces within European government. Interviews reveal that civil servants in other parts of the European Commission such as DG MOVE, the Commission's department dealing with transport, DG CLIMA, dealing with greenhouse gas reduction and DG Environment, in charge of reducing air pollution, considered electrified transport as a solution to clean up Europe's transport system. In addition, NGOs and consumer associations and other European interest organizations, but also Members of European Parliament and European industry organisations started to consider electric car as an alternative for clean transport. These actors started to build a network of close observers of the solutions now to be institutionalized, and of their environmental effects.

As the first policy instrument on European level, the EGCI promotes an alternative narrative that challenges the institutional conditions of existing automobility. In 2007, it is the first European support instrument that formulates and decisively supports electric car technology as a promising alternative for the combustion engine car, both for its environmental and potentially for its economic benefits. Through its application, the instrument showed 'performative' character: resources were allocated on electric and hybrid car R&D, which fostered a development competition that would unfold during and after the economic crisis. The instrument anticipated electric mobility as a control problem for car makers and distributed R&D resources to main car makers and suppliers. The way the programme was conceived reflects the classic idea of research and innovations policy as a push mechanism that encourages technologies to gain maturity and spread into the market. DG R&I concentrated on electric mobility as an automotive technology to support *because* it was marginal as a niche, and perceived as not yet close to market at the time.

With the beginning of the crisis in late 2008, the EU Commission's narrative underwent a substantial re-interpretation: support for the electric car was now framed as an industrial policy instrument to overcome the car makers' sales crisis and bridge financial gaps. Retrospectively, the DG R&I officer established a closed link between the running of the programme and the crisis. Money was urgently needed, and the Commission seized the first fund that was available because it was already set up as a financial programme. *"I think [...] the EGCI was started because of the crisis... Industry couldn't, on the one hand, get short-term funding, medium-term funding for R&D of the next product, of the next innovation, and they might have been forced, or tempted, to cut the long-term investments to try and fund the shorter time. And with the research we are also trying to bridge that gap*" (Interview 13). This re-allocation of resources predetermined that the electric car support, initially intended as long term innovation policy, could not be separated from what would become a broader mid-term industrial policy framework during the crisis. The link between long-term environmental innovations support and short-term rescue of the industry was thus first and foremost political, pragmatic and crisis-induced. But it established the core argument for European and national institutions which made the electric car the anchor point and recipe for necessary industrial restructuring.

Collective problematisation: electric car as a crisis remedy

The soon to be called economic crisis in late 2008 caused severe sales setbacks for European manufacturers, and hit even more severely the numerous suppliers that depend essentially on continuous production and thus demand from their clients, the large car makers. As an immediate reaction, DG Enterprise and Industry as the department responsible for industrial and economic policy inside the European Commission, defined a policy strategy that pushed for investments in the electric car as a solution to the crisis and a remedy to save the automotive industry from collapsing. Existing research support from the European Green Cars Initiative was bundled as part of an action plan that defines support for green cars, defined as eco-efficient conventional and electric cars, as the European way to best handle the crisis.

In February 2009, after several European member states had given short-term aids to their automotive industries, the Commission considered that a long-term strategic orientation for the sector was necessary to solve not only the recent, but the underlying structural crisis in the sector: stagnating sales, overcapacities in Europe and rising global competition. DG Enterprise & Industry sought a means to link short-term help into a long-term governance programme to strengthen the sector's competitiveness, built on innovations in low emission vehicles. Consequently, the 30-staff automotive unit in the DG Enterprise & Industry created an encompassing support programme in the beginning of 2009 which further contributed to the collective diffusion of the industrial framing of the electric car. It places the electric car in the context of an increasingly coordinated, if not interventionist, European automotive industrial policy. A responsible policy officer in DG Enterprise & Industry, interviewed in early 2010, recalls the situation: "*So this is more or less February last year [2009], we have also the change of the Commission, so you can imagine for political reasons a new commissioner [Tajani] would like to have some visible action. So the new commissioner Mr. Tajani is coming, what does he have? He has the second year of the crisis, first signs of recovery especially on the financial side, but, well you cannot continue just on the green cars initiative. [...] We need a new quality, we need a new approach, and for that, we had in February last year a meeting of ministers.*" (Interview 8). In addition to the obvious urgency decision-makers felt at the time, the description suggests between the lines that a strong competition between DGs was also a factor of motivation to create that policy. A new Commissioner, and DG Enterprise & Industry as the Commission's voice of industry wanted to take the lead and coordinate a European crisis response for this key sector of European value creation.

DG Enterprise & Industry's initiative was thus born with a strong political motivation to define the sector's future development. It was intended to give orientations and should be, in that sense, deliberately an industrial policy guided by a vision for the whole sector. Just as the research policy described above, it illustrates how imagined futures on the micro-level, shape future government of the sector. A policy officer in charge describes the reflections as deliberately strategic, comprehensive and, at the same time, respective of persisting market differences: "*What should this long-term orientation be? Well they [the ministers, J.H.] agreed, our industry is a technology leader. We will not produce less costly in Europe than in Asia, so this road of competition is closed to us, we need to remain technology leader. Now which technologies? Of course we are very good in premium cars, but we are also very good in clean cars, which is partly pushed by the European legislation [CO_2 Regulation, J.H.]. So this should be the way that we favour, and that's totally in line with the climate change objectives, with the quality standards, so that makes sense with other European policies, and this is how you had the strategy on clean and efficient vehicles, that's April last year [2010].*" (Interview 8).

The result of these strategic discussions were new policy instruments, more financial support and thus, cumulatively 'more European government' of the automotive sector including more active organisations. The 'European strategy for clean and energy efficient vehicles' (ESCEEV) was launched at the beginning of 2010. The head of the DG Enterprise & Industry's automotive unit and co-author of the strategy at administrative level, justifies it as a necessary measure to save and reinforce the industry. This, in itself, seems to have been an ultimate goal for this part of the European Commission that had elaborated a separate policy for the sector during collaborative hearings of interested parties such as the first CARS 21 negotiations of 2009. He suggests that the European Investment Bank (EIB) played a key role in the definition of the strategy. It articulated technology support as a criterion for a successful exit of the crisis.

"We realized that 500 million are not enough, we not only need research, but a strategy. And the EIB asked us to have a strategy [...] they asked that we define a strategy on which investments should be financed. Which technology. So all the measures that will be developed were going to be relatively significant." (Interview 9.)

Under the auspices of the EIB, these new instruments aimed at providing investment security for automotive companies. The strategy prescribes an investment focus on conventional eco-efficient *and* alternatively fuelled cars, reinforcing the performative impact of such instruments in times of high uncertainty, especially concerning future car technology: *"You hear very very different forecasts, the reality to is that nobody really knows because the approach is not yet decided; in a sense that they are testing things with vehicles which are a first try... "* (Interview 8). In a situation where the market could not decide and firms could not invest, DG Enterprise & Industry thus implemented the shared problematisations of the crisis through electric car support as a remedy to revitalize the European automotive market. The head of unit confirms that the EIB had significantly raised the total sum of loans to the car industry in the crisis year: 10 billion Euro were accorded to car makers in 2009 as opposed to 2 billion Euro in 2008, which represents about 25% of the EIB's overall credit volume (confirmed in interview 9). Importantly, these were loans to R&D in the field of green car development. Credits worth 866 million Euro were allocated to car makers in a scheme dedicated to 'clean transport', as the EIB announced in April 2009 (GreenCarsCongress 2009). This funding scheme included all existing technological powertrain alternatives, but included a strong focus on the battery electric vehicle.[82]

In sum, the new shared narrative on European industrial policy and additional instruments based on green and electric cars had created additional institutional structures of European government in, and beyond the sector. This created an unprecedented destabilization of the dominant role of combustion engine and the importance of so-called efficiency technologies. By privileging radically innovative technologies as an instrument of economic policy, European public authorities jointly implemented a specific 'imagined future' of the European car market. This could threaten the car makers' dominant position defining

---

[82] The aim was to de develop a market for alternatively fuelled vehicles: develop standards, encourage the market entry in (alternative) technologies that would be marketable and best adaptable in the long term: "It [the strategy, J.H.] says that research is not sufficient, we need standards, we first need priorities, we have to choose the technological options that are really beneficial in longer term" (Interview 9). The strategy consists of two pillars, one to support ecological conventional powertrains, preparing the transition, and the second one to support electric drive, the innovation objective.

future market supply. At a time where public loans could impose conditions of technology and market development, this very specific and ambitious development vision would produce a control problem for the other players such as the car makers themselves or national governments, if they did not seize full control of the development and commercialization of electric cars. The more a successful implementation of innovative technologies was bound to public funding, the less car makers would be in control of investment processes. While the industry, at a very vulnerable moment, was uniquely open to strategic choices of investment priorities that could imply a long-term reorientation, or even the rupture of an existing technology path, the destabilization of the sectors' conception of control provoked conflict. As the following sections will show, this semantic shift towards public-private innovation coordination on the European level provoked conflict between national governments and also between market incumbents and challengers. Both trends confirm the Fligsteinian view established in Chapter 2 that institutional change in sectors' governance towards a more European government only came about along with a power struggle and a change of the dominant conception of control.

Conflicting instrumentation: national crisis policies (Germany and France)

In the beginning of 2009, European member states competed with the EU on a control conception in the sector that would give priority to national policy solutions. This is because the crisis unleashed a movement of nationalization of politics in reaction to secure domestic value creation. Many governments see the automotive sector as a key field to ensure employment, infrastructure and demand for cars. Governments of countries in which car makers and large suppliers were established, particularly France and Germany, supported domestic car sectors through various financial instruments including direct loans, R&D support and purchase incentives. In both countries, state-subsidized part-time work – in which salaries of workers are subsidized by the state – was applied in many automotive companies. Through close cooperation of public authorities with large firms, car makers' different and competing strategies shaped each country's answer to the crisis. Investments into low emission and electric vehicles were part of this answer.

In contrast to French car makers, German firms were not prepared for a shift to electric vehicles. German car makers had built their entire business model on internal combustion engines, and struggled to identify competitive advantages other than in highly specialized battery research. The German government initially reacted to the sales crisis through maintaining demand for new car sales in the short-term. In a 'cash-for-clunkers' scheme, for nine months in 2009 the state granted 2500€ to each car buyer replacing their used car with a new one, guaranteeing demand for car makers.[83] The programme lacked ambitious environmental criteria[84] boosting specific innovative alternative technologies, and mainly accelerated the renewal of the car fleet by anticipating purchase decisions (Blöcker/Hildermeier 2015).

In the mid-term, the government gradually created a more explicit link between crisis recovery measures and electric cars, focusing on Research&Development support. A so-called recovery package (Konjunkturpaket I, 2009), contained a 500 million Euro support for R&D on electric mobility. But funding for e-car development was clearly concentrating on domestic car makers implementing innovations, and, at the same time, maintaining their international competitiveness. My own calculations on available data on the allocation of recovery funds to firms reveal that Daimler received €63.9 million (about half of the allocated public subsidies for electric power train development), BMW €26.8 million, VW €17.6 million, and Audi €4.1 million R&D funding between 2009 and 2011.[85] Other public and public-private support programmes were added, in sum contributing to a focus on existing dominant players such as car makers,[86] and existing forms of automobility.

International competition (Michaux 2010), particularly from France, forced government and industry representatives to enter into a dialogue on how elec-

---

[83] Five billion Euro were provided to boost demand with an individual 2500 Euro bonus. Success was exceptional: 1,932,929 new cars had been bought. However, measures were short-term: While in 2009, 3,807,175 vehicles were sold, 2010 showed a sales decrease of 23.4% to 2.916.260 new cars (Blöcker/Hildermeier 2015).

[84] However, in order to protect industry and sales, no further restrictions on the emission reduction through the offer were taken. In environmental terms, this rapid renewal of the car fleet would have been a unique opportunity to reduce emissions across the whole car fleet, whereas most other instruments such as CO_2 limits or others only affect newly sold cars. This intention became visible with a change of wording as soon as the instrument was in place: Although the government had officially labelled it 'Umweltprämie' (environmental bonus), this term was soon replaced by 'Abwrackprämie' by the public, designating it literally to 'cash for clunkers'.

[85] Sources: Government data base on publicly co-funded projects www.foerderdatenbank.de and overviews compiled by individual ministries, cf. Environment Ministry: http://www.erneuerbar-mobil.de/de/projekte/foerderprojekte-aus-dem-konjunkturpaket-ii-2009-2011/pkw-feldversuche.

[86] This strong focus in terms of funding allocations has been questioned by environmental groups. VCD, Germany's association for transport and environment, criticized that Porsche was allocated 2.8 mill. Euro for a demonstration project from 2012, in which only 3 vehicles (Porsche Boxxter 918) were to be converted into electric cars. The objective of the demonstration project was to "reach maximum speed of 200 km/hour and accelerate" (DUH 2011). VCD rightly criticizes that the demonstration effect of this costly experiment is rather limited for the user.

tric cars should be developed. New cooperative industrial policy structures emerged, such as the public-private national platform on electric mobility from 2010 onwards. This coordinated industrial policy space resembles expert groups such as CARS 21 on European level (discussed in Chapter 4); equally marginalizing environmental, consumer and trade unions interests. Nevertheless, this public-private cooperation in setting industrial policy strategies, reinforces the observation that the sector's government had transformed.

Through the platform, industry had committed to 4 billion Euro investments in electric car technology and a competitive goal for the automotive sector: 1 million registered e-cars were to be sold by 2020, a share corresponding to 2.3% of the current fleet (assuming a regular growth of the 2011 car fleet at 41.7 million to 43 million in 2020). The idea that these electric cars were to be developed by domestic industry and sold to customers as individually owned cars was clearly part of the strategy formulated in the programme. With a few exceptions, the national answer to the electric vehicle as a new collective crisis remedy relied much more on conservative narrative of automobility and sought to secure market control. A shift away from traditional forms of automobility could slowly emerge in regional industrial clusters across the country to host a number of EV demonstration programmes. But these remain strongly influenced by car makers' headquarters, as their geographic locations in Stuttgart (Daimler), Munich (BMW/Audi) and Wolfsburg (Volkswagen) suggest. Yet, several EV projects created potential for path change as Chapter 5.2. will analyse.

The French government adopted a more balanced approach, supporting long-term demand and supply of low-emission vehicles. As a short-term crisis measure, the government supported car makers by direct credits: Renault and PSA received a 300 billion Euro loan each and another 500 million was accorded to Renault Trucks at a low interest rate. "In return, the two manufacturers committed to invest in R&D and to preserve employment and production in France. The aim was to protect the French industry from delocalisation and to modernise the national sector to ensure the competitiveness [...] of factories." (Hildermeier/Villareal 2011: 11). A platform of industrial and government representatives (Etat Généraux de l'Industrie) formulated an additional "low-carbon vehicles plan" to be implemented in October 2009 (Plan Véhicule électrique 2009). In contrast to Germany, the French recovery package was inherently linked to the creation of a new sector on low-emission and electric cars. It was "designed to ensure the relevance and to promote the relocalisation of production and the creation of a new sector based on electric technology. To that end, the government agreed to finance a part of the conversion of the factory in Flins (near Paris) to produce the ZOE, the Renault's future main electric car, whose manufacture is supposed to employ new qualified workers." (Hildermeier/Villareal 2011: 11). Visibly, French car makers tried to secure their competitive advantage in the European car market by investing early in innovative technologies. Electric engines can be more easily built into small-sized cars and create environmental advantages over the whole car fleet. As volume producers specialized in small segments, Renault's and PSA's vehicles emit less on average than that of their German counterparts. Accordingly, the French president Sarkozy announced, at the Paris "Mondial de l'automobile" of October 2009, that the country would invest in decarbonized vehicles, which include battery vehicles, hybrid cars and other alternatively fuelled vehicles.

During the crisis year 2009, the French government and car makers thus created a considerable dynamic of competitive electrification, placing the electric car as a central innovation to secure the automotive sector''s competitiveness. The French government thus acted in coherence with the EU Commission's efforts, and was inclined to have influenced them through regular talks during the crisis (Interview 8). Strongly supported by Renault, France was the first state in Europe to opt for a public buying scheme in 2009. Led by the group La Poste, several firms guaranteed to buy 30,000 Renault Kangoo Zero Emission cars, of which about half were sold at the time of writing. The official objective was 2 million electric (including hybrid) cars by 2020 - which represents about 5% of the French overall car fleet. Government and industry upheld an industrial as well as an environmental framing of the problem: the introduction of the bonus malus system had already been discussed during the Grenelle de l'Environnement, a French energy and climate law required by European legislation by 2007. Renault had already invested 4 billion Euro in the building of electric cars – drawing on battery production capacities and know-how from its partner Nissan – and saw a considerable comparative advantage against German competitors. In sum, the French industrial policy efforts were more decisive in terms of technology, but nearly as conservative as German politics in terms of car use: Electric cars were aimed to be sold to private customers. An interesting exception is the association of institutional buyers such as La Poste, which realized a scenario of integrating electric utility cars into professional fleets, essentially electric Renault Kangoos for mail delivery.

European member states' efforts to nationalize low-carbon and electric vehicle support as industrial policy during the crisis transformed the sector's structures. Governments' emphasized the industrial framing of the electric car, i.e. its potential economic value, over its potential environmental benefits. While those two narratives had existed parallel at the beginning of the crisis, the two national examples show how electric car politics turned the electric car into an industrial benefit, ever more disconnected from environmental considerations. Increasing Research&Development support for electro-mobility strengthened the cooperative character of sectoral governance on all political levels, because the efforts were mainly driven by political imperatives and not by internal market demand. This increasing cooperation diminished car makers' strategic autonomy in the emerging market for low carbon and electric vehicles, and thus their dominance as rule-makers in the European car market and their impact on nationalising automotive policies. From 2009 onwards, their strategic development through technology and future competitive assets depended, at least in an earlier stage, much more on cooperation with public authorities at regional, national or European level. At the same time, firms from other sectors such as telecommunication and energy developed an increasing commercial interest in the electric car. In sum, despite national attempts to prevent a further Europeanisation of the sector's organizational structure from 2009 onwards, to the extent that cooperative policy-making emerged as a pattern on all decision-making levels, the car sector's conception of control started to transform towards a cooperative, pan-European structure. The next subchapter highlights how this impacted the stability of the automotive car market in Europe.

The car market's architecture transforms: new players emerge

Collectively established and instrumented as a crisis remedy, the electric car started to transform the automotive market and reactions differed. Some actors expected a unique market opportunity for a European mass market of electric cars that would make it competitive with the leapfrogging Asian industry. Others focused on the risk the electric car production represents for the traditional automotive value chain focused on the combustion engine car, in which firms would lose the basis of their activity and consequently employment. Facing the risk of losing their share in the value chain forced formerly dominant players to seek collaboration in order to seize control and started to actively co-define the evolving new conception of control. This subchapter exposes the initial institutional consequences as signs of a structural change in the whole automobile path.

Technologically, the electric car posed a particular threat to European car makers. The electric engine drastically reduces technological complexity of the vehicle as a product. An ICEV's powertrain and gearing mechanism consists of about 1400 components, opposed to an electric engine which has about 210. Future losers of the transformation towards a market for electric cars would be supply firms that produce car components of combustion engine cars not compatible with an electric car: small and medium enterprises, but also car makers not investing in electric cars (for example Italian Fiat). Winners of the transformation would be battery firms. In an electric vehicles' value chain, 35% of the value created would be related to the car battery itself. The largest battery producers come from Asia (Samsung: Korea, Sony and Sanyo: Japan; also the Chinese company BYD produces batteries and cars). In 2009, observers feared a new monopoly was emerging, as the three largest battery producers owned 60% of global production (Jullien 2011:258).

As a consequence, former incumbent market players such as the car producers but also large suppliers risked losing market value. IAO/PWC estimated in 2010 that German car makers' share in car value could decrease from 63% of the conventional combustion engine to only 15% of the electric engine (IAO/PWC 2010: 36). Given the unfavourable distribution of knowledge and capacities on building e-car components on the one hand, and political pressures in Europe to regain competitiveness on the other hand, car makers were forced to open up to intra-industry collaboration. Fostered through public research support, industrial R&D cooperations on the electric car multiplied after the crisis. From 2008 onwards, OEMs have cooperated with battery producers, depending on the degree to which the OEM outsourced battery production. Generally car makers had three options to deal with external know-how:

- buy batteries for production (procurement)
- establish joint R&D projects to develop own capacities
- jointly produce batteries or even electric vehicles with foreign firms.

Table 2 gives an overview of cooperation of German OEMs with battery suppliers as of the beginning of the market transformation in 2010 (Jürgens et al 2010: 260). Many projects were co-financed by public investments and of short or medium-term duration. By 2014, some consolidation can already be seen as to the supply chain of batteries to manufacturers, for example when Daimler sold its shares in Tesla and closed down domestic battery cell production with LiTec.

OEM	Battery supplier	Start of cooperation	Type of cooperation	Objective
Audi	Sanyo	2008	Development (1 Mrd € by VW)	Lithium-Ion Batteries
BMW	Continental AG (DE)	2008	Procurement	Conti supplies batteries since 2008 to BMW for BMW7 ActiveHybrid
BMW	Johnson-Contros-SAFT (FR)		Procurement	
BMW	Cobasys (US)		Procurement	
BMW	SB LiMotive (Bosch + Samsung) (DE-COREA)		Procurement	
BMW	A123Systems (US, cell producer)		R&D	
BMW-Mini	AC Propulsion (US)		Procurement	AC propulsion provides electric powertrain. LI Batteries from Taiwanese firm 'E-One-Moli'
Daimler/GM	Continental AG (DE)	2008	R&D cooperation	LI batteries for Mercedes Benz S 500 Bluehybrid
Daimler/PSA	JohnsonControls (US)-SAFT(FR)	Temporary	Procurement	Provided batteries to Daimler before Continental started battery series production
Daimler	Evonik Industries (DE)	2008	R&D	Daimler aimed to secure its own bat-

				tery production, joint venture 'Deutsche Accumotive'
Daimler	BYD (CN)		R&D	Shenzhen BYD and Daimler New Technology Ltd founded R&D centre on batteries in China, BYD produces batteries and e-cars
Daimler	Tesla (US)	2009	Procurement and R&D	Tesla delivered battery for smart ed; Daimler had shares in Tesla
Mercedes-Benz	Hitachi (J), LiTec (D), CObasys		Procurement	Different types of batteries
Smart	MesDEA AC Propulsion, '18650', LiTec		R&D	Different types of batteries
VW	Sanyo Electric (J)		R&D of different types of batteries, 800 mill. Dollar	Build capacity of 1 mill. by 2015, 2.4-3.4 mill. by 2020
VW	Toshiba (J)	2010	Development	
VW	BYD (China)		Development	
VW	Varta Microbattery		Procurement	

Table 2: Cooperations between car makers and battery manufacturers from 2009/2010. Source: Jürgens et al 2010: 259f.

New competitive pressure from overseas accelerates the transformation of the European market. As a consequence, the increasing global competition on electric cars enhances the Europeanisation of the leading car markets in European member states. While European OEMs had just begun to motorize China and conquer the Chinese car market as one of the largest and most rapidly growing worldwide[87], the Chinese government decided to massively invest in domestic production of electric cars[88] in order to strengthen their local industry. This represented a substantial threat to European firms: China invested in a future technology market European OEMs were not competitive on, and replaced foreign imports through local products, especially domestic batteries[89]. In addition, electrifying transport would help tackle increasing air pollution problems in Chinese megacities. The European Commission used these developments as an argument for harmonization of those plans by the European Union. The head of the DG Enterprise & Industry's automotive unit puts it clearly: "*The danger is in Asia. The Chinese market has become larger than all the European markets together, and in 2025, the Chinese market will be bigger than the European plus the American plus the Chinese market. So, there is a problem of size, and even if Germany is a large automotive country, the VDA knows that Germany alone cannot influence the Chinese market. We have to do this together, this is to say either with the French, maybe with the Japanese, and sometimes maybe with the Americans. But not by yourself.*" (Interview 9)

In addition to global competition, internal market competition by challengers further contributed to the restructuring of the car market in Europe. The electric car's technological characteristics as a 'battery on wheels' created an oligopoly of electric energy producers and providers. Especially the building and operation of electric vehicle charging points provided a potential new market, even less controllable for car makers. Numerous collaborations emerged between OEMs and energy providers, following nationally different configurations of interest. For example, in France, car makers faced one single state-owned energy provider (EDF), while in Germany's more liberalized markets four large providers, RWE, Vattenfall, E.On und ENbW compete with demonstration projects on EV charging networks (Jullien 2011: 262f). In the early market phase, the character of the collaborations varied: firms aimed at obtaining

---

[87] In 2014, China's total vehicle fleet encompasses ca. 110 mill. vehicles. According to forecasts, it may reach between 200-250 mill. units in 2020, and 400-550 mill. units in 2030.

[88] Michaux (2010:2) considers the Chinese government plan, to reach 500 000 clean vehicles from 2011 (compared to 10 000 in 2009), i.e. 10 % of annual as unrealistic. The government aims at 6 million in 2020.

[89] In addition, China seeks strategic leadership in the production of LIB batteries, of which it holds a 22% share in 2010.

knowledge on usability and users' acceptance, at gaining know-how in order to develop possible business models, or simply gaining publicity by installing charging polls at representative spots in city centres.

Charging infrastructure reveals a fundamentally new dimension of the electric car as a product that the combustion engine car did not require in the same manner: the electric car is locally and spatially limited, being 'dependent' on infrastructure. Different technological characteristics explain this new importance of locality:

- Electric cars have less autonomy (= the range feasible without recharging on average driving pattern). At the current state of technological development, their range is around 150 km depending on model, temperature, car equipment etc.

- The density of charging infrastructure becomes crucial to assure the needed range for daily use.

- Charging time varies from normal to quick charging infrastructure, but determines availability of the product.

- Infrastructure providers need to assure customers that cars can run, park, be charged in cities, and that space is provided.

These characteristics determine new possibilities of car *use* that fundamentally differ from traditional forms of automobility in terms of the vehicle's autonomy, charging time and thus availability, and speed limits. For the first time, and in difference to industrial and environmental politics before the crisis (Chapter 4), governments in many countries globally had supported an innovation that compromises these cultural conditions of car use and started to promote acceptance of alternative forms of automobility.

The changes in the EU's automotive market set the basics for a different European government of the automotive industry and beyond, merging automobile transport with an increasingly integrated transport system. Former challengers gained importance in shaping the emerging electric car market: regions and cities as owners of space authorize for use, charging, parking, registration of electric vehicles. Charging infrastructure providers (utilities, local providers) guarantee EV use. Put in Fligstein's terms, analysis has shown that the new conditions of spatiality and EV use constitute an entry point for challengers into the transforming car market. As a consequence, in 2011, the political and economic investments in e-car development had started to transform the European government of the car industry. Car maker's hegemony diminished as institutionally anchored hierarchical vertical relations of supply for the production of ICEVs were partly replaced by horizontal R&D collaborations, in which partners were equal.

But instead of a rapid institutional transformation, we observe gradual institutional change. The expected mass market for electric cars did not take off as some initial enthusiastic forecasts had assumed. Electric cars sales registered from 2011 onwards remain marginal. By January 2013, a total of 7,500 battery electric cars were registered in Germany, compared to 64,995 hybrid EVs. With a total fleet of 43,4 million, the share of pure EVs is still at 0.017%, rising to 0.14 when hybrids are considered. In France, since 2010, 10,400 EVs have been sold, i.e. 0.027% of the total fleet of 38,138,000. However, electric cars are often leased, not sold. The AAA, a private data base, selling automotive market data to industrial clients and to the European Commission, states in November 2012 that 13% of all cars in use are electric in Germany, versus 35% in France.[90]

The main reason for which the transformation of the European automotive market happened gradually and remains incomplete, despite organizational shift in key European market, is that different 'imagined futures' for the market are still competing. Initial support policies had not questioned the assumption that electric cars would best fit private individual car use, i.e. that other contexts of mobility and shared use are possible. EV registration numbers instead reflect that there were multiple ways electric cars were integrated into the existing markets. The higher market share of EVs in France, for example, can be explained by public buying schemes and car-sharing schemes. Car-sharing offers, for private persons or company use, illustrate a possible new form of use that provides a more realistic and appropriate way to achieve the politically required mass market use of electric cars. These trends, presented in the remainder of this chapter, suggest evidence on how recent and on-going electric car demonstrators have impacted institutional development. New forms of use could develop into a new institutional trajectory, the crisis of which had not been anticipated by politics and car makers.

---

[90] Own calculation based on data from AAA/AVERE for EV sales and CCFA data for total registrations and http://www.france-mobilite-electrique.org/bilan-des-immatriculations-de-vehicules-electriques-en-europe,4043.html?lang=fr.

New framings and multiple government structures: From electric cars to electro-mobility

Further institutional changes can be observed after the first impact of the 2009 economic crisis was weakening and some economies including the car industry experienced signs of recovery. Multiple demonstration projects on the electric car were rolled out, experimenting with traditional and alternative use and business cases integrating electric vehicles into existing transport systems and markets. This new experimental market situation gave room for a debate on environmental effects and more efficient transport policy based on the electric car. The narrative on low emission vehicles and different forms of automobility, marginalized during the 2000s and postponed during the crisis due to recovery measures (Chapter 4), could now unfold and gain legitimacy the more alternatively fuelled, hybrid and electric cars were on the market.

At the same time, because the EU, national governments and also private companies co-funded R&D and demonstrations, innovation policies multiplied on different decision-making levels. Different new technological path options started to compete for funding, creating a new potential source of conflict and a further reason to Europeanize policy for the European Commission. However, while DG Transport developed a vision to harmonize technological development in the European transport sector in its 2011 White Paper for Transport, stressing that "Coherence at EU level is vital – a situation where (for example) one Member State opted exclusively for electric cars and another only for bio-fuels would destroy the concept of free travel across Europe" (European Commission 2011:5), this vision is based on the principle of technological neutrality and therefore opens up different potential institutional futures instead of opting for one.

A systematic analysis of national and EU-funded projects and their impact has not been published at the time of writing. An exploratory research was therefore conducted aimed at understanding what type of electric car research has been publicly financed; and if this public engagement allows possible scenarios to be identified by which electric cars could transform market and industry. The analysis is based on the theoretical assumption outlined in Chapter 2 that policy instruments are not neutral devices but 'perform' a new institutional reality – setting the basis of sustainable transport for different European governments, and a new type of mobility behaviour based on electric vehicle use.

A first estimate reveals that the EU co-funded a high number of small and medium-sized projects distributed unequally across member states. According to estimates, the EU funded 320 Research, Development & Demonstration projects on electric mobility with a total of 1.9 billion Euro from 2007 and (July)

2012. 65% of these projects were publicly funded, about 1.24 billion Euro, mainly by EU funding schemes. *Demonstration projects* only accounted for about one third of funding (470 million Euro) were spent on demonstration projects.

Germany and France most benefit from R&D and Demonstration funding (Germany 38.5% of total budget, France 10.7%)[91]. Germany has by far the largest number of R&D and demonstration projects (65 R&D, 53 demonstration projects) while the second largest country, France, has 20 R&D projects and 9 demonstration projects. The map of demonstration projects across Europe suggests that funding has been attracted to already existing industrial clusters, so that electric car clusters are found where combustion engine clusters are already located. Eastern Europe, the Baltic States and Greece that have not run any EU co-financed electric car trials so far.

---

[91] All cited figures are taken from JRC 2013.

Figure 6: Distribution of publicly financed EV demonstrators
red dots: state-financed, large green dots: country co-financed, small green dot: region
co-financed. (Source: JRC EV Radar; http://iet.jrc.ec.europa.eu/ev-radar/)

On the European level, over 18 funding schemes were initiated and managed
by different parts of the Commission between 2007 and 2013. They covered
several aspects on electric car testing in cities, but overlapped in general objectives and spread funding over differently chosen cities and regions in Europe.
Projects vary considerably in budget, size and scope; some were technology-
specific.[92] The largest scheme was Green E-Motion with an overall budget of
42 million Euro out of which 24 million Euro come from the EU, developing
standardization solutions for electric car charging services along with European
demonstrators. Another collaboration project, E-BRIDGE, is an example of
efforts to produce sustainable electric-car use through substitution effects: it is
specifically dedicated to electrifying existing car-fleets. The European Commission streamlined support structure from 2014 onwards, giving priority to
integrating electric vehicle technologies more broadly into overarching research areas and transport challenges such as urban environments, mobility
behaviour or the European transport economy. Being intentionally less pre-
scriptive on the topics and focus, three large programmes will additionally support electric mobility in the future.[93]

The analysis[94] of innovation support instruments on European level shows increasing support for the electric car as a means to make transport more efficient. However, these instruments do not reflect a coherent vision of the role an

---

[92] In the period 2007-2013, eight projects investigated hydrogen and fuel cell technologies in
passenger cars, buses and infrastructure. Others concentrated on battery electric vehicles, in city
infrastructure (CIVITAS), development of automotive clusters and SMEs (ENEVATE), ICT
(ICT4EVEU, MOLECULES, Smart CEM), intelligent grids (MERGE) and cross-border deployment (MOBI.Europe).

[93] *Smart Cities* allocated 200 mill. Euro for 2 years of collaboration on converging themes of low
energy districts, integrated infrastructures and sustainable urban mobility. This programme responds to the growing importance of cities as integrators of e-mobility to urban transport development, including logistics, freight, and infrastructure. *Green Vehicles Initiative* (public-private
partnership, PPP) focuses on the energy efficiency of vehicles and alternative powertrains and
covers additional vehicle types. *Mobility for Growth* aims at comprehensively comparing different modes of transport in economical, behavioural and technical aspects including e-mobility as
part of the car/roads section with a total EU budget of 106.5 million Euro.

[94] A more extensive version of this exploratory analysis is published in Hildermeier, Julia (2016):
Which role should the electric car play in Europe's cities? An analysis of publicly funded
demonstration projects 2007-2013. International Journal of Automotive Technology and Management, Vol. 16, No.1, pp.90 – 107.

electric car should play in European markets. Therefore, in a second step, individual demonstration projects were compared in terms of vision and scope, in order to grasp the possible visions that could emerge from current or past demonstration projects.

Box E: Exploratory research: European financing of electric car development ?

A data base[95] of 130 EU co-funded e-mobility projects were systematically compared. Which visions of electric mobility were implemented through these trials? What type of actors (industry, users, local authorities, and public transport) participated? To what degree were these co-funded projects promoting a vision of sustainable electric mobility development?

Demonstration projects were ranked by real-life exposure of tested electric vehicles, i.e. the degree to which EVs are used and demonstrated in a day-to-day environment. This could provide information on possible different forms of electric car use. The resulting typology categorizes trials into five ideal-types defined below. 128 demonstration projects[96] have thus been classified by the following types:

A) Prototype testing: extended R&D: simple, safe and inexpensive tests of a vehicle prototype under controlled conditions. Some include or focus on examination of charging infrastructure. Testing users' feedback allows 1:1 comparisons to be made with combustion-engine vehicles in use, but has very limited real-life experience.

---

[95] The analysis was based on three principal sources: a) The European Commission's Joint Research Centre issued a report on European electric vehicle Research and Demonstration funding including a database covering all projects from 2007 until July 2012, giving an overview of all EU electric vehicle support initiatives launched within or parallel to the 7th framework-programme. The JRC kindly provided this list and a more detailed list of all partners, private and public, participating in each project. b) More recent work of the newly established European Electro-Mobility Observatory (EMO). This public-private monitoring body has produced two reports. One gives an "overview of national and regional European electric-mobility pilot programmes and projects" (issued in March 2013); the second gives an overview on European programmes and projects funding these trials, updated at the end of 2013. The EEO has listed all 19 European overarching funding programmes that allocated resources to E-mobility trials in cities since the early 2000s. c) Data collection was completed by attendance of formal meetings and informal talks with actors from the Electric Mobility Observatory (Brussels), the JRC (The Hague), and DG MOVE of European Commission.

[96] Two projects out of 130 could not be classified due to lack of information on the character of demonstrations.

B) Captive fleet tests including: EV tests in commercial environments integrating EVs into full fleet operations of the company or a public transport or utility fleets with fixed journeys (i.e. waste collection or school transport), limited degree of controllable real-life exposure, some substitution effects of utility vehicles' use, and some use of infrastructure/charging at the point of parking/departure (for example on company territory) or end of trip of the vehicle.

C) User tests: renting or leasing out a number of EVs to private customers for a limited period, testing real life use of vehicles by providing them to a customer or a customer group. These tests allow complete and long-term comparative user/customer studies on demand, use, problems etc. of one type of different vehicles, but require more complex and extensive charging infrastructure including recharging at home / point of departure, work and/or public.

D) Intermodal tests: include real-life testing with a large and heterogeneous vehicle fleet and different use options, linking it to public transport infrastructure, and allowing extended studies of users' mobility chains and needs. Different use profiles are tested (business, private, shared/individual use) simultaneously and these can include point-to-point or stationary car-sharing; depending on sufficiently broadly spread infrastructure. Intermodal demonstrators seek to realize a systematic vision of the integration of new types of mobility- combined with electric driving in a city, but also in semi-urban areas. They include complex charging and parking infrastructure.

E) Coordination projects: Consist of information platforms, awareness raising and business development. They support electric vehicle development mainly through coordinating commercial collaborations between different (local) companies. They also incite use of public schemes through information and publicity.

The analysis (figure below) of all EU co-funded projects by project type shows: 37% of all EU co-funded projects involve user-tests using EVs in real-life circumstances. This confirms that the largest share of EU-demonstration funds for e-mobility are appropriately allocated for the intended purpose, i.e. analysing and improving users' acceptance of electric car technology under local circumstances in various European cities. The largest share of EU co-funded projects thus concentrates on passenger car trials examining private e-car use.

The third largest share of EU co-funded projects (22%) is focused on commercial applications of electric cars (captive fleets). This share shows that participating firms consider commercial use an important market entry point for electric cars. However, the projects' potential impact on mass commercialization is

limited to the size of commercial fleets, the frequency of use in logistic operations as well as companies' efforts to electrify their fleets. A further limitation
of commercial e-car use is, however, that electric engine technology is less
developed in the utility vehicle sector than in that for passenger cars. While the
number of projects in this segment is reasonable, many of them could more
explicitly address sustainability criteria and seek substitution effects of combustion vehicle based journeys, through using electric vehicles for most-driven
journeys.

However, a large amount (27%) of demonstration projects are in fact extended
R&D prototype-testing or grid development. This means, in one third of the
cases, tested EVs are not tested under real-life conditions or according to users'
daily needs. This is problematic for future electric car development: Real-life
demand for use of these vehicles, users' adaptability and their integration into
existing transport markets is not, or only indirectly, taken into account. If one
third of demonstration projects demonstrate car technology only, and not its
use, no inferences can be made whether this technology is adapted to current or
future market circumstances and could improve the transport situation.

The analysis shows that 6% of projects are intermodal, i.e. link tested electric
vehicles to public transport applications, through joint travel passes or specific
hubs at key intersections linking different transport means such as train stations. These demonstrators integrate the individual or shared car use as one
mode of transport equal to others in an integrated transport system. Electric
vehicles are well suited to be part of intermodal transport systems as they can
be connected to a smart and traceable charging infrastructure; are ideal for
short- or medium-distance use that cover the large part of daily mobility (80%
of daily vehicle trips are below 65km[97]); and increasingly are offered in car-
sharing fleets for occasional use. As part of an integrated transport system,
using electric cars in a more efficient transport system combines environmental
with efficient on-demand use patterns. Some electric car test projects develop
interconnectivity of tested electric cars with other parts of the transport system
or sharing-schemes of other vehicles (scooters/bikes). This includes special
offers, business and pricing models for customers as well as extended coordination among participating companies (see benchmark examples below).

The 8% share of overarching coordination projects, i.e. projects that enable
coordination, give information, set up trial infrastructure etc. reflects the need
for a local governance of these projects.

---

[97] https://ec.europa.eu/jrc/en/publication/eur-scientific-and-technical-research-reports/individual-
mobility-conventional-electric-cars

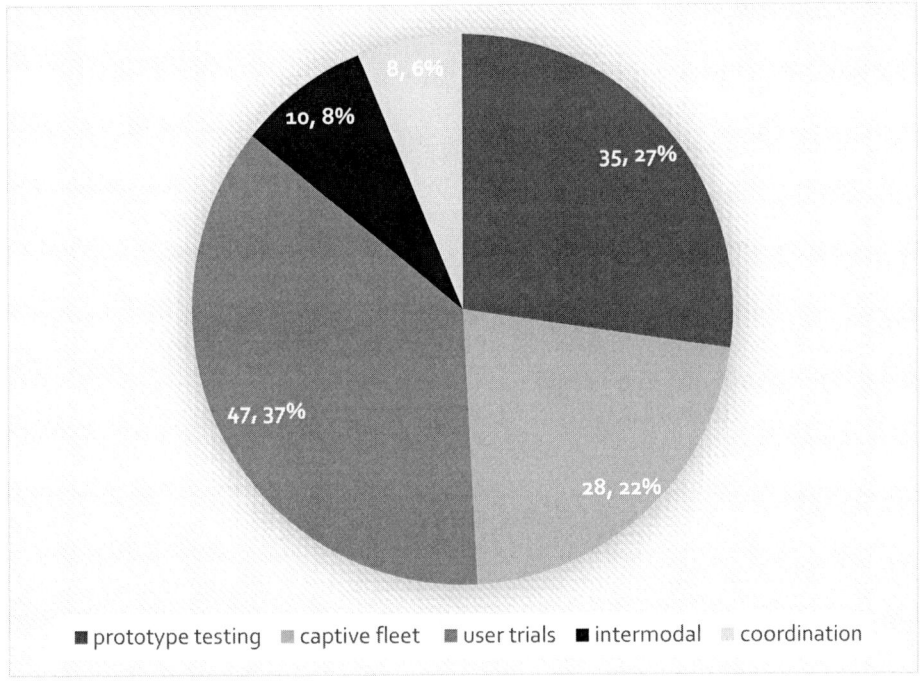

Figure 7: Number of projects by type in EU funding period 2007-2012, absolute numbers and percent shares, source: Hildermeier (2014, 2016)

As a result, the distribution of project types indicates that different visions of future electric vehicle-based transport emerge and are likely to be performed as the number of demonstrators around Europe will increase. Trade unions' early reflections on the changing status of the car begin to materialize. This narrative, marginalized so far, has gained relevance in a new post-crisis policy configuration as they are implemented by the regions and cities that play an increasingly important role in an emerging European government of transport.

Even if no dominant vision emerges of how electric cars should enter the future market, some of the emerging scenarios could exist parallel such as individual and commercial car use. At least a small part of demonstration projects is inspired by the idea that electric cars, due to their limited autonomy and their dependence on flexible charging infrastructure, are apt to serve as publicly shared cars. As such, they may be combined with other means of transport within the public transport system. The vision of intermodal transport in which electric cars can be used as shared cars, has emerged after the crisis as one option among several.

The alternative framing of the electric car as enhancing different and new forms of mobility – labelled here as electro-mobility – spread beyond demonstration projects back from the regional level to European government. In parallel to post-crisis research-funding, the European Commission had re-invigorated industrial politics with a second round of CARS21 negotiations (cf. Chapter 4). This was mainly a project by DG Enterprise & Industry, through which CARS21 threatened to become an enlarged justification platform for DG Enterprise & Industry's industrial policy as it had been in the mid-2000s. Therefore, DG Climate and Energy, for example, was very sceptical to the re-opening of the CARS 21 process. The policy officer in charge comments: "There was the CARS 21 first round of discussions, the industry had a very strong role there, and from our point of view maybe too strong. So we had, let's say, a negative view of the CARS 21 as a process, and it made us very worried also that this relaunch of CARS 21 – because that is one of the objectives of this thing – what does it actually mean." (Interview 6). To prevent CARS 21 turning into a pure industrial consultation body, they imposed a condition on the consultations of the European Strategy for Clean and Energy Efficient Vehicles to integrate possibly critical environmental stakeholders in the consultations. "We wanted NGOs included in the process" (Interview 6). The re-opening of CARS 21 enlarged and formalized the extension of the network of actors that influence sectoral decision-making processes. In contrast to the first round of the High-Level Group in 2005, post-crisis CARS 21 was much more heterogeneous. In more recent years, however, the platform lost relevance. However, it had lost much of its purpose, and has remained as an observation exercise for the Commission rather than a decision-making arena.

In sum, during the crisis, politics on the electric car had extended the sector's governance patterns to a heterogeneous multi-level structure. Policies were formulated by interpretations of the crisis by European administrative staff, national governments, and industrial experts. Interpretations had shifted from an understanding of the innovation of a technology research and environmental problem to an industrial problem. In 2010, the EU Commission had concentrated a large part of its automotive policy on low carbon and electric car development and demonstration projects had begun to develop its own market dynamics. The depicted evolution produced a rupture in the European car sector's trajectory.

Conclusion 5.1. A new conception of control emerges

Chapter 5.1. illustrated a new phase in the European automotive sector's institutional transformation process. Sectoral actors' reactions to the perceived sales crisis in 2008/09 produced space for challengers to question the pre-existing conception of control: increasing investments in the electric vehicle and with it, alternative forms of car use questioned car maker's capacity to remain technological leaders in the market, and thus the core of the existing conception of control. Shared narratives on electric vehicles as part of intermodal transport systems, marginalized before the crisis, entered the space on the European, national and regional government level. As a result, the e-car debate allowed the implementation of policy instruments such as demonstration funding that accelerate a process of transformation that already had started before the crisis.

Applying a view on European government of industries as market by (changing) conceptions of control, the debate on the electric car during and after the crisis appears as a competitive quest between firms and politics for a new legitimate institutional order in the sector. This semantic competition of economic and ecologic framing of the innovation in a unique context of lack of legitimacy had considerable institutional impacts: financial support for R&D and strategic policy programmes on the electric car multiplied. In comparison to the emergence of the CO_2 regulation before the crisis (Chapter 4), the car market's transformation after the crisis is more disruptive: The high degree of uncertainty urged governments and the European institutions to compensate for missed innovation opportunities to correct the on-going sales crisis by publicly pushing an innovation. Whereas before 2008, a critical interpretation of environmental politics had been gradually accepted and provided the basis for more coordinative policy-making, interpretations of the electric car as crisis recipes vary and have been competing since.

But while car makers benefited from Research, Development and Demonstration support, evidence shows that there is no clear vision on how the electric car could be integrated into the European car market at the time of writing. It remains to be seen (taking into account the time lap by which innovations diffuse to the market) if technological innovations spill over into the market, and produce significant change in the supply and demand. Due to this remaining dissonance between structural shift and prevailing collective narratives, the years following the crisis have been marked by a paradoxical situation: a shift in R&D and production has been politically forced, and its impacts are so far occasional, unstructured and not market driven. No mass market uptake of electric cars can be seen that would decide on a new power balance. The electric car has not (yet) produced a collective semantic that could replace the individually owned passenger car.

Publicly co-funded demonstrators, however, have already produced organizational changes that alter the car industry's rules of the game, and therefore its conception of control. Car makers do not dispose of the means to control technology or market development as before 2008. They have also lost control over defining sectoral government patterns, which gradually evolved into cooperative and multi-level structures along with the CO_2 and electric car conflicts. In the semantic and structural vacuum after the crisis, new players, challengers in Fligstein's terms, appeared on the market and pursued new business models that contested the electric car's continuity.

As Chapter 5.2. will show, this invokes the dimension of automobility that had so far remained uncontested by both environmental politics and the electric car debate, but emerged in some demonstration projects around Europe: new forms of car use. Due to a dominant industrial framing of the electric car debate in and after the crisis further reflections on possible new forms of mobility linked to the electric car had not appeared before 2011. Clearly, car makers as incumbents on the market did not have an interest in launching this debate. Rather, privately-initiated demonstration projects, new business models and mobility solutions transform the market. As these expand, path rupture has given way to path creation and a new conception of control emerges that includes a different set of dominant players. Challengers' market initiatives and ambitious demonstration programmes have allowed the 'invisible third' of the automotive market to appear: the consumer. Challengers offer new business models contesting the conception of individual ownership, paving the way to a new path of electrified (auto)mobility.

5.2. From automobility to sustainable transport: enactment of new visions

The introduction of the electric car created an obvious 'control problem' car makers cannot solve alone. Public support instruments for the electric car produced business opportunities for market challengers. These challengers were transport operators, consumer groups, cities and regions, and firms from different non-automotive sectors such as infrastructure and energy providers that offer new business models based on the electric car. But to what extent does their appearance constitute elements of a stable new institutional order? This chapter demonstrates, based on two examples, how these offers challenged characteristics of the existing automotive conception of control. First, demonstration projects accorded a new decision-making role to cities and regions as actors and transformed the established hierarchies in the car industry and beyond: Berlin, Paris and other European cities decided on the installation of charging infrastructure, accompanying measures to allow electric car use in cities (use of bus lanes etc.). Second, the consumer started to play a central role in the making of innovative products. Challengers consequently focus on the urban young that show different mobility patterns and needs. This new customer segment does not *own* but *uses* cars. Both examples illustrate how features of the new market question the last pillar of traditional automobility, consumption. Customer acceptance is the crucial factor for the success, and the implementations, of different conceptions of automobility underlying the emerging sustainable transport sector and its new emerging path.

Electric car-sharing offers become commercialised

The first surprise success of public car-sharing has been Daimler's urban car-sharing scheme Car2go, initiated by the car maker in collaboration with the autorental company Europcar, during the crisis, in 2009. The service provides short-term rental of Smart cars in a free-floating manner: drivers can rent cars, pay for the ride; and park the car anywhere they want in a designated urban area. Tested in the city of Ulm, near Daimler's headquarters, Car2go has expanded since into 28 European and North American cities as of 2014, sharing 11,500 Smarts, among which 1200 are solely battery-driven (Gerpisa/Tech2Market 2014). Equipping the Car2go fleet with small cars meets several demand purposes: As the service provides an additional public short rental scheme for users whose household may already own a larger car, the occasional second car tends to be smaller, (especially in cities with a high private car motorization rate such as Ulm).

Building a small car fleet is also beneficial for premium car maker Daimler to meet European regulation: a Smart fortwo emits 88g CO_2 per km on average. Diffusing a fleet of small cars into the market helps the firm to achieve the emission quota for fleets to meet European legislation on CO_2 limits of passenger cars.[98] Benefitting from the supercredit mechanism of the revised CO_2 and car regulation in 2013, which valorises electric cars even more, and generally expecting stricter European average limits in the future, the firm can thus bene-

---

[98] Firnkorn/Müller (2011) show that the project can reduce emissions in the long term by substituting private cars and by integrating battery vehicles into the local car fleet.

fit from the commercialization of sufficient small vehicles to achieve a more favourable overall CO_2 average. In addition, car-sharing schemes are an appropriate experimental platform for electrification of car fleets. Gradually, Car2go is replacing combustion-engine Smarts by electric Smart ed, depending on the density of charging infrastructure. In three cities, Copenhague, Amsterdam and Stuttgart, infrastructure and public support has permitted full electric fleets to run. What had started as an experiment on shared car use, can develop into a successful scheme which reinterprets traditional car use. Cars increasingly play the role of the 'public individual car' (Honsel 2011) in the sense that they are individually rented but not owned. In order to provide short-term car rental service, Daimler cooperates with a traditional actor in long-term car rental, Europcar. Car2go is a challenging product, but run by two established market actors that observe possible emerging new business models.

Not all challengers in the market survived the competition of bringing electric cars to market combined with new modes of use. Another early challenger of large car companies was Californian start-up Better Place: the firm tried to enter the market by providing a joint charging and battery solution. Better Place's business model relied on extending EVs' limited range by building battery swap stations along highways to quickly swap batteries instead of re-charging cars. The firm collaborated with electric car builders such as Renault which made the Fluence, equipped with battery swap systems. Renault offered a battery leasing system serviced by Better Place on top of an electric car. However, as EV sales remained marginal, the replacement service of batteries did not diffuse as planned, only few countries bought Better Place's infrastructure. After first expansions into Denmark and Israel, the company had to declare bankruptcy in 2014. The start-up's idea to overcome drivers' range anxiety had failed.

Successful demonstrators suggest that instead of copying traditional automobility with new technological means (for example battery swap), different forms of use of the electric car seem more plausible to consumers. An example of a successful challenger of the traditional car industry and car use is the Parisian Autolib' scheme. Its emergence shows how a challenger aptly made use of the semantic vacuum in which the traditional car use had remained after the crisis.

Box F: Autolib' – challenging urban automobility

The firm is a subsidiary of French multinational logistics company Bolloré that has invested 1.5 billion Euro in the production of the lithium-polymer battery in the last 15 years. The company benefited from the City of Paris's call for a public car-sharing scheme in 2009 to demonstrate its competing technology, the lithium-polymer battery, in self-developed electric cars ("Bluecars"). With the objective of reducing car traffic congestion and pollution in the city, two major problems in Paris[99], the City of Paris had decided to offer an electric car-sharing service. The person responsible at the City of Paris justifies the need for this additional system as follows: *"Our objective was to offer a mobility service for occasional trips. For example, when you need a car to go shopping and bring back a bulky object to your flat"* (Interview 37). The city sought to install a *stationary*, electric-car-based one-way service that in contrast to traditional car rental, allows one-way journeys as the car could be parked somewhere else. An additional criteria was that the service be auto-sufficient, i.e. that no additional public staff was required. Further, anticipating an enlarging electric car market in view of Renault's investments, the city asked that charging infrastructure should be accessible for charging other electric cars not provided by the service[100].

Helped by public authorities, the new public e-car renting scheme created conflict with dominant actors on the traditional transport market. With Autolib', Paris deliberately created and funded a car use that competed with existing car rental and taxi services. Both actors on the urban transport market had a legal battle against the scheme's introduction: ULPRO, the French association of short-time car-rental firms (Union des Loueurs professionnels), claimed that Autolib' was unrightfully subsidized as a commercial competitor. It judged the services' public-private status as unfair competition: In fact, the City of Paris had offered Autolib' a 12 year contract, which in exchange took the full operational responsibility for running the service and providing car, charging infrastructure and service. "Autolib' has benefited from 50 million Euro from the City of Paris, 130 million Euro from the European Investment Bank and 70 million Euro from Ile-de-France's *collectivités*, all of which subsidizes a service that competes with existing car rental firms without any compensation

---

[99] As Hildermeier/Villareal (2014) specify, Paris pollution levels are problematic. "According to a European observatory for road traffic pollution that delivers comparable data for European cities, Berlin's pollution levels have been moderate and continuously lowered since the mid-2000s. In contrast, Paris' scores were high and rising (Air Quality in Europe, 2013). Struggling to keep EU limits of 35 days in excess of 50 microgram particulate matter (PM10)/m³, the French capital urgently needs to limit its particle emissions (AirParif, 2012)." (Hildermeier/Villareal 2014:6). French Mayor Hidalgo recently published a package of measures to tackle this problem, including prohibiting the use of Diesel vehicles in the city centre.

[100] Autolib's infrastructure is based on 3000 stations, co-financed by Paris and participating cities of the Ile-de-France region.

having been discussed or offered", a top executive manager of France's largest car rental firm ADA claims (Interview 3).[101] In the same line of argument, he criticizes the price of charging and parking stations granted to Autolib' as unfair, compared with the amount car rental firms pay to park their rental cars on the streets. The law suit was ruled out by the court with the argument, that Autolib' was a different form of car rental than traditional car rental even used short term, and thus co-existence and competition was legal. The fact that the service remained a promotion of automobility, even if shared and electric, provoked contestation not only from potential competitors, but also from environmental stakeholders. Green party deputies in the Paris Senate protested against its introduction. Several districts[102] of Ile-de-France refused to install the service on their territory.

The implementation of first e-car-sharing schemes in metropolitan areas such as Autolib' in Paris provided a new arena for a debate on the usefulness of electric cars. Interest groups in favour of public transport, and the Paris Green Party (Hildermeier/Villareal 2014), gained voice, arguing that electric cars are not and should not be an alternative to public transport, as the electric car can cause just as much congestion as any other vehicle. The conflict on the most efficient use of the electric car in urban areas built a new semantic context in which the car was no longer considered an industrial product but a means of transportation. Criteria to evaluate its societal value were not employment creation and added value, but possible links to urban transport systems and efficient use. Driven by a conception of the future car market that prioritizes fewer cars, promoters of public transport and consumer and environmental organizations have generally remained sceptical towards electric car schemes, such as the German Transport Club (VCD). They require that public attention focusses more on the question of electric *mobility*, than on the car itself.

Public electric car-sharing schemes such as Car2Go and Autolib' combine new technology with shared forms of use. The more they expand as alternatives to individual car use, the more they develop an institutional impact on traditional car markets. Both solutions benefit from collaborating with cities to implement their schemes. The decision of the City of Paris to support this challenger against other offers from established public transport and automotive firms, has set the conditions for a successful niche development. It has allowed Autolib'

---

[101] The mentioned amounts refer to research, development and implementation of the cars and charging infrastructure. They could so far not be confirmed by other independent sources.
[102] Montreuil, Gentilly, Le Kremlin-Bicêtre, Ivry, Vincennes, Le Pré-Saint-Gervais, Aubervilliers, Saint-Denis, Clichy-la-Garenne.

to challenge established car maker's at a weak point, their collaboration with public administration, and the provision of integrated charging and rental services with the car itself. In contrast to other car makers, Bolloré could provide a complete package, i.e. the infrastructure, the car and the service, already in 2011. It important to note that Autolib' benefitted from being backed by a multinational company and investor: As a logistics company and battery developer with no experience in car building or e-car-sharing service, Bolloré had bought companies that provided the missing building blocks in order to be able to provide a whole electric car *system*: The company bought IER, providing charging infrastructure and Pininfarina, the Italian car assembler producing the Bluecar. With this backdrop, Autolib' could pay all additional personnel costs the City of Paris could not finance, which may have been the main argument that made the company win the competition.

In addition to growing visibility and market shares, public e-car-sharing creates different forms of mobility and thus transforms consumption. This overarching innovative character suggests these challengers and their business models could constitute a new institutional trajectory for the car market. However, taking a closer look at Autolib', the question as to whether the new service really provides new patterns of mobility, remains unanswered at the moment, because proof that the new mobility solution actually meets real demand for mobility is still missing. According to the few available independent studies, consumers' growing acceptance of Autolib' since 2013 as an additional means of public transport can be explained by its adaptation to local features such as low motorization rates, high traffic congestion and pollution, little parking space and small urban distances in Paris urge consumers to look for publicly managed alternatives (Autolib' metropole 2014, 6-t-recherche 2014). However, it is still unclear if the scheme really responds to the city's initial transport policy objectives, as no official evaluation has been carried out so far. Critics promoting public transport feel that their initial concerns are confirmed. The mayor of Paris's assistant has overtly criticised the service's results the first time in 2013, taking up the earlier discourse of the Green Party: "We do not reach objectives. In reality, Autolib' seduces public transport passengers. Autolib' does not replace cars" (cited in Razemon 2013). Indeed, the available data leads to a rather paradoxical conclusion: The car-sharing scheme is especially popular in those districts where the alternatives, in terms of modes of transport (access to public transport), are especially high, namely in central Paris (Autolib' Metropole 2013). Do users want to replace uncomfortable public transport with a temporary public private car? In this case, the scheme would have encouraged more rather than less car use. In all, the much discussed introduction of public electric car-sharing such as Autolib' shows a possible but not yet stabilized new configuration of car use, remaining on a temporary and contested governance compromise between public authorities and the service provider. One condition for success is if it will be able to accurately meet the mobility needs of metropolitan drivers.

The other condition will be its exportability. So far the case study has focused on Paris as a laboratory for public e-car-sharing. With public support from the city government, the world's first large metropolitan stationary e-car scheme could build a publicity platform supporting the expansion of the business model into other metropolitan areas of the world. This can have structural consequences for the configuration of emerging e-car markets'. In 2013, Autolib' expanded to Lyon and Bordeaux and integrated local car-sharing schemes. In May 2014, the service expanded to Indianapolis, USA. At a closer look on the Bolloré group's strategy, it becomes clear that Autolib' forms part of a larger systemic vision to provide mobility and energy storage solutions in a joint infrastructure for cities: At the same time, Bolloré has extended its vehicle range to electric buses and trams. In 2014, the firm was in negotiation with Singapore and the Cambodian tourist site Angkor Wat. The green image or green tourism development of the latter seem to be a profitable platform for the investor to provide electric vehicle-sharing systems and charging infrastructure[103]. Behind Autolib's shared mobility solution, the Bolloré group pursues strategic research in mobile energy storage solutions in batteries. An Autolib top executive confirmed in an interview that the company's strategic target was not to provide mobility but to sell the battery: *"Our objective is to deliver public service, to market this solution in the international context and finally to sell our batteries. I remind you that the major strategic issue nowadays in the world is energy storage."* (Interview 4)

Contributing to institutional path creation, the case of Autolib' suggests that shared mobility seems to be a cornerstone of a larger business concept which builds a future government of sustainable transport across Europe and beyond. The electric car is being exploited as a means of transport and energy storage.

---

[103] Branded by a corporate label 'blue', the group's systemic strategy is grounded on three pillars: energy production (solar energy, houses), storage (batteries) and vehicles (tram, bus, car, boats) that can be, but do not have to be shared. For Bolloré, the expansion of systemic solutions of energy and mobility supply in (Asian) metropolitan areas is a huge and crucial market. (www.blue-solutions.com). The company has inherited a series of companies from its former colonial freight transport empire, such as 'La Compagnie du Cambodge', today a financial holding. Network and charging stations builder, IER holds 47.5% of stock options. http://www.compagnie-du-cambodge.com/fr-fr/la-societe. Given this background, the massive protest due to allocating the project to a MNC such as Bolloré, known for his radical investment strategies and ambitions, takes a different dimension beyond the City of Paris.

This trajectory reflects as much the interest of different challenging industries with which car makers had to collaborate since the crisis, as it reflects the need for new forms of car use. Looking at the emergence and the context of different instruments and strategies such as public e-car-sharing demonstrators, raises the question if Autolib' and Car2Go can be characterized as challengers in Fligstein's sense: the two large successful car-sharing schemes persist as subsidiaries of profitable multi-national corporations (MNC). Both of these MNCs try to develop the emerging car-sharing use and possible future automobility in the sense of their corporate strategy: accordingly, Daimler does not compromise individual car use as such, whereas Bolloré seeks to develop stationary car-sharing for mobile energy storage. The only typical startup in Fligstein's sense of the challenger, Better Place, failed to impose its business model in the market. The new e-mobility services are not profitable yet, and are still benefiting from public subsidies and their parent companies.

Furthermore, the analysis of the project's institutional context reveals that the commercial interests behind Autolib' had clear priority over that of providing mobility. In 2009 during the call for tender, the offer had run against two other consortia, one of which had proposed a car-sharing service of 'intermodal' character, being integrated in the existing public transport scheme. There would have been a different solution potentially better at meeting the needs of mobility, and the interests of different actors already involved in the Paris transport market. "Three out of five applications were considered closest to meeting these requirements: First, the '4city' consortium led by SNCF (Service Nationaux de Chemins de Fer, French national railway company), with Vinci Park[104], Daimler with Smart ed from Car2go as vehicle supplier, Avis, a French short- and long-term car rental company, and the RATP, Paris's transport company[105]. According to their competing proposal, the use of the public electric car would become part of an intermodal public mobility service to be created. To this end, public transport season tickets should include the right to use the electric car during a specific journey (....) The second candidate 'VTLIB' (Veolia urban transport) proposed the Peugeot-Ion based on the Mitsubishi iMIEV as a shared electric car." (Hildermeier/Villareal 2014 : 7).

In sum, commercial e-car-sharing as a business model has emerged as a market alternative, but does not seem commercially stable (yet). The emergence and persistence of challengers gives an idea of their potential impact on the future car market. The role of 'market integrators', those firms that produce, maintain

---

[104] The Vinci group is active in public and private transport, infrastructure, water and energy.
[105] RATP is the major collective transport provider in Paris, operating bus, metro, train and tramway in the city and its outskirts.

and legitimate the final product over a whole value chain and develop related innovations could actually shift from car makers to energy or technology providers such as Bolloré. This section revealed that different visions compete on how to integrate future shared electric mobility into urban transport systems. In fact, projects prioritize transport efficiency meeting mobility needs to a different degree. The following section contrasts Autolib' with a different case which contains elements of a more innovative path of future (electric) car use.

Electro-mobility as intermodal urban transport

Demonstration projects on electric mobility can be considered an instrument implementing a vision on the future role electric cars should play in urban transport. If the above-cited examples implement multinationals' strategies to explore shares in emerging car-sharing markets (Car2go), and to promote future storage systems (Bollore), a small share of projects, about 8%, is pursuing the goal of embedding the electric and shared car into urban transport systems as shown above. Similar to the non-successful candidature to the City of Paris's call for an electric car-sharing system, these experiments seek to imply the vision of intermodality, connecting electric car use to the use of collective public transport such as metro and buses via a common use card, supported by a smartphone application on best transport choices by different criteria. They deliberately reformulate the place of the car in people's daily transport choices, replacing its cultural relevance and significance as the only means of transport that can ensures one's total autonomy into that of a flexible means to connect to different equal alternatives. In this sense, their implementation as experiments goes beyond a simple challenge of the conception of individual car use. It implements an entirely different vision of how transport should be organized: *"All transport means should circulate electrically with electricity from renewable sources. With your mobile phone you have access to bus, trains or cars – the bill arrives at the end of the month, you pay for the electricity you used."* (Canzler/Knie 2011: n.d.).

The electric-car-sharing experiment BeMobility in Berlin provides an illustration of the performative power of e-mobility demonstrators as instruments to implement different visions of (auto-)mobility. It had been designed deliberately as a project that would disembed electric car use from the dominant hegemonic view. As a pre-market experiment issued from public-private collaboration between Deutsche Bahn, a mobility research think tank and the city of Berlin, it has financed the German governments' electric car programmes from 2009 onwards. It has remained an (albeit expanding) demonstrator until today.[106] In its first phase (2009-2011), the demonstrator aimed at the gradual electrification of Deutsche Bahn's existing station-based, i.e. round-trip electric car-sharing system named Flinkster.

Box G: Different forms of car-sharing

Round-trip
Classic car-sharing has existed for several decades, services offered a car to be used and brought back to its point of departure. This model is referred to as 'round-trip' car-sharing.

Point-to-point or one-way car-sharing
allows customers to park the used car at a different location. These locations can be anywhere in a designated area, a model referred to as *free-floating*. An example is Car2go.

Stationary
When parking locations are transformed into stations where (electric) cars are (charged when) parked. In this case, the system is referred to as stationary (Autolib').

In the context of political pressure for results in a not yet existing electric car market, the experiment encountered organisational problems. When the project was to be started, only very few electric cars were available, and none by German car makers who had just started to invest in electric car development. This illustrates the project's visionary character in 2009. The car fleet operator DB Fuhrpark, Deutsche Bahn's subsidiary and rental car fleet operator, had to buy cars one by one from different international providers, so that the project began on a smaller scale than planned with 18 Toyota Plug-In Hybrid Prius and additional electric Smarts. Later, Citroen C-Zeros were added to a total of 47 vehicles. In addition, 135 customers used the electric car, Deutsche Bahn public bicycles and Berlin's entire public transport network via a user card (mobility

---

[106] Berlin-Brandenburg had been designated one of the demonstrator regions for electric mobility development since August 2009. Until November 2011, it had been funded with 4.6 mill. Euro. I have estimated the overall cost of the project at ca. 8 mill. Euro, as government co-funds experiments at 50% of their total cost. My estimates (Hildermeier/Villareal 2014) are based on the project's first phase's final report (BeMobility 2011) and government information from www.foerderdatenbank.de. The project has expanded into Germany's smallest federal state (Saarland) and will equip the capital and its surroundings.

card) between June and September 2011.[107] In order to provide test customers with intermodal options, project partners developed a joint smartphone application to allow customers to select their most appropriate transport mode along their criteria of choice (cheapest, quickest, most ecological journey). From 2012 onwards, customers had the additional option of using Berlin's first one-way electric car-sharing Multicity offered by Citroën, which was not station-bound: the 100 C-zeros, that were to reach 500 in 2015, can be parked anywhere, or at charging stations, in Berlin's central public transport zone.[108]

The demonstrator involved only a small number of customers and thus had limited visibility. But it has been driven by an ambitious vision of urban transport since its start. Beyond offering an additional public (electric) car-sharing system, it seeks "to establish new multimodal mobility concepts and to integrate electric vehicles into public transport" (BeMobility, 2013). Addressing Berlin's urban transport system as a whole, the idea is to link the technological product innovation (hybrid or electric cars) with a behavioural transformation that has been observed in Europe's urban areas: customers' raising acceptance of sharing cars instead of owning them (see below). The project's authors in Berlin's Think Tank co-financed by Deutsche Bahn could thus implement "a vision of a smart, user-friendly urban mobility system that combines elements of collective and individual transport" (Ruhrort et al. 2014:288), a vision that has been promoted by sociological mobility research (Knie et al., 2012, Sheller and Urry, 2002).

The strategic question of energy storage solutions for the future that drives Bolloré's expansion strategy has also inspired BeMobility's second project phase from 2012 onwards. On Berlin's EUREF technology campus, where the project is located, the intelligent use of the project's electric cars as mobile energy storage is tested locally, they connect to the campus smart grid. Having combined new use forms with a new type of car, the third pillar of the project author's vision includes electric cars as energy storage devices, in order to provide and enhance more efficient energy infrastructure in the city. Since the beginning, the Flinkster and the Multicity fleet have been charged with renewable energy. One of the project's coordinators thus emphasized in an interview (Interview 40) that the project's unique selling point was the integrated vision

---

[107] For 78 €/month, clients could purchase a monthly public transport ticket and a 50 € voucher for the car-sharing system "e-Flinkster". In addition, rental rentals were free for 30 minutes per trip. Users had access to 20 parking spaces (Contipark) and 100 public charging stations in the city. By the end of the project's implementation, 40 electric and hybrid cars were available for rental.
[108] Information on available vehicles (location, battery status) could be retrieved via the smartphone application and a web interface (Ruhrort et al 2014: 4).

of the electric car at the intersection of transport, flexible use and new forms of energy use. Environmental objectives could thus have a positive effect of creating more efficient transport: "The rationale behind such a vision is that the smart combination produces a system attractive enough to form a user-friendly alternative to private car ownership and use. Using BEVs as an integral part of such a system has the additional potential of reducing transport emissions and potentially paving the way for zero-emission transport based on renewable energy sources." (Ruhrort et al 2014:288).

The project's vision of intermodal, emission-efficient public transport including public and shared e-cars has been discussed by scholars in the context of changing mobility needs and a new mobility culture (Keichel/Schwedes 2013); especially among the urban young. Bratzel (2011) conducted research on the shrinking car use and 'affection' to cars. Two thirds of car-sharers in Germany are younger than 36 years (Hildermeier/Canzler 2014:197). Exploring future generations' use and preferences for transport, Schönduwe et al (2012) identified mobility patterns and needs of Berlin's teenagers. They concluded that "Young people use available transport modes according to their needs and are open towards an efficient combination of different means of transport. [...] It isn't the private car that is important to young people but rather independence and flexibility. If alternative mobility services provide those attributes, the private car and its alternatives are not mutually exclusive." (Schönduwe et al. 2014:5). Thus, the shared car could develop into an additional means of transport. This assumption is undermined by the fact that the market for car-sharing is growing in large automotive markets such as France and Germany[109] (Shaheen and Cohen 2007, Lindloff et al. 2014). In Germany, especially the free-floating spontaneous car-sharing, born with smartphone applications and localisation of customers, has been growing exponentially (bcs 2014). While some assumed, this could be a manifestation of the need for flexible and shared *cars*, others were hesitating and interpreted this shift as the need for more flexible and varied *mobility options.*

The degree to which this ambitious and comprehensive project can constitute a vision for future mobility policy depends of different factors. The question is if it really meets mobility needs. Transport sociologists and geographers examine different interpretations of the same observed trend: In larger cities with scarce parking spaces, longer daily distances and congestion problems, car-sharing can be a valuable option to lower car use and, in the long term, ownership

---

[109] This results from an unpublished study made by GERPISA and T2M for the Pôle Interministériel de Prospective et d'anticipation des mutations économiques (Pipame), French Government, October 2014.

(Lanzendorf/Schönduwe 2013). The cities of Paris and Berlin have generally encouraged the launch of different car-sharing initiatives in order to replace the need for a second car. However, with the rise of different car-sharing services, potentially 'perverse incentives' as to public transport have been discussed: The rapid expansion of car-sharing services; round-trip and free-floating (bcs 2014) raised the question in academic and public debate: Do "these services pose a threat to existing public transport or [do] they contribute to the development of a more eco-friendly transport system (Bock, 2013, Firnkorn and Müller, 2011)?" (Ruhrort et al 2014:3). Since intermodal demonstration projects are still scarce and do not imply mass use, empirical results cannot be generalized. First investigations on the BeMobility project, however, identified different types of possible future e-car-sharing users: "There are at least two key target groups for such services: one being persons with a high affinity to PT [Public Transport, J.H.] and/or bike and strong environmental orientations, the other being a 'multi-optional' group with affinity to all urban modes of transport including the car." (Ruhrort et al 2014: 18).[110] User research accompanying first experiments allows testing assumptions on changing mobility behaviour in cities, and evaluating the potential interest and future driver's profiles of e-car-sharing systems.[111]

Independent of use, however, intermodal demonstration projects signal important opportunities for strategic reorientation to firms. Therefore, even in pre-market stage, intermodal projects such as BeMobility affect the transport sector's institutional configuration locally. As the project's final report points out, BeMobility realized previously unseen inter-sectoral cooperation. Requiring a high share of collaborative R&D, it allowed participating firms to develop strategies and products by which a potentially emerging market could be explored. Participants could gain experience and knowledge by co-developing parts of the required service, the smartphone application or infrastructure with companies from other sectors. Gathering user data through the smartphone application seems to have been most attractive for all partners, as the interviewed project coordinator explains. This common data base allowed each partner to evaluate the feasibility, for example on customers' acceptance of the charging infrastructure (RWE, Vattenfall). The project also allowed assumptions on car sharing user behaviour to be tested and fed them back into mobility

---

[110] Given Berlin's exceptionally low motorization rate, and a high bias in the analysed user sample '(male, well-educated, above-average income)' (Ruhrort 2014: 18), these results can only be generalized within strict limits.

[111] This approach is much more precise than inferring characteristics from a so-called 'Generation Y' and test them in different market environments, an approach which is popular in management research.

research. The Deutsche Bahn could investigate customer acceptability of new 'off the rail' commercial services such as car-sharing. Thirdly, the project created a model for a market niches based on alternative electric car use. As a demonstrator and R&D instrument, BeMobility explores future market options conceptually. Based on local conditions and needs, it tests and extends possible path options for future forms of automobility, while producing the knowledge and material to evaluate them. In this sense, this type of intermodal demonstrator project they can be considered performative: Through its implementation, it can create future structures of use and consumption. BeMobility diverges explicitly from the conventional conception of automobility.

As with Autolib', BeMobility can be considered a niche competitor even if it has not entered the commercial stage. The main reason is that it is developed, as is Autolib', by the German national railway company Deutsche Bahn. Deutsche Bahn has been operating a car-fleet 'Flinkster' and continuously offered its off-rail mobility services by car-sharing at train stations. They also operate a public bike fleet in many larger cities. As for Bolloré, Deutsche Bahn's motive for investing in car-sharing is to undermine car maker's traditional oligopoly on the car market, and offer instead as a 'mobility provider' where car makers struggle to meet complex user demands combining different mobility needs. As with Bolloré, Deutsche Bahn challenges the car market with new user concepts. This strategy has been observed sceptically by critics, pointing out that Deutsche Bahn, as a public officer responsible for e-mobility development coordination observes, benefits from the fact that Berlin is a highly competitive territory. No car maker has its headquarters in the capital (Interview 41). The second case illustrating an even more radical challenge of traditional automobility, again, suggests that on the automotive market, challengers are multinationals from different sectors that develop and test business models to compete for value in a transforming market for electric mobility.

The preceding examples showed that the electric car has been ascribed various complementary and/or competing roles in future transport. Demonstrators range from status quo tests to a variety of ambitious commercial and non-commercial electric car projects in Europe. Investments of car makers and challengers started to produce important shifts in the sector's government:

- Innovative tests of shared (electric) car use are created in local environments. They are determined by local specificities.

- Large companies and/or small subsidiaries fund long-term undermining of the car oligopoly, including MNCs from energy, rail and logistics sectors.

- Experiments could develop some performative effects as use patterns can be shaped through the ideas behind different demonstrators. As different user profiles emerge, projects seem to promote the opening of the future car market towards a heterogeneous, differentiated offer of transport modes, adapted to individual demand.

The fourth development will be examined in detail in the next and last section of this subchapter: with more innovative local demonstrators, regions and cities will play a decisive role in the deployment of electric car use and become key players in a European government of sustainable transport which formerly relied on national governments and European industrial policy frameworks.

Transforming hierarchies: Regions and cities as 'innovation makers'

Cities and regions will be more important in the future automobile market, a fact which was observed by an automotive supplier lobbyist in Brussels already in 2012 (Interview 19). The cases revisited above confirm this observation. Regions as market actors could enhance the transformation of the future car market by integrating the car into its public transport context: The more a challenger's business model, such as car sharing, deviates from the classic car use pattern, for example through intermodal connections offered, the more it empowers cities and regions as new actors. The organizational shift in the sector's innovation governance since 2008 towards co-decision and multi-level decision-making processes involves European cities, regions and even local transport firms which launched numerous experimentations to integrate the electric car, as a shared or rented short-term car, into their transport systems. Given the different spatial requirements of electric car use, local authorities automatically are concerned as decision-makers and gain considerable market shaping power. They have acquired control – and shape the future sustainable transport market's conception of control accordingly. They decide on the implementation of charging infrastructure, on according parking space for the use of shared cars. They can further allow incentives such as free parking and bus lane use[112]. The new key role for cities and regions as potential market shapers is also ambiguous. Cities are still bound to government imperatives as usually they do not dispose of the sufficient resources to fund coherent electric car

---

[112] Across Europe, many examples of cities as market shapers have emerged with the roll-out of EV demonstrators. In Oslo, EVs can use bus lanes, making use particularly attractive for work commuters. London has levied a congestion charge for combustion engine cars in city centres, giving privileged access to users of hybrid or electric vehicles.

infrastructure development. Both of the interviewed responsible staff in Paris and Berlin administrations highlighted this problem (Interviews 37 and 41).[113] Of the European projects analysed by type of institutional partners, local authorities represent 14 % of all project partners.

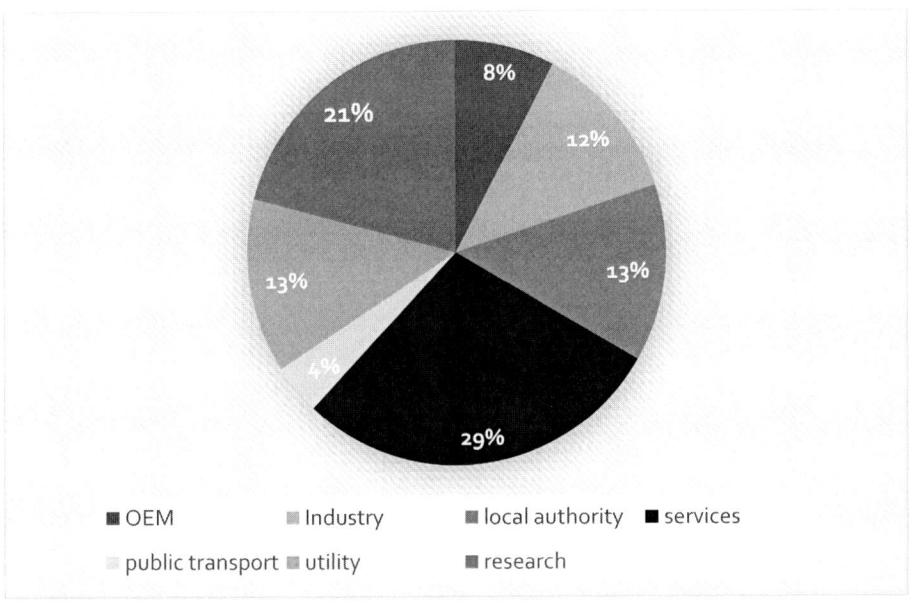

Demonstration project partners (n=814)

Figure 8: Demonstration project partner types. Source: own calculation (Hilder-meier 2016:102)

The government of sustainable transport innovations based on the electric vehicle requires reconsidering the principle of subsidiarity between European, national and regional levels of decision-making. Between cities, decision auton-

---

[113] The working realities of the decision makers at local authorities are not comparable to those of strategy planners in interested companies. Interviews both in Paris and Berlin confirmed these differences clearly. Berlin's representative describes his lack of resources regarding the EU's large-scale electric car support project 'Green E-Motion' with which European electric car market was supposed to be established: "I do not see any sense in participating. Siemens has an 8 mill. Euro budget, I have a budget of 140,000 Euro for four years. (...) For all that we are supposed to do in this project: Conferences, accompanying research.... I can hardly even cover my travel costs. So in the end, I don't go at all..." (Interview 41).

omy on electric car services varies along administrative competences and administrative cultures. In Paris, the city itself had formulated the need for an additional car-sharing system, co-financed the set-up of charging infrastructure and has subcontracted the building of the service to Bolloré. It has thus prepared the territory for this challenger's successful niche expansion, at the expense of other challengers that were excluded from competition in advance. In contrast, Berlin has opened up its territory for competition. Public administration has long been rather sceptical towards the planned mass introduction of electric cars. However, the open competition unfolded some perverse incentives as public-private collaborations to develop and test e-cars increased, and coherent market development seems difficult. As each district had authority to collaborate with energy providers, different charging systems began to be created in different districts rendering coherent use impossible. By late 2012, Berlin's Senate responsible was criticizing the lack of consistence in charging infrastructure development: "Today, we have about 100 charging points in Berlin, probably a bit less. There is an RWE and one Vattenfall charging point, one for ENBW, and every customer can use only one of them. This is absurd, especially in public space. An indispensable condition for me is access to charging without discrimination: No matter which company I am a customer of, I have to be able to charge my car at every charging point." (Interview 41). Recognizing urgent need to standardize, the city developed a map of needed charging infrastructure across the city.

The empowerment of cities and regions through demonstration projects has increased their visibility among the automotive sector's established government institutions on European level. The European 'Committee of Regions' (representing the regions as decision makers and interest groups in Brussels) reinforced this transformation of market hierarchies since the crisis. The Committee forged an 'automotive crisis intergroup' in 2009 with the intention of coordinating the (automotive) regions' needs and recovery after the crisis. It was mainly carried by the initiative of the French Region Bretagne, hosting production infrastructure of Peugeot (Interview 25). The initial support for innovations in industrial clusters has partly converged with support for intelligent and integrated local transport politics after the crisis.

In sum, the cities' and regions' increasing political and economic relevance constitutes the forth element of the emerging European government of sustainable transport. In an emerging e-mobility market, cities and regions represent an additional type of new public player that was not present in the traditional automobile configuration. The setting up of public charging infrastructure, car-sharing systems and the integration of electric vehicles into the transport system enable them to secure control of an emerging market conception, and emerge as legitimate players in new European government structures.

Conclusion 5.2. New path options develop

Chapter 5.2. illustrated that in the years following the crisis, a new wave of experimentations has questioned the third institutional pillar of automobility, i.e. the historically grown and culturally embedded pattern of car use. The analysed market niches and demonstrators contest the conception of individual car ownership and its cultural superiority. On-going experimentations and public support programmes suggest the emergence of new paths along several technologies and use patterns. Empirically, it is likely that different forms of automobility will co-exist in the near future. Parallel developments suggest that the new services should not be interpreted as a linear shift towards a new institutional path, but as the emergence of different scenarios of which none is dominant at the moment. This is because even if organizational and semantic shifts could be clearly observed, possible new path options have not entered mass market. But they constitute the micro-foundations of a new European sustainable transport government.

Summarizing the empirical results of this study in the light of my research question: How did the new path in Europe's automotive and transport sector emerge? Chapters 4 and 5 analysed different sequences of transformation of the European car sector's institutional trajectory and identified patterns of path creation emerging into a new institutional configuration.

Chapter 4 showed that in the conflict on CO_2 emission reduction of cars and vans, cooperative forms of governance replaced car makers' dominance in bilateral and informal decision-making in the European legislative process. With the 2008 emission standards replacing the car makers' voluntary agreement, a formalized negotiation arena was constituted, hosting a more heterogeneous network of stakeholders and establishing a slightly more balanced practice of future legislation. The result was an organizational shift in the sector from private to semi-public control, and the collectivization of a framing of the emission problem as one of democratic and economic responsibility and transparency. Emission standards changed car makers' product and strategy planning throughout the 2000s causing some shifts towards collaborative government. But keeping the debate as technology-focused as possible, car makers tried to secure their market control by introducing eco-efficient innovations into com-

bustion engine products and maintaining a narrative of automobility as the solution to increasing environmental problems.

Only in the context of the perceived severe sales crisis in 2008, (Chapter 5), did
initial investments to introduce alternative engine technologies, especially the
not even mature electric car, become the heart of a new narrative of European
industrial policy. Replacing the collective narrative of environmental innovations, a debate arose on how the sector could overcome its sales crisis and
structural problems of saturated domestic markets and overcapacities. The new
problem framing the necessity of electric cars development rapidly became a
dominant collective narrative among key public authorities, firms and national
governments. New visions, embedding electric car use into different mobility
patterns and linking it to public transport encouraged a shift to a multi-level
government in which new players such as market competitors, cities and consumers gained control and shaped the market, provoking the car makers' loss
of decision-making power. The demand regime, which European automotive
sectors took for granted, has changed. Different successful demonstrators illustrated the fact that consumers play a more active role in defining which different scenarios of electric mobility will diffuse into the car market.

A new sectoral order is about to emerge. Path rupture was defined as the destabilization of a structural and semantic sectoral hegemony. Path creation is the
emergence of a new institutional order. But does the creation of a path, lead to
stable institutional configuration? If structural changes have emerged in regulation and technology, the transformation of automobile use patterns so far has
not been a mass phenomenon. Different narratives for the role electric cars
could play currently compete, and drivers' transport choices have yet to be
evaluated.

Two empirical restrictions to the identified trends could argue against this
study's findings and have to be mentioned here.

1) Changing mobility patterns differ in economic and geographical contexts: The choice for transport alternatives is somewhat biased as most
   research and most projects are conducted in urban areas where visibility and density of transport is already very high. It has however been
   shown that the rural and semi-urban population is in larger need of
   shared transport alternatives to the individual car (Wells et al. 2014).
   Different geographical and demographic conditions suggest divergent
   trends towards new forms of mobility, differing from individual automobility.

2) Established car firms (incumbents) try to control the described transition through strategic adaptation. But observing different trends in con-

sumer behaviour makes product development and market anticipation more difficult for firms. As a consequence, almost every car maker has developed schemes in which electric cars can be rented, or shared at public stations, some are diversifying into (electric) scooters or other products. These remain a marginal activity so far, but can be seen as an important symbolical investment. On a small and local scale, Volkswagen started a local station-bound car-sharing service in Hannover with 200 Golf BlueMotion diesel cars named *Quicar,* and additional customized offers with cars from other segments for families or commercial use, in 2011. Labelled *DriveNow,* BMW offers a free-floating use of Mini cars in several German cities in direct competition to Daimler's car2go. Peugeot has opted for a comprehensive mobility package (*Mu),* comprising a rental service for all types of vehicles on demand: (electric) bikes, small cars and light utility vehicles, and scooters. This offer illustrates an opening towards different vehicle types and markets in which car makers need to become mobility operators.

These trends show that a new institutional order cannot emerge without a coherent narrative that justifies structural changes described, and links the three institutional dimensions of the industry: production, regulation and consumption. For a stable new path to emerge, a collective narrative is needed that makes sense of new technologies, politics and markets in a coherent manner to all actors involved. Chapter 6 will elaborate this by concluding on the empirical study.

6. Conditions of path creation - 21st century (auto-)mobility

"There is no doubt about the direction we're going in, the only doubt is the speed of this development, that, we do not control. We are supporting everything that allows to gradually develop sales of electric vehicles [...]"
(Vincent Bolloré, founder of Autolib', cited in autoactu.com, 10.9.2014)

This last chapter identifies future paths of (auto-)mobility and their conditions of emergence as possible futures of the European car market. Within the limits of the empirical study, these can be generalized to a model of path creation in general. Results will be interpreted against the background of a broader shift from liberal to more cooperative European governance and economic policy – still inspired mainly by market principles. The observed mechanisms are placed in the theoretical framework. How can ideas change markets and open up different institutional futures in the sector? How did emerging narratives co-evolve with organizational shifts in different areas of the industry? Finally, the empirical results will be evaluated in the light of the study's theoretical objectives. Can imagined futures provide a new micro-foundation for institutional trajectories?

How ideas change markets: future paths of (auto-)mobility

Empirical evidence supports the assumption of path creation. The car sector's institutional order emerging after the crisis begins to show coherent patterns. These patterns will determine to which degree OEMs' dominance will be transformed in the future - and which actors, based on which justifications, will control and shape the sector's future trajectory. The empirical analysis has shown that each of the sector's domains, regulation, supply and demand, have evolved, but also increasingly overlapped over the last 20 years:

- Emission reduction law has politicized and extended coordinative governance structures on European level
- Innovations in alternative powertrains attract more and diverse actors (governments, regions, firms) and more public and private investments
- Significant competition has emerged between old and new players

The identification of patterns requires the researcher to reduce historical complexity. Industrial development is a complex process in which developments are not linear and not always directly linked to one cause. In order to highlight this, one may speak of 'co-evolution' of different institutional configurations that may in the future develop into one 'institutional trajectory'. Since environmental policy had been problematized in the European automotive sector, different narratives on emission-reduction and later on the electric car have co-evolved with a transformation of the sector's organizational structure. Comparing the different sequences identified, each narrative implies a different pace of transformation. The pace of gradual but consistent change accelerated with the 2008 crisis; when dynamics of change converged.

- In the CO_2 debate, critics put forward a different framing with regard to emission reduction, but this understanding did not question the concept of automobility. The emerging narrative focused on emission-efficient automobility, implying that problems can be solved based on incremental change and improvements of the internal combustion engine.

- The crisis brought about a shared narrative of the electric car as a solution to the sector's global competitiveness problems. This framing has translated into many national subsidy programmes on electric vehicles.

- In parallel, through implementation of demonstration projects, an alternative understanding of emission-efficient mobility emerged based on alternative automobility including technological and behavioural change towards different forms of car use. It implies a more radical deviance from traditional automobility as it formulates new needs and forms of car use as the public car.

The preceding (micro-level) analysis shows that the transformation of the automotive industry consists of a series of collective framing processes, by which interested actors promote a specific view of the emission problem. If these narratives are shared and translated into instruments and, by consequent adaptation of firms' and authorities' interaction, they can produce organizational change in the market. Path rupture occurs consequently if terms of negotiation change. For example, when different framings emerge that define problems in a different way, suggesting new answers and therefore new policy instruments. Consequently, path options can only be indicated, while uncertainty always remains. From the time of writing in 2014, two possible path options have emerged.

Electric automobility

The more conservative path option consists of integrating electric cars as individually owned cars into the existing vehicle fleet. Current market research presents this as a realistic scenario. Fojcik and Proff (2014) have studied customer's willingness to buy electric cars in combination with participating in car-sharing options. Their study shows that people will keep buying cars, rather than replace them and rely on public car-sharing options only. However, car-sharing can be an attractive additional option to buying an electric car. In Germany, electric cars are very price-sensitive and currently about 5,000 to 10,000 Euro more expensive than comparable combustion engine cars (Fojcik/Proff 2014). One limit to this and similar studies (Ruhrort et al. 2014) is that potential user groups in which surveys are conducted are not always representative.[114] A second limit is that consumers' acceptance of e-car technology cannot be generalized. It depends, again, on the density of charging infrastructure and thus availability of mobility as a service. While most of the charging would be done at home and/or at work, public infrastructure will still be needed especially to cover longer distances. This depends on the use scenario. It may not be a coincidence that car makers so far have assumed that private charging would be preferable and sufficient, as home charging behaviour corresponds to the private ownership pattern of cars.[115] In general, the challenge for car makers in this future scenario is to maintain control over the definition of car use. They have so far managed to keep the idea of innovation (altering the powertrain in the car) semantically decoupled from ideas on different car use.

Electric automobility as a path option is not yet stabilized. Its gradual and experimental character is illustrated by the fact that car firms test different types of electric-car related solutions, to keep options open and to shape the preferred option for the firms' participation in the future market. Niche competitors' services such as Autolib' or Car2go suggest different visions of future car use. Car2go represents a form of use in which car use is public but, due to individual flexibility in using and parking the car, still resembling the individual driving pattern. Bolloré has opted to enter the car-sharing market by subcontracting to cities and regions, which implies a publicly co-managed infrastructure, urban

---

[114] Proff/Fojcik 2014 conducted surveys in the area of Duisburg/Essen, a metropolitan Ruhr area in which car ownership is higher than in Berlin.
[115] BMW had conducted a first study on charging behavior with 540 Mini customers in 4 large global cities. 89 % of customers indicated that they would not need public charging infrastructure for their daily car use, charging at home or work being sufficient. Source:
http://www.heise.de/autos/artikel/BMW-Studie-Aktionsradius-von-E-Autos-reicht-aus-1128621.html?view=print, accessed 17/12/2014.

planning, regional development and a less flexible use of the car as it is station-bound. However, Autolib' also sells BlueCars to private customers and professional end-users, keeping the individual automobility path open. In the same line of argument, Bolloré has recently engaged in a partnership with Renault to produce different small electric cars. Car-sharing platforms may become a mere marketing tool in order to sell electric cars and the battery. This illustrates the limits of the electric automobility development path.

Electric multimodality

A number of electric car experiments discussed in the empirical analysis have opened up the possibility of a 'multimodal electric transport path' for urban European areas and beyond. Promoters of electric mobility as 'systemic' transport innovation suggest a different narrative of future automobility that can be named electric multimodality mobility. Long-term transport and industrial policy objectives align using electric vehicles, preferably fuelled with renewably sourced electricity, as a means to better integrate private and collective transport with open access to all journey options via mobile devices.[116] Projects such as BeMobility require intermodality, i.e. the combination of transport means, and open access to mobility as key conditions of future car use. In this path, automobility is no longer a synonym for car ownership but signifies a personal journey, independent of whatever transport means is used. This path is innovative: not only in technology but also concerning use, transport and urban planning and in redefining the role of the car in transport as a whole. It is open to other transport modes; and consequently evolving with them as part of a larger transport system. It is embedded in European transport policy objectives, formulated as follows: "[...] the paramount goal of European transport policy is to help establish a system that underpins European economic progress, enhances competitiveness and offers high quality mobility services while using resources more efficiently." (European Commission 2011: 6). However, also this path is limited by two conditions:

- Connectivity: integrated information services such as mobile applications and real-time information are crucial for intermodal services. This path is tied to their technological development and requires users familiar with mobile devices.

---

[116] Multimodality refers to the use of various transport means to cover mobility needs. 'Intermodality' can be understood as a specific category of multimodality, i.e. the combination of different means of transport for one journey. The car, therefore, becomes one of the means of transport used.

- Infrastructure: intermodal transport connects cars and bikes to existing transport (public transport, bikes) and, if electric, appropriate charging infrastructure (stations). Either this option will remain confined to dense urban areas, or the surrounding structure will have to evolve accordingly.

These two different path options for the European automotive market compete. It remains to be seen if one narrative could dominate or convince others, or if a diverse market of several co-existing forms of automobility will remain. This will depend on the evolution of consumer demand. With over 75,000 electric vehicles sold in 2014 (representing a 48.5% increase over 2014[117], sales are going to exceed 1 million in 2025 at least (Transport&Environment 2014), so even a conservative development scenario establishes hybrid and electric as a market reality in the mid-term.

This study does not aim at delivering forecasts, rather, from the economic and political history of these two path options, it aims at deriving the institutional conditions of path creation. These will determine if future path options become reality. Nevertheless, a few empirical conclusions can be drawn at this stage. A general condition for all future development paths is the rising *regional differentiation*. Across all path scenarios, regional characteristics will be much more important than in 20th century automobility. Car makers are forced to revise their market projections. Individual car ownership was characterized by its *universality*. Because of its relative independence in technology and use, regional characteristics such as infrastructure density (supply stations) and transport modes were perceived as less constraining than they are for electric car use. Charging infrastructure and geographical conditions will remain a critical factor for market uptake. Car use can no longer remain a universalized individual projection that car makers frame and then design products. The user, so far the 'invisible third' in the market, becomes visible and articulates different needs and use patterns. In addition to economic and social segmentation of user groups, regional and generational segmentation will play a more important role. In sum, regional geographic characteristics of car use, ownership, charging infrastructure and density of transport alternatives will condition every future scenario of electric-car use. Due to regional differences, a multitude and co-existence of scenarios is therefore even more probable in the short-term.

In the mid-term, however, this study shows that a profound transformation towards electric multimodal transport will take place, driven by changes in urban centres. In semi-urban and rural areas, electrification of individual car

---

[117] http://cleantechnica.com/2015/12/27/europe-ev-sales-up-49/

use is likely to take off more slowly, depending on how fast the range anxiety and cost come down, and infrastructure will develop. Current debates have produced a structural transformation of the sectors' conception of control. Even if empirically this change is not yet visible as an outcome of an on-going transformation, in indicators such as car sales, changes have taken place in other areas: the mindset of the involved actors, the terms of discussion, the arenas of debate, and the narrative linked to mobility have changed. These set structural conditions for path change. The rules of rule-making in the sector, i.e. the conditions of reproduction of dominance have profoundly changed. The characteristics of 20th century automobility, i.e. the assumption that consumers like to possess and drive cars, that combustion technology will prevail and that OEMs determine the demand through supply (and state the reverse), can no longer be reproduced. The control conception of automobility which industry has forged will evolve. The question is whether this transformation will be more gradual than radical, at least in the near future,

The analysis has also shown why establishing a mass market for EVs as a condition for defining a new path reflects in itself thinking in dimensions of 20th century mobility. In the old conception of control, the car as a universal product was dominant because of its mass consumption. Electric cars and their integration into public transport, however, have changed this criterion since the new product has different non-universal characteristics but favours efficient forms of use. As a consequence, mass marketization of electric cars is not necessarily a representative criterion of evaluating the new paths of electrified transport, especially electric multimodality. On the contrary: expecting parallel developments as in the 20th century automotive configuration means reasoning in terms of industrial policy, as many governments do, instead of reasoning in terms of efficient transport.[118]

But there is more to path creation. The empirical analysis suggests that the automobility path emerged in a larger semantic and structural context of liberal economic politics on the European level. If so, there might be further conditions of successful institutionalization of alternative institutional trajectories: path creation requires a larger shift in European economic governance.

---

[118] Some observers have indeed made this distinction. Jullien argues, that the electric-car debate shows more consistency than critics expected precisely because of infrastructure adaptations the innovation has required over the last few years. "[...] even though the bubble of expectations [after the crisis, J.H.] burst, those actors who were at the forefront remain and are joined by others. [...] slowly, the ecosystem the EV needs emerges. Parking spaces, charging stations, batteries, vehicle standards, relevant usage patterns and feasible pricing: on all levels, the questions of 2014 are not the same as those five years ago." (Jullien 2014:2)

A new European economic governance?

The way the environmental question was dealt with in the automotive sector reflects the rise and fall of liberalist economic politics in the European economic governance. The first debates on CO_2 regulation in the sector, and on emission reduction in a larger sense, were led in the context of a rising acceptance of voluntary approaches. Chapter 4 showed that several attempts by parts of the Commission that were preferring an interventionist top down approach, imposing CO_2 limits and sanctions by law, or later, through a vehicle tax, were stopped during the decision making process by different member states and the car industry. Car makers in particular disposed of excellent informal relations with the DG industry, and decided in a quasi-bilateral manner on a voluntary approach to emission reduction which environmental policy makers in the Commission were forced to accept. As a symbol of horizontal governance approaches, the Commission had advocated voluntary agreements as an instrument to be favoured when dealing with industrial sectors in its White Paper of Governance (2001). The Lisbon Agenda of 2001 had justified these types of cooperative policy approaches as a part of a larger liberal economic policy agenda, which aimed at increasing Europe's competitiveness and thus to increase industry's flexibility to act. Liberal policy-making had also diffused into the EU's environmental programmes. Dezalay argues that the observed neoliberalist turn concerned environmental politics in general, not just those concerning the automotive industry. "The history of European environmental policy is an example of a broad neo-liberal counter-offensive which has provoked a profound restructuring of the state's tools of intervention in politics, in Europe and beyond" (Dezalay 2007: 67). In semantic coherence with the larger context, car makers had aligned their market control strategies by arguing for voluntary efforts in reference to sustainable development goals and reporting practices. This way of arguing verifies what Dezalay has observed for European environmental policy from the 1990s in general: "Large multinational companies and consultancies become the dominant actors in this market of sustainable development which serves them as a laboratory for disqualifying the interventionism of the Welfare State." It can be said that around the year 2000, the sectors' conception of control comprehended a neoliberal idea of governance that had diffused into the automotive market by politics aligned to the supply only, not to demand.

This analysis suggests that the economic crisis in 2008 encouraged a shift back towards more cooperative politics in European economic policy, i.e. building a middle ground between liberal and interventionist forms of governance. The European Commission's belief in the benefits of conferring with industrial stakeholders might have diminished with the failure of the CO_2 emission agreement in 2008. From then on, automotive sector politics returned to cooperative governance as it had been observed in the 1970s/80s with regard to the environmental and competition domains. First, consultations on different representative and working levels were institutionalized through CARS 21 in 2006-2007. The 2008/2009 crisis called governments and the European Investment Bank on stage as those organizations that could help re-vitalize sales and secure employment depending directly or indirectly of the car industry. This is especially true for countries hosting car manufacturers, but also for those that host a large supply industry or production sites.

The crisis was interpreted by the European Commission as a need to restructure - in a cooperative effort with industry - the whole sector and support the mass introduction of alternative technologies. Chapter 5 showed that publicly co-financed R&D, but also demonstration projects have started to develop important institutional and market effects in metropolitan areas. Public authorities emerge as project partners, levels of decision-making have multiplied. Co-operative decision making, and the consent of public authorities, are a condition for the future development of institutions in the car sector. Formerly dominant car makers need to work at all decision-making levels to secure control. The 2013 CO_2 negotiations, following up the precedent set by the 2009 CO_2 law, were then pursued in a cooperative style in which a heterogeneous network of stakeholders participated in the negotiations. As far as emission policy is concerned, future governance is likely to remain cooperative. Cooperative regulation practice has diffused towards other areas of the transport sector and industry such as the electric vehicles.[119] Radical innovations that go beyond institutional control necessitate consensus rather than competition in order to build a common future market. Partly conditioned by the loss of technological and thus strategic control, partly forced by competitors and authorities, car makers did not succeed in aligning their conception of control to a more coordinative policy-making (as they tried by arguing for an 'integrative approach'). Importantly, however, the case study does not imply that with more cooperation, stakeholders gained equal influence over political decisions. Rather, industry players still seem more influential than environmental or consumer groups.

---

[119] Technical harmonization of standards, for example of charging infrastructure and electric vehicle plugs has been one of the major problems of consensus-building, in which French and German market actors competed to become standard setters for Europe. This conflict recalls patterns from the introduction of the catalytic converter, see Chapter 1.

Further work will have to show whether this turn can be expected for all European markets, as this touches the limits of a one-sector case study. However, Carter et al. argue on the basis of a comparison between four different industrial sectors that similar shifts can be observed for sustainable development politics in the EU. Today, the umbrella term 'sustainable development' encompasses many environmental regulations and has increasingly become a tool of competition policy. "Notwithstanding the diversity of problematizations and instrumentations of Sustainable Development to which this has given rise, we claim it has nevertheless, and increasingly, been subordinated to the norm of competitiveness as enshrined in 'the Lisbon Strategy' of 2000." (Carter et al 2014: 167)

The study confirmed that in-depth case studies are an appropriate method to understand how policy concepts as such are being drafted, enacted and what consequences they provoke. Any shift towards a different kind of environmental policy needs to be analysed from practices on the micro-level. Carter et al argue: "If the 1990s were indeed marked by significant changes, the supposed rigidity of 'the bureaucratic model' of regulation, as well as its current obsolescence, must be questioned in the light of this policy's actual implementation. Similarly, the supposed victory of an unambiguous economic doctrine promoted around SD will also be questioned." (Carter et al. 2014: 166).

The degree of involvement of public authorities and administration in economic policy practices will determine future paths of automobility. If a larger role is left to market forces, it seems to be more likely that the path of electric automobility will develop. The more governments, regions and the EU authorities interfere and fund alternative mobility demonstrators, the more likely it is that the second path of multimodality could shape future markets.

The role of ideas in capitalist economies

This study showed that ideas can change markets. Indeed, the collective framing of the electric car as an investment into a not yet mature innovation represents features of what Beckert called a 'rationality fiction'. Actors' expectations of the future state of the market impacted sectors' institutional configurations. Two rationality fictions in particular appeared in the analysis as drivers of path creation throughout the last 20 years:

- the idea that emission reduction would improve the automotive sector's environmental and economic performance

- that the electric car would secure a competitive future and that the 2008/09 crisis was the appropriate moment to adapt sectoral policy.

These shared understandings among dominant actors of the sector were interpretations of the present in the light of an aspired future in which the market would be stable and founded on a globally competitive and value-creating innovation. Both ideas translated into instruments which then shaped the future market and are likely to shape a future path of the sector. This sheds light on the role of instruments as 'translators' of ideas. Chapters 4 and 5 showed in which sense they are performative and shaped new institutional configurations as they were enacted.

The impact of CO_2 standards as an instrument of regulation set the conditions for path rupture. The standards as a political instrument translated environmentalists' and consumers' expectations of improving car emissions into a mechanism encouraging sales of less polluting new cars. The suggested mechanism is one of sanctioned and transparent reduction. The standards translate the collective idea, or expectation, that emission reduction will be realized if publicly controlled and comparatively pursued among firms, pushed by a strong financial incentive. Their implementation not only shaped the terms of future negotiations, but also opened up a debate on best technological solutions to solve the problems: The electric car emerged as the most realistic option. In that sense, the standards' performative character shaped an unforeseen solution. Categories and practices in which the (emission) problem were formulated (technological strategies), produced a solution that was no longer under car makers' initial control: Car makers, in 2008, did not have a strong interest in promoting the electric car. Rather, emission reductions produced a favourable context, in which Asian competitors promoted alternatively fuelled cars worldwide, creating a new reality in which European firms have to compete. The strict regulation, and car makers' consequent investments, opened up 'futures' beyond limits of the present conception of control. These changes accelerated investments into new (e-car) technologies that question the previously stabilized path. It contested the narrative of technological control by carmakers and suggested transparent coordinated public private governance patterns and institutionalized conflict negotiation arenas.

The financial support instruments for the demonstration projects on electric cars, from 2009 onwards, accelerated the gradual process of transformation of legitimacy patterns prevailing in the automotive sector. If individual car possession and use so far had been an unquestioned assumption for market development, the suitability of electric cars for urban distances, and especially shared use in public and private fleets, promoted different scenarios of car use as a possible future. Energy and parking space providers, rail operators and electric car makers invested in projects, developed business models and forced the conventional car industry to also develop mobility services in order to remain competitive. The instrument of demonstration projects, initially thought to reinforce the traditional car industry by increasing sales, opened up a different market future by allowing different vehicle use scenarios and a shift from discussing electric cars to electric mobility and electrified transport. The political instrument turned out to be performative in that they allowed different ideas to become reality.

The results of this study also confirm the theoretical concepts and the research design chosen. The emerging institutional paths identified on the macro-level were constituted from collective framings and instruments (following rationality fictions) at the micro-level. The micro-level analysis revealed that there is no such thing as self-reproducing structures as institutionalist literature presumes. If these are reproduced, market actors do this actively through deploying instruments that reflect a given conception of control. The market-shaping power of rationality fictions explains how the narrative of the electric car as a recipe for the sector's global survival could unfold a collective effect on the existing conception of control. Rationality fictions as ideas on how the future should look inspired public policy makers and companies to adapt their strategies. To study how fictions translated into organizational shifts which bring about path change, we need the concept of performative character of instruments. The empirical study further suggests that path creation needs a favourable environment and historically contingent events, such as the crisis, to allow framings to translate from micro-challenges to macro-configurations, which then open up different market futures. These findings give room to further develop the theoretical framework on path creation. This is done by means of a theoretical conclusion in the following section.

How do institutional orders stabilize? The micro-foundations of path creation

Historical trajectories are a macro-level analytical category applied ex-post to historical configurations. Paths can only be clearly identified over longer periods of time. Uncertainty over development remains, especially in sequences of potential path rupture and the creation of new trajectories. The creation of a new institutional path is not a linear process. For the sake of exploring the concept's theoretical explanatory value, the analysed events can be schematized into three sequences on the macro-level. Each sequence of events contains different dynamics of stabilization and destabilization across different fields of sectoral activity. A conception of control is therefore a constantly re-negotiated and never stable, as the analysed sequence of events illustrates.

(1999 - 2008) Gradual destabilization:

The 2000s saw a destabilization of a given institutional order that occurred gradually. Increasingly strict emission norms triggered a transformation in governance patterns and prepared the ground for destabilization which occurred through competition of alternative solutions.

(2008 - 2011) Path rupture:

During the crisis, alternatives such as the electric car were supported quickly and extensively, though uncoordinatedly through linking to short-term economic recovery programmes to enable a longer-term innovation. This shift involved more decision-making levels: While the EU Commission tried to harmonize policies, national governments sought to support national champions and entered into a race for electric car technology development, while cities and regions started to implement new technology and use forms. Path rupture occurred as an adaptation to a new narrative on all decision-making levels, with competing rationality fictions.

(2011 - Present) Path creation:

The industrial framing and implementation of support instruments in the crisis resulted in a slowing down of competition of market scenarios for the future European automotive sector. Car makers compete with other new players and direct challengers on rivalling business models on electric car use, while different actors on all decision-making levels create strategies and planning on electrified transport. The need to cooperate in order to develop an emerging market, and face global competition, have become stronger.

The following table shows that path creation can be interpreted as a diffusion process of alternative narratives, and corresponding organizational shifts, into different areas of an industry, or control: governance, technology and markets.

Historical Sequence	Actors		
	Politics	*Industry*	*Users*
Destabilisation (1998-2008)	X		
Path Rupture (2008-2011)	X	X	
Path Creation (2011 -)	X	X	X
	Regulation	*Technology*	*Market*
		Sectoral Domain	

Table 3: Scheme of patterns of path creation: environmental conflicts in the EU car industry

We can derive necessary conditions without which path creation is not likely to occur:

- All institutional dimensions of the sector need to be included.

- Path change only occurs if changes in each sectoral area are connected. This might be because of a historical contingency such as a perceived moment of crisis or global shifts in competition.

- Semantic and structural changes need to be coherent across all sectoral dimensions

In order for institutional orders to be (de-)stabilized, semantic and structural transformations need to be coherent with each other. Political instruments, communication media such as reports and statements, and the organization of negotiation arenas are powerful means to incorporate semantics into structures. This can maintain and or change a given institutional order, but only if the resulting control instrument is coherent in its normative content (Le Ga- lès/Lascoumes 2004) with an emerging order. Therefore, narrative coherence is a necessary condition for path creation: A shared narrative must be sufficiently comprehensive as to include governance, supply and demand, in order to justi- fy a new institutional path.

Stability of institutional orders is by definition limited, as the empirical analysis shows. This is true for the conception of automobility, as the history of various alternative mobility projects since the 1970s reminds us (Chapter 1). Control- seeking instruments such as the voluntary agreement, already contained the roots of destabilization, as unveiled in Chapters 4 and 5. The same relative stability can be expected for a new stabilizing order: If the market for electric cars will dominate in one specific form of use, for example free-floating car sharing such as Car2go, it is likely that other competitors will challenge this model.

The idea that criticism is inherent to an institutional order is indeed part of Fligstein's history of 20th century capitalism as a succession of conceptions of control (1990). In his terms, the evolution of one conception of control towards another shows that each conception of control already contains the possibility of its criticism. It is even the precondition of their transformation and succession, and, in very general terms, the precondition and driver of the evolution of political and economic institutional development. If at the same time, constant institutional evolution was characterized as an essential part of capitalist economies, the consequence may surprise us: If institutional orders always contain their criticism, one could derive that in order to persist, dominant firms and authorities should tolerate, rather than absolutely control or oppress, challengers and their business models. The definition of 'challengers' in Fligstein's terms can thus be extended to the political and economic sphere: Challengers are not only market competitors but also political authorities, interest groups and experts who criticize the control strategies of incumbents. Consequently, it can be concluded that any future institutional order will be all the more stable, the more open it is to non-dominant actors and alternative narratives.

The remainder of this chapter outlines its conditions of path creation as first elements towards a theory of path creation. Building on the empirical analysis, the process of structural and semantic consolidation of a new path is generalized. In sum, four conditions for path change are sufficient to create path change.

1. Contained alternatives

Macro-patterns, accordingly, always contain margins of action for their challengers (structure) and tend to absorb their critics (narratives). A condition for path creation is therefore, that these marginalized or contained alternatives are present and can emerge at specific points in time. This sheds light on a theoretical paradox: A path needs a dominant structure and a narrative to emerge as such. But at the same time, we could observe that absolute dominance provokes path ruptures. Path stability appears to depend rather on the right balance between tolerating alternative framings and justifying dominant models, a theoretical hypothesis to be analysed in further case studies.

2. Moments of crisis and path rupture

Institutionalism postulates that crises are times of path rupture, but consider them external events. The analysis has falsified this assumption. Each crisis is differently constituted by underlying conflicts in governance, supply and demand. They differ in character, as sectoral configurations are historically unique. A moment of what sectoral actors perceive to be a crisis does not create path change. Rather, crises can be seen as moments of structural opening to deconstruct existing legitimating narratives. They help already existing alternative ones to emerge. The 2008 crisis can be considered as catalyst of a new path on electric and shared mobility, but not as its cause. Consequently, crises are a necessary, but not sufficient condition to path creation. A crisis can cause path rupture, but not every disruption is productive and can create a new path. The analysis by micro-foundations proves that crises and ruptures are not external to an institutional setting - they are made in the sense that actors interpret their consequences and anticipate them through instruments.

3. Interaction on the micro-level determines path creation

This is why institutionalism so far could not explain the process by which new paths emerge. The micro-foundations are the ways in which market and politics interact on conflicts that constantly emerge in any institutional trajectory. Solving these problems by specific instruments that are justified in specific ways, actors decide each time on the degree to which they maintain or deviate from a given path. Consciously or not, their problem framings, strategies or instruments call upon given patterns of legitimation dominant players have set in a sector. Fligstein's concept of a conception of control, a dominant shared narrative and accordingly organized sectoral institutions, does not deliver a sufficient explanation for how ideas change markets. Micro-foundations such as collective framing, conflict solving and the empirical reconstitution of interaction fill this gap.

4. Semantic and organizational co-evolution

Reciprocal influence between alternative framings and organizational shifts emerged as a key characteristic of processes of path creation. I concluded that, as a condition of path creation, they need to be coherent and collective in order to convince the dominant majority of actors to act differently, to adapt instruments and strategies to, for example, electric mobility support. My analysis has identified different factors of explanation of institutional change that transition theory (Geels et al. 2011) does not specify. The history of the automobile path provides evidence why coherence is a necessary condition to create new institutional structures: before 2008, path rupture was not possible. It follows that path creation is as much a semantic process, i.e. a result of interpretative action by market and political actors, as it is an organizational one, conditioned by prevailing market structures and hierarchies.

Embedded policy analysis - limits and gains

Linking overarching concepts such as institutional stability and change to a study on the micro-level analysis necessarily produces shortcomings that a single large case study cannot overcome. Part of the problem is that research combining public policy and industries/markets, and linking existing concepts, is not common. This study addressed a field of research that has just emerged, without defined boundaries or a consistent epistemological core. This approach entails methodological limits and gains. An embedded policy analysis can unite economic and political dynamics in one analysis. This study contends that path change occurs by combining inherited given social structures (the past) and imagined futures (the future). This is where institutionalist research and approaches of market sociology meet. An embedded policy analysis can, in situations of path rupture, provide elements to predict future scenarios. Institutionalist studies of industries (Hall/Soskice 2001, Jullien/Smith 2014) articulate this need. Due to its micro-level approach and the focus on semantic and organizational context in markets and politics, an embedded policy analysis can produce results that would have been overlooked by a macro-level perspective. The emergence of institutions explains what is not visible from the outside. The analysis could thus uncover the logic of an institutional process that has not been described as such so far: That environmental politics prepared a gradual shift in power-relations inside the industry, on which cultural change in mobility patterns could settle in order to provoke major shifts in markets, industry and consumption patterns at the same time.

The influence of representations of the future can be generalized. From the strong impact of the shared narrative on the electric car, we can derive that in many markets, technological innovations are expected to improve existing products and are likely to change markets even before being sold or in use. Inversely, the risk in emphasizing the power of actors' expectations in the analysis is to create room for subjectivist analysis. Especially dealing with innovations, whose impacts are always subject to estimates, conducted by experts, interest-driven forecasts by individuals or consultancies tend to influence terms of thinking and reference. The concept of rationality fictions includes the definitional power of expertise.

Conclusion

This study is a contribution to research on institutional trajectories. It suggests complementing the lack of micro-foundations in path theory with existing sociological theories of framing and instrumentation. By building conceptual bridges between sociological market research and institutionalist political economy, this approach could give insights into how industries or markets change from within. External shocks such as the global financial crisis of 2008 are thus mere catalysing events of transformations that are already on-going. The case study of the European car sector showed that path creation is, in fact, an endogenous phenomenon made by market and political actors. The role of ideas is central for the emergence of new institutional paths, as market actors' objectives are inspired by representations of a desired future, for example more efficient forms of automobility. Further research on imagined futures in different markets will be relevant in order to anticipate future developments, for example environmental conflicts and how to govern them.

Changes in socio-cultural patterns alone are not sufficient to induce path ruptures, for example away from the individual passenger car towards shared forms of automobility. Path creation occurs only when generative rules of the sector's hierarchy reproduction are changed. New patterns of legitimacy of market shaping firms, products, and forms of use and practices of governance had to be accepted in order to allow alternative ideas to gain ground. Consequently, a new path's stability will emerge if these rules are coherently reproduced. The legitimacy of expectations about the future are as an important explanation factor to path creation as is the historical context. Consequently, in order to better understand processes of path creation, historical institutionalist analysis should include actors' semantic or cognitive orientation to representations of the future.

These findings were demonstrated within the limits of a single-case study illustrating path ruptures and creation due to environmental conflicts in the European car industry. Further research is necessary to confirm these conclusions. First pieces of research comparing different industrial sectors historically have been conducted parallel to this study (Jullien/Smith 2014). The demonstration of possible institutional futures requires a certain reduction of their empirical complexity: Parallel legislation, diverse political and market actors, industrial dynamics on the national and local level certainly have impacted the empirical dynamics, but have been taken into account. This choice was made deliberately in order to identify the impact of the most direct influence factors to path creation. As social actors' rationality is limited to expectations of desired futures, any possible future state of the industry depends on the degree to which actors pursue these expectations.

This study sought to characterize institutional processes of path creation not the macro-level, where the concept has been defined, but on the micro-level of interaction. The way the research question is formulated produces a second limit worth addressing. While empirical analysis confirmed that collective narratives and instruments produce organizational change, it is evident that the impact of these changes can only be identified retrospectively on the macro-level with hindsight and in comparison with previous historical patterns. Given that the empirical field researched includes quite recent events, this study is limited to determine potential scenarios. The degree of uncertainty – empirically – is high. It would therefore be useful to update this research in the future and discuss empirical developments against its current findings. A further theoretical challenge is the indication that path creation can also lead to more than one trajectory in the future. Here, again, empirical analysis suggests more complexity than the initial macro-level concepts contain. A first hint at solving this problem conceptually is to clarify the fact that institutional paths always already contain 'alternatives' as marginalized narratives, or different organisational forms such as competing business models or niche regulations. Historical analysis showed that paths are in fact not stable but are a continuously negotiated compromise between a dominant institutional compromise and alternative solutions.

The role of ideas in shaping markets is crucial. Necessary conditions for path creation are that collective framings of how products, markets and market law will work, become shared narratives. The semantic and structural coherence of these alternatives is key to overcoming existing path dependency. This case study showed that new narratives (constructions of automobility) go along with coherent organizational changes (sectoral restructuring). Institutional trajectories are the realization of new shared narratives. As social and semantic constructions of the future, they shape capitalist economies and actors' options to transform them.

References

[6t]-Bureau de recherche (2014) : L'autopartage en trace directe: quelle alternative à la voiture particulière ? Résultats de la première enquête sur l'impact d'un service d'autopartage en trace directe (le cas d'Autolib').
http://6t.fr/blog/fr/lautopartage-en-trace-directe-quelle-alternative-voiture-particuliere/. Accessed 9/4/2015.

ACEA (2005): Efforts to Reduce CO_2 Emissions from Passenger Cars. Presentation by Hermann Meyer to Transport & Environment's Conference "Clean Cars 2010", Brussels, January 20, 2005.
http://www.transportenvironment.org/sites/default/files//docs/presentations/200 5/2005-01_clean_car_seminar/2005-01_p7_efforts_to_reduce_CO2_emissions_from_passenger_cars_meyer.pdf. Accessed 9/4/2015.

ACEA (2013): Statistical Pocket Guide. Brussels.
http://www.acea.be/uploads/publications/POCKET_GUIDE_13.pdf. Accessed 9/4/2015.

Aigle, Thomas, Ante Krstacic-Galic, Lutz Marz, & Andrea Scharnhorst Andrea (2008): Busse als Wegbereiter. Zu einem frühen Markt für alternative Antriebe. Discussion Paper SP III 2008-102. Wissenschaftszentrum Berlin für Sozialforschung. http://bibliothek.wzb.eu/pdf/2008/iii08-102.pdf. Accessed 9/4/2015.

Aigle, Thomas;, Holger Braun-Thürmann, Lutz Marz,Kerstin Schäfer,& Marc Weider (2007): Mobil statt fossil: Evaluationen, Strategien und Visionen einer neuen Automobilität, WZB Discussion Paper, No. SP III 2007-106.
http://bibliothek.wzb.eu/pdf/2007/iii07-106.pdf. Accessed 9/4/2015.

Air Quality in Europe (2013): Compare the Current Air Quality in Different European Cities. http://www.airqualitynow.eu/comparing_home.php. Accessed 19/8/2013.

AirParif (2012): La qualite´ de l'air en 2011 a` Paris. Mai 2012.
http://www.airparif.asso.fr/_pdf/publications/Rbilan75_2011.pdf. Accessed 19/8/2013.

Aldrich, Howard (2010): Beam me up, Scott(ie)! Institutional Theorists' Struggles with the Emergent Nature of Entrepreneurship. Howard E. Aldrich. In: Sine, Wesley & Robert David(2010). Institutions and Entrepreneurship, p. 329ff.

Altvater, Elmar (2006): Das Ende des Kapitalismus wie wir ihn kennen. Münster: Westfälisches Dampfboot.

Amable, Bruno & Yannick Lung (2008): The European Socio-Economic Models of a Knowledge-Based Society. Main Findings and Conclusion. Working Papers of GREThA, n° 2008-26. http://ideas.repec.org/p/grt/wpegrt/2008-26.html. Accessed 9/4/2015.

Artur, Brian (1984): Increasing Returns and Path Dependence in the Economy, Ann Arbor: University of Michigan Press.

Autolib' Metropole (2014): Annual Report 2013. http://www.autolibmetropole.fr/le-rapport-dactivite-autolib-metropole-2013/. Accessed 9/4/2015.

Automotive News (2014): Toyota Moving Away From EVs in Favor of Hydrogen Fuel Cells. http://www.autonews.com/article/20140520/OEM05/140529984/toyota-moving-away-from-evs-in-favor-of-hydrogen-fuel-cells. Accessed 13/12/14.

AVERE (2007): European Commission Consultation "Reducing CO_2 Emissions from Cars", Contribution to Stakeholder Hearing, 10.7.2007. http://ec.europa.eu/reducing_co2_emissions_from_cars/. Accessed 31/10/2013.

Bandelow, Nils C.; Kundolf, Stefan & Kirstin Lindloff (2014): Agenda Setting für eine nachhaltige EU-Verkehrspolitik: Akteurskonstellationen, Machtverhältnisse und Erfolgsstrategien. Berlin: edition sigma, 2014.

bcs (Bundesverband CarSharing) (2014). Carsharing Boom Continues, Press Release 27.2.2014. http://www.carsharing.de/sites/default/files/uploads/presse/pm_carsharing-bilanz_2013_englisch.pdf. Accessed 9/4/2015.

Beckert, Jens (2013): Imagined Futures: Fictional Expectations in the Economy. In: Theory&Society. Volume 42 (May 2013), 3, pp. 219-240.

Beckert, Jens (2014): Capitalist Dynamics. Fictional Expectations and the Openness of the Future. MPIfG Discussion Paper 14/7. Max-Planck-Institut für Gesellschaftsforschung, Köln http://www.mpifg.de/pu/dp_abstracts/dp14-7.asp. Accessed 9/4/2015.

BeMobility - Berlin elektroMobil (2011): Gemeinsamer Abschlussbericht des Projektkonsortiums. Unpublished.

Blöcker, Antje & Julia Hildermeier (2015): Income Polarisation, Rising Mobility Costs and Green Transport. Contradictory Developments on Germany's Automotive Market. In: Bruno Jetin (ed.) The Global Automobile Demand after the "Great Recession". Vol. 1. Automobile Demand in Mature Countries. Palgrave Macmillan, pp. 105-126.

Boavida, Nuno et al. (2013): Technology Transition Towards Electric Mobility – Technology Assessment as a Tool for Policy Design. Paper presented at the 21st Gerpisa Conference, June 2013, Paris. http://gerpisa.org/node/2085. Accessed 5/11 /2013.

Bogner, Alexander & Wolfgang Menz (2005): Das theoriegenerierende Experteninterview. Erkenntnisinteresse, Wissensformen, Interaktion. In: Bogner, Alexander; Littig, Beate; Wolfgang Menz (eds.), Das Experteninterview – Theorie, Methode, Anwendung. Wiesbaden: VS Verlag für Sozialwissenschaften, pp.33-70.

Bourdieu Pierre (1997): Le champ économique. In: Actes de la recherche en sciences sociales. Vol. 119, septembre 1997. pp. 48-66. http://www.persee.fr/web/revues/home/prescript/article/arss_0335-5322_1997_num_119_1_3229. Accessed 9/4/2015.

Boyer, Robert & Michel Freyssenet (2003): Produktionsmodelle: Eine Typologie Am Beispiel Der Automobilindustrie. Berlin: Ed. Sigma.

Bratzel, Stefan (2010): Die Innovationen der globalen Automobilkonzerne. Eine Analyse der Zukunftstrends und Innovationsprofile der 19 bedeutendsten Hersteller. Bergisch-Gladbach.

Bratzel, Stefan (2011): Das Auto aus Sicht der jungen Generation. Statussymbol oder nur Funktionsgut ? Eine empirische Studie zu Einstellungen und Verhaltensmustern von 18 bis 25-Jährigen in Deutschland. FHDW Center of Automotive. Vortrag AutoUni, Marketing und Vertrieb aktuell, Marketing und Vertrieb aktuell, Wolfsburg, 18.01.2011.

Braun-Thürmann, Holger (2005): Soziologie der Innovation. Themen der Soziologie. Bielefeld: transcript verlag.

Buhr, Regina, Weert Canzler,Andreas Knie,& Stephan Rammler (eds.) (1999): Bewegende Moderne. Fahrzeugverkehr als soziale Praxis. Berlin: edition sigma.

BUND (2007): Deutsche Autohersteller und die Reduzierung von CO2 bei Neuwagen. EU-Klimafahrtenbuch 2012 für PKW. http://www.bund.net/fileadmin/bundnet/publikationen/klima/20070314_klima_eu_klimafahrtenbuch_klimafakten.pdf. Accessed 9/4/2015.

Calabrese, Giuseppe (ed.) (2012): The Greening of the Automotive Industry. Basingstoke: Palgrave Macmillan.

Callon, Michel (1979): L'État face à l'innovation technique. Le cas du véhicule électrique, Revue française de science politique, vol. 29, n° 3, pp. 426-447.

Callon, Michel (1986): The Sociology of an Actor-Network. The Case of the Electric Vehicle. In: Callon, M., Law, J., & Rip, A. (1986). Mapping the Dynamics of Science and Technology: Sociology of Science in the Real World. Macmillan, pp. 19-34.

Canzler, Weert (1996): Das Zauberlehrlings-Syndrom. Entstehung und Stabilität des Automobil-Leitbildes, Berlin: edition sigma.

Canzler, Weert, Andreas Knie (2009): Grüne Wege Aus Der Autokrise. Vom Autobauer Zum Mobilitätsdienstleister. Berlin: Heinrich-Böll-Stiftung. Strategiepapier. https://www.boell.de/de/content/gruene-wege-aus-der-autokrise. Accessed 9/4/2015.

Canzler, Weert, Andreas Knie (2011): Einfach aufladen. Oekom Verlag.

Canzler, Weert; Andreas Knie, , & Otto Berthold (1993): Das Leitbild Automobil vor seiner Auflösung? Zum Widerspruch von motorischer Ausrüstung und realem Nutzungsverhalten. Schriftenreihe / Wissenschaftszentrum Berlin für Sozialforschung, Forschungsschwerpunkt Technik - Arbeit - Umwelt, Abteilung Organisation und Technikgenese, Berlin, pp. 93-105.

Canzler, Weert & Andreas Knie (1994): Das Ende des Automobils. Fakten und Trends zum Umbau der Autogesellschaft, Heidelberg: C. F. Müller.

Canzler, Weert & Andreas Knie (2014): Post-fossile Mobilität. Zukunftstauglich und vernetzt unterwegs. Politische ökologie, Band 137, München: oekom.

CARS 21 (2005): First Meeting of "CARS 21" group. MEMO/05/117, 21(April). http://europa.eu/rapid/press-release_MEMO-05-117_en.htm?locale=en. Accessed 9/4/2015.

Carter, Caitriona Clarisse Cazals, Laura Michel,Julia Hildermeier,& Axel Villareal (2014): Sustainable Development Policy. 'Competitiveness' in All But Name. In: Jullien, Bernard & Andy Smith (eds.), 2014. The European Government of Industries. Markets, Institutions and Politics: Routledge, pp. 165-189.

Chanaron Jean-Jacques & Yannick Lung (1995): L'économie de l'automobile, Paris : La Découverte.

Christensen, C.M. (1997): The Innovator's Dilemma. New York: HarperCollins Publishers.

Cini, Michele (1996): La Commission européenne: lieu d'émergence de cultures administratives. L'exemple de la DG IV et de la DG XI In: Revue française de science politique, 46e année, n°3, 1996. pp. 457-473.

CLEPA – European Association of Automotive Suppliers (2008): CLEPA Press Release on the CARS 21 High Level Conference, Brussels, 29 October 2008. http://www.clepa.eu/strategic-issues/cars-21/, accessed: 5.11.2013.

Cochoy, Frank (1999): Une histoire du marketing: discipliner l'économie de marché. Paris: La Decouverte.

Cohen, Michael, James March & Johan Olson (1972): A Garbage Can Model or Organizational Choice. Administrative Science Quarterly. London: Sage, 17/ 1, pp. 1-25

Corbin, Juliet & Anselm L. Strauss (1990): Grounded Theory Research: Procedures, Canons and Evaluative Criteria. Zeitschrift für Soziologie, 19(6), p. 418-427.

Crouch, C. & H. Farrell (2004): Breaking the Path of Institutional Development? Alternatives to the New Determinism. In: Rationality and Society 16(1), pp. 5-43.

Degallaix, L. (2007): BEUC Comments on the Commission's Communication on the Cars 21 Report.
http://ec.europa.eu/reducing_co2_emissions_from_cars/doc_contrib/beuc_cars 21_en.pdf. Accessed 9/4/2015.

Desrosières, Alain (2000): La politique des grands nombres: histoire de la raison statistique. Paris: la Découverte.

Deutsche Bundesregierung (2007): Integriertes Klima- und Energiepaket (IEKP). http://www.bmub.bund.de/fileadmin/bmu-import/files/pdfs/allgemein/application/pdf/gesamtbericht_iekp.pdf. Accessed 15/12/2014.

Deutsche Umwelthilfe (DUH) (2011): Anhörung im Verkehrsausschuss am 25. Mai 2011. „Nachhaltige Elektro-Mobilität und Klimaschutz". Stellungnahme der Deutschen Umwelthilfe e. V. zu den BT-Drucksachen 17/3479, 17/1164, 17/2022 und17/3647. http://www.duh.de/3939.html. Accessed 17/12/2014.

DeWalt, Billie & Kathleen M. DeWalt, (2002): Participant Observation. A Guide for Fieldworkers. Walnut Creek: Alta Mira Press.

Dexter, L. A. (1969): Elite and Specialized Interviewing. Evanston: Northwestern University Press.

Dezalay, Yves (2007): De la défense de l'environnement au développement durable, *Actes de la recherche en sciences sociales* 1/2007 (n° 166-167), p. 66-79
www.cairn.info/revue-actes-de-la-recherche-en-sciences-sociales-2007-1-page-66.htm. Accessed 17/12/2014.

Dierkes, Meinolf, Lutz Marz, & Thomas Aigle (2009): Die automobile Wende. Analyse einer Innovationslandschaft. In: R. Popp & E. Schüll (Eds.), Zukunftsforschung und Zukunftsgestaltung. Beiträge aus Wissenschaft und Praxis. Berlin, Heidelberg: Springer. pp. 323-340.

DLR (German Aerospace Center Institute of Transport Research) (2004): Preparation of the 2003 Review of the Commitment of Car Manufacturers to Reduce CO_2 Emissions from M1 Vehicles. Identifying and Assessing the Reasons for the CO_2 Reductions Achieved Between 1995 and 2003 (December 2004). http://ec.europa.eu/clima/policies/transport/vehicles/docs/a_11742_en.pdf. Accessed 17/12/2014.

Dobbin, Frank (1994): Forging Industrial Policy: the United States, Britain, and France in the Railway Age. New York, NY [u.a.]: Cambridge Univ. Press.

Dudenhöffer, Ferdinand (2010): Batterietechnologie für automobile Anwendungen und ihr Wertschöpfungspotenzial für Europa. In: IFO-Schnelldienst 11/2010,p. 19-27. https://www.cesifo-group.de/ifoHome/publications/docbase/details.html?docId=14568017. Accessed 17/12/2014.

European Commission (1992): Report of the Commission of the European Communities to the United Nations Conference on Environment and Development. Office for Official Publications of the European Communities, Luxemburg.

European Commission (1995): A Community Strategy to Reduce CO2 Emissions from Passenger Cars and Improve Fuel Economy. Brussels. http://europa.eu/legislation_summaries/other/l28055_en.htm. Accessed 09/04/2015.

European Commission (1999): Commission Recommendation of 5 February 1999 on the Reduction of CO2 Emissions from PassengerCcars. COM 1999/125/EC of 5/2/1999. Brussels. http://eur-lex.europa.eu/legal-content/EN/TXT/HTML/?uri=CELEX:31999H0125&from=EN. Accessed 09/04/2015.

European Commission (2000): Communication from the Commission to the Council and the European Parliament - Implementing the Community Strategy to Reduce CO2 Emissions from Cars First Annual Report on the Effectiveness of the Strategy. COM/2000/0615 final. http://eur-lex.europa.eu/legal-content/EN/TXT/HTML/?uri=CELEX:52000DC0615&from=EN. Accessed 09/04/2015.

European Commission (2001): European governance — a White Paper. Brussels. http://europa.eu/legislation_summaries/institutional_affairs/decisionmaking_process/l10109_en.htm. Accessed 09/04/2015.

European Commission (2002): Taxation of Passenger Cars in the European Union - Options for Action at National and Community Levels (COM(2002) 431 final). Brussels. http://eur-lex.europa.eu/legal-content/EN/ALL/?uri=CELEX:52002DC0431. Accessed 09/04/2015.

European Commission (2005): Proposal for a Council Directive on Passenger Car Related Taxes (COM(2005) 261 final). Brussels. Retrieved from http://eur-lex.europa.eu/LexUriServ/LexUriServ.do?uri=COM:2005:0261:FIN:en:PDF. Accessed 09/04/2015.

European Commission (2006): Cars 21. A Competitive Automotive Regulatory System for the 21st Century. Final Report. http://ec.europa.eu/enterprise/sectors/automotive/files/pagesbackground/competitiveness/cars21finalreport_en.pdf. Accessed 09/04/2015.

European Commission (2007a): A Competitive Regulatory System for the European Automotive Industry. CARS 21 Final Report. http://ec.europa.eu/enterprise/sectors/automotive/competitiveness-cars21/cars21/. Accessed: 31/10/13.

European Commission (2007b): Communication from the Commission to the Council and the European Parliament. Results of the Review of the Community Strategy to Reduce CO2 Emissions from Passenger Cars and Light-Commercial Vehicles Suggestion on Co2 Standards. Brussels, 7.2.2007 COM(2007) 19 final. http://eur-lex.europa.eu/LexUriServ/LexUriServ.do?uri=COM:2007:0019:FIN:en:PDF. Accessed 09/04/2015.

European Commission (2008). CARS 21 - Conclusions and Report. Mid-term Review 2008. http://ec.europa.eu/enterprise/sectors/automotive/documents/consultations/2008-cars21-mtr/index_en.htm. Accessed 09/04/2015.

European Commission (2011): White Paper. Roadmap to a Single European Transport Area – Towards a Competitive and Resource Efficient Transport System . Brussels, 28.3.2011 COM(2011) 144 final. URL: http://eur-lex.europa.eu/legal-content/EN/TXT/PDF/?uri=CELEX:52011DC0144&from=EN. Accessed 09/04/2015.

European Commission (2014): Reducing CO2 Emissions from Passenger Cars. http://ec.europa.eu/clima/policies/transport/vehicles/cars/index_en.htm. Accessed 6/12/2014

European Council (2006): Renewed EU Sustainable Development Strategy, Council of the European Union, 8.6.2006, Communication from the Commission to the Council and the European Parliament 6 Results of the review of the Community Strategy to reduce CO2 emissions from passenger cars and light-commercial vehicles {SEC(2007) 60} {SEC(2007) 61} COM/2007/0019 final. http://eur-lex.europa.eu/legal-content/EN/TXT/HTML/?uri=CELEX:52007DC0019&from=EN. Accessed 09.04.2015.

European Economic Community (1991): Council Directive 91/441/EEC of 26 June 1991 amending Directive 70/220/EEC on the approximation of the laws of the Member States relating to measures to be taken against air pollution by emissions from motor vehicles. OJ L 242, 30.8.1991, pp. 1–106.

Fédération Internationale de l'Automobile (FIA) (2014): About us. http://www.fia.com/about-fia. Accessed 17/12/2014.

Firnkorn, J. & M. Müller (2011): What Will be the Environmental Effects of New Free-floating Car-Sharing Systems? Ecological Economics 2011, 70/8, pp. 1519-1528.

Firnkorn, J. and M.Müller. (2012). Selling MobilityIinstead of Cars: New Business Strategies of Automakers and the Impact on Private Vehicle Holding. Business Strategy and the Environment 21(4), pp 264-280.

Fligstein Neil (1990): The Transformation of Corporate Control, Cambridge: Harvard University Press.

Fligstein Neil (1996): Markets as Politics: A Political-cultural Approach to Market Institutions, American Sociological Review, vol. 61, n° 4, pp. 656–673.

Fligstein Neil (2001): The Architecture of Markets: An Economic Sociology of Twenty-first-century Capitalist Societies, Princeton: Princeton University Press.

Fligstein, Neil (2001): The Process of Europeanization. Politique européenne n° 1, no. 1 (March 1, 2001). pp 25–42.

Fligstein, Neil (2002): Markets as Politics. A Political-Cutural Approach to Market Institutions. In Readings in Economic Sociology, Blackwell readers in sociology ; 8, ed. Nicole Woolsey Biggart. Malden, Mass. [u.a.]: Blackwell, pp. 197–218.

Fojcik, T.M. & H. Proff (2014): 'Accelerating market diffusion of battery electric vehicles through alternative mobility concepts', International Journal Automotive Technology and Management, Vol. 14, Nos. 3/4, pp. 347–368.

François, Pierre (2011): Vie et mort des institutions. Paris: Presses de Sciences Po.

Freyssenet M. (ed.) (2009): The Second Automobile Revolution, Basingstoke and New-York: Palgrave Macmillan.

Geels, Frank, Rene Kemp, Geoffrey Dudley & Glenn Lyons (eds.) (2011): Automobility in Transition?: A Socio-Technical Analysis of Sustainable Transport. London: Routledge.

Gerpisa/Tech2Market (2014): Étude prospective relative aux « nouveaux services de mobilité offerts par les usaes novateurs de la voiture » Rapport Intermediaire 1. Etude commissionnée par Pôle Interministériel de prospective et d'anticipation de mutations économiques (Pipame). Not published.

Glaser, Barney G. (2002). Constructivist Grounded Theory? Forum Qualitative Sozialforschung / Forum: Qualitative Social Research, 3(3), Art. 12, http://nbn-resolving.de/urn:nbn:de:0114-fqs0203125. Accessed 9/4/2015.

Gläser, Jochen & Grit Laudel (2006): Experteninterviews und qualitative Inhaltsanalyse, 2. Aufl. Wiesbaden: VS-Verlag.

Goertz, Gary & James Mahoney; (2006): A Tale of Two Cultures: Contrasting Quantitative and Qualitative Research. In: Political Analysis (2006) 14, pp. 227–249.

Goffman, Erving (1974): Frame Analysis: An Essay on the Organization of Experience. New York u.a.: Harper & Row.

Gold, R. (1958): "Roles in Sociological Field Observation." Social Forces, 36, pp. 217-213.

GreencarsCongress (2009): European Investment Bank Approves €866M in Loans for Cleaner Cars; Majority to Nissan and Jaguar. 12.4.2009. http://www.greencarcongress.com/2009/04/european-investment-bank-approves-866m-in-loans-for-cleaner-cars-majority-to-nissan-and-jaguar.html. Accessed 28/10/2013.

Greenpeace (2008): Driving Climate Change. How the car industry is lobbying to undermine EU fuel efficiency legislation. http://www.greenpeace.org/belgium/PageFiles/16797/drivingclimatechange.pdf. Accessed 28/10/2013.

Grieco, Margaret & John Urry (2011): Mobilities New Perspectives on Transport and Society. Farnham; Burlington, VT: Ashgate.

Hall, Peter (1986): Governing the Economy: The Politics of State Intervention in Britain and France. Oxford University Press.

Hall, Peter & David Soskice (2001): Varieties of Capitalism. The Institutional Foundations of Comparative Advantage. Oxford: Oxford Univ. Press.

Hellmann, Kai-Uwe (2007): Marken machen Märkte: Eine funktionale Analyse des Zusammenhangs von Märkten und Marken. In: Beckert, Jens et al. (ed.) 2007. Märkte als soziale Strukturen. Campus-Verlag, pp. 183.

Hildermeier, Julia (2013): Autolib': Elektroauto statt U-Bahn. Klimaretter Online. http://www.klimaretter.info/mobilitaet/hintergrund/13902-autolib-bilanz. Accessed 28/10/2013.

Hildermeier, Julia (2014): E-car-Sharing als Pariser Weltschlager. Klimaretter Online. http://www.klimaretter.info/mobilitaet/hintergrund/17103-e-car-sharing-als-pariser-weltschlager. Accessed 28/10/2013.

Hildermeier, Julia (2016): Which Role Should the Electric Car Play in Europe's Cities? An Analysis of Publicly Funded Demonstration Projects 2007-2013. International Journal of Automotive Technology and Management, Vol. 16, No.1, pp.90 – 107.

Hildermeier, Julia & Axel Villareal (2014): Two Ways of Defining Sustainable Mobility: Autolib' and BeMobility, Journal of Environmental Policy & Planning. http://dx.doi.org/10.1080/1523908X.2014.880336.

Hildermeier, Julia & Weert Canzler (2014): Editorial. International Journal of Automotive Technology and Management, Vol. 14, Nos. 3/4, 2014, pp. 195-202.

Hildermeier, Julia & Axel Villareal (2011): Shaping an Emerging Market for Electric Cars: How politics in France and Germany transform the European automotive industry. ERIEP, Number 3, on line since 12 December 2011, URL : http://revel.unice.fr/eriep/index.html?id=3329. Accessed 28/10/2013.

Honsel, Gregor (2011): Das öffentliche Automobil. Technology Review, November 17, 2011, pp. 62-65.

Hoogma, Remco, Rene Kemp, Johan Schot & Bernhard Truffer (2002): Experimenting for Sustainable Transport. The Approach of Strategic Niche Management. London: Spon Press.

Hutter, Michael et al. (2010): Forschungsprogramm der Abteilung Kulturelle Quellen von Neuheit. WZB Discussion Paper SP III 2010-401. Berlin.

IAO Fraunhofer & PWC (PriceWaterhouseCoopers) (2010): Elektromobilität. Herausforderungen für die öffentliche Hand. http://wiki.iao.fraunhofer.de/images/studien/elektromobilitaet-herausforderungen-fuer-industrie-und-oeffentliche-hand.pdf. Accessed: 17/12/2014.

ICCT (International Council for Clean Transportation) (2015): From Laboratory to Road. A 2015 update. http://www.theicct.org/laboratory-road-2015-update. Accessed 17/12/2014.

IEEP/TNO/CAIR (2005): Service contract to carry out economic analysis and business impact assessment of CO2 emissions reduction measures in the automotive sector. REF: B4-3040/2003/366487/MAR/C2. Final Report. By Patrick ten Brink, Ian Skinner, Malcolm Fergusson, Dawn Haines. http://ec.europa.eu/clima/policies/transport/vehicles/docs/cars_ia_final_report_en.pdf. Accessed 9/4/2015.

International Council on Clean Transportation (ICCT) (2012): Global Transportation Energy and Climate Roadmap. http://www.theicct.org/sites/default/files/publications/ICCT%20Roadmap%20Energy%20Report.pdf. Accessed 9/4/2015.

IÖW/future (eds.)(2009): Ranking der Nachhaltigkeitsberichterstattung. Berlin und Münster. http://www.ranking-nachhaltigkeitsberichte.de/. Accessed 9/4/2015.

Jöhrens, Julius & Julia Hildermeier (2015): Umweltinnovation im Pkw-Bereich: Kann die Politik Technologiesprünge erzwingen? In: Schwedes, Oliver; Canzler, Weert; Knie, Andreas (2015): Handbuch Verkehrspolitik. München: Springer, pp. 649-676.

Jullien B.; Y. Lung & C. Midler (2012): L'épopée Logan, nouvelles trajectoires pour l'innovation, Paris: Dunod.

Jullien, Bernard (2010): La Seconde Révolution automobile et ses contours, Sociétal, n° 70, p. 54-61.

Jullien, Bernard (2011): ICaTSEM. Institutional Change and Trajectories of Socio-Economic Models. Deliverable D4.3. WP4 – Sectoral studies of institutional configurations and industrial dynamics - Final Report. http://icatsem.u-bordeaux4.fr/sites/icatsem/IMG/pdf/icatsem_deliverable_d4.3.pdf.

Jullien, Bernard (2014): Véhicule électrique : un quiproquo sur le tempo. In: Chronique du 15.9.2014, www.autoactu.com.

Jullien, Bernard& Yannick Lung (2011): Industrie automobile: la croisée des chemins. Paris: la Documentation française.

Jullien, Bernard & Andy Smith (2010) 'Conceptualizing the Role of Politics in the Economy: Industries and their Institutionalizations', Review of International Political Economy, First published on: 19 October 2010 (iFirst) http://dx.doi.org/10.1080/0969229100372361.

Jullien, Bernard & Andy Smith (2012): GEDI Project Draft Working Paper. Unpublished.

Jullien, Bernard & Andy Smith (eds.) (2008): Industries and Globalization: The Political Causality of Difference. Palgrave Macmillan.

Jullien, Bernard & Andy Smith (eds.) (2014): The European Government of Industries. Markets, Institutions and Politics: Routledge.

Jürgens, Ulrich & Thomas Sablowski (2008): Sektorale Innovationsprozesse und die Diskussion über deutsche Innovationsschwächen. HBS-Edition Wirtschaft und Finanzen Nr. 204. Düsseldorf.

Jürgens, Ulrich, Antje Blöcker,Julia Hildermeier (2010): ICATSEM Report. Deliverable 4.3. The German Automobile Industry. Earlier and unpublished version for Jullien, Bernard (2011): ICaTSEM. Institutional Change and Trajectories of Socio-Economic Models. Deliverable D4.3. WP4 – Sectoral studies of institutional configurations and industrial dynamics - Final Report. http://icatsem.u-bordeaux4.fr/sites/icatsem/IMG/pdf/icatsem_deliverable_d4.3.pdf.

Kawulich, Barbara B. (2005): Participant Observation as a Data Collection Method. Forum Qualitative Sozialforschung / Forum: Qualitative Social Research, 6(2), Art. 43, http://nbn-resolving.de/urn:nbn:de:0114-fqs0502430. Accessed 9/4/2015.

KBA - Kraftfahrtbundesamt (2014): http://www.kba.de/DE/Statistik/Fahrzeuge/Neuzulassungen/neuzulassungen_n ode.html. Accessed 9/4/2015.

Keay-Bright, Sarah (2000): European Environmental Bureau. European Environmental Bureau (pp. 1–84). Brussels. Retrieved from http://www.eeb.org/publication/2001/ACEA-10-final-complete.pdf. Accessed 9/4/2015.

Keichel, Marcus & Oliver Schwedes (2013): Einleitung. Plädoyer für eine neue Mobilitätskultur. In: Keichel/Schwedes (Eds.): Das Elektroauto. Mobilität im Umbruch. Wiesbaden: Springer Fachmedien.

Kemp, René, Frank Geels, Geoff Dudley (2012): Introduction. Sustainability Transitions in the Automobility Regime and the Need for a New Perspective. In: Geels, F. W., R. Kemp, G. Dudley, & G. Lyons (2012): Automobility in

Transition?: A socio-technical analysis of sustainable transport. New York: Routledge.

Knie, A., S. Kramer, C. Scherf & F. Wolter (2012): 'E-Carsharing als Bestandteil multimodaler Angebote', Internationales Verkehrswesen, Vol. 64, No. 1, pp.42–45.

Knoll, Lisa (2012): Über die Rechtfertigung wirtschaftlichen Handelns CO2-Handel in der kommunalen Energiewirtschaft. Wiesbaden: VS Verlag für Sozialwissenschaften.

Kocka, Jürgen (2013): Geschichte des Kapitalismus. München : C.H. Beck

Krstacic-Galic, Ante & Lutz Marz (2011): Konsenschancen des energietechnologischen Paradigmenwechsels : das Beispiel der Wasserstoff- und Brennstoffzellentechnologie. Berlin: Wissenschaftszentrum Berlin für Sozialforschung gGmbH.

Lanzendorf, M., & R. Schönduwe (2013): Urbanität und Automobilität: Neue Nutzungsmuster und Bedeutungen verändern die Mobilität der Zukunft. Geographische Rundschau, 65, 6, 34-41.

Lascoumes, P. & P. Le Gales (2007): Introduction: Understanding Public Policy through Its Instruments—From the Nature of Instruments to the Sociology of Public Policy Instrumentation. Governance, 20: 1–21.

Lascoumes, P. & P. Le Gale (2012): Sociologie de l'action publique. Paris: Armand Colin.

Lawrence, Thomas & B. Roy Suddaby (2006): Institutions and Institutional Work. In S. R. Clegg, C. Hardy, T. B. Lawrence, & W. R. Nord (Eds.) Handbook of Organization Studies, 2nd Edition: 21 5-254. London: Sage. Pp. 215-254.

Legewie, Heiner (2005): Rezension: Jörg Strübing (2004). Grounded Theory. Zur sozialtheoretischen und epistemologischen Fundierung des Verfahrens der empirisch begründeten Theoriebildung [63 Absätze]. Forum Qualitative Sozialforschung / Forum: Qualitative Social Research, 7(2), Art. 1, http://nbn-resolving.de/urn:nbn:de:0114-fqs060210. Accessed 9/4/2015.

Leithäusl, Stefan (1998): Kommunikationsstrategien in der Autowerbung : vergleichende Analyse der Werbekampagnen für die Mercedes-Benz-C-Klasse und den Ford Scorpio. Fernwald : Litblockín

Lenschow, Andrea & Katja Rottmann (2005): 'Privatising' EU Governance: Emergence and Characteristics of Voluntary Agreements in European Environmental Policy. Paper Prepared for Scientific Workshop 'Soft Modes of Governance and the Private Sector – The EU and the Global Experience'

(Darmstadt, 1-3 November 2005). http://www.mzes.uni-mann-heim.de/projekte/typo3/site/fileadmin/research%20groups/6/Papers_Soft%20Mode/Lenschow%20Rottmann.pdf. Accessed 9/4/2015.

Lindloff, Kirstin, Nadine Pieper, David Woisetschlaeger, Nils Bandelow (2014): Drivers of Carsharing Diffusion in Germany: an Actor-Centred Approach. Int. J. Automotive Technology and Management, Vol. 14, Nos. 3/4, 2014, pp. 217-245.

Littig, B. (2008): Interviews mit Eliten – Interviews mit ExpertInnen: Gibt es Unterschiede. Forum Qualitative Sozialforschung/Forum: Qualitative Social Research, 9(3), Art. 16. Retrieved from http://nbn-resolving.de/urn:nbn:de:0114-fqs0803161.

MacKenzie, D. & Y. Millo (2003). Constructing a Market, Performing Theory: The Historical Sociology of a Financial Derivatives Exchange. American Journal of Sociology, 109, 107–145.

Mahoney, James & Kathleen Ann Thelen (2010): Explaining Institutional Change : Ambiguity, Agency, and Power. Cambridge [u.a.]: Cambridge Univ. Press.

Malerba, Franco (2007): Innovation and the Dynamics and Evolution of Industries: Progress and Challenges. International Journal of Industrial Organization 25(4): 675–99. http://www.sciencedirect.com/science/article/B6V8P-4KYXHJR-1/2/9fe640a40b4784c92b6ebe89622146bf, accessed February 26, 2010.

Marz, Lutz & Ante Krstacic-Galic (2010): Valorisierung durch "Problem/Solution-Framing". Das Beispiel der deutschen Wasserstoff- und Brennstoffzellen-Community. Discussion Paper SP III 2010-403. Wissenschaftszentrum Berlin für Sozialforschung. http://bibliothek.wzb.eu/pdf/2010/iii10-403.pdf. Accessed: 31.10.13.

Mayring, Philipp (1990): Einführung in die qualitative Sozialforschung, München.

Meißner, Heinz-Rudolf (2011): Vortrag "Elektromobilität - Gestaltungsnotwendigkeit des Strukturwandels", IGM Albstatt, Klausurtagung, 18.11.2011, http://www.fastev-berlin.org/fo_ergeb.htm. Accessed: 15/12/2014.

Merten, Thomas (2009): Branchenkritierien Automobilhersteller. IN. IÖW/future (ed.): Anforderungen an die Nachhaltigkeitsberichterstattung: Kriterien und Bewertungsmethode. Berlin und Münster, Juni 2009, 43-52.

Meyer, John W. & Brian Rowan (1977): Institutionalized Organizations: Formal Structure as Myth and Ceremony. In: American Journal of Sociology. Vol. 83, 1977, pp. 340–363.

Michaux, F. (2010): Monographies des plans nationaux d'action en faveur de l'électro-mobilité. Dans le cadre des Entretiens européens à la recherche de la voiture propre. Confrontations Européennes. 14-15 avril 2010, Paris. http://www.confrontations.org/images/confrontations/IMG/pdf/Monographies_plans_nationaux_voiture_propre_Francois_Michaux.pdf. Accessed: 15/12/2014.

Mitchell, William J; Chris Borroni-Bird, Lawrence D. Burns (2010): Reinventing the Automobile: Personal Urban Mobility for the 21st Century. Cambridge, Mass.: Massachusetts Institute of Technology.

Mom, Gijs (2004): The Electric Vehicle: Technology and Expectations in the Automobile Age. Baltimore: John Hopkins University Press.

Morguen-Toursel, Marine (2004): Les structures de représentation de l'industrie automobile en Europe. Un foisonnement de réseaux aux stratégies multiples? In: Dumoulin, Michel (ed) (2004): Economic networks and European integration. Peter Lang.

Morguen-Tousel, Marine (2009): L'action collective des élites économiques. Contribution at Congrès AFSP 2009, thématique 33, Axe 3 Les produits de l'action collective.

Orsato, R.J. (2006): Competitive Environmental Strategies: When Does it Pay to be Green? California Management Review 48: 127–143. DOI: 10.1225/CMR334

Orsato, R.J. & Wells, P. (2007b): U-turn: The Rise and Demise of the Automobile Industry. Journal of Cleaner Production, Vol. 15, pp. 994-1006.

Orsato, R.J. & Wells., P. (2007a) The Automobile Industry & Sustainability: Introduction. Journal of Cleaner Production, Vol. 15, No. 11-12, pp. 989-993.

Orsato, R.J.. (2009): Sustainability Strategies: When Does It Pay to Be Green? Palgrave MacMillan: Basingstoke.

Pardi, Tommaso (2011): La révolution qui n'a pas eu lieu: les constructeurs japonais en Europe (1970-2010). Thèse pour le Doctorat de Sociologie. Tome II. Not published.

Parkhurst, Graham, René Kemp, Marc Dijk,& Henrietta Sherwin (2012): Intermodal Personal Mobility: A Niche Caught Between Two Regimes. In: Geels, F. W. et al (2012). Automobility in transition? A Socio-Technical Analysis of Sustainable Transport. New York Routledge. Pp. 308-335.

Pel, Bonno, Geert Teisman,& Frank Boons (2011): Transition by Translation. In: Geels, F. W., Kemp, R., Dudley, G. & Lyons, G (2012): Automobility in Transition?: A socio-technical analysis of sustainable transport. New York: Routledge. pp. 250-267.

Peters, Jürgen (2007): Untitled. Intervention at Restructuring Forum. The Challenges of the Automotive Industry. Towards a European Partnership for the Anticipation of Change. 17/18 October 2007. Minutes, p.15. http://ec.europa.eu/employment_social/restructuing/forum_en.htm, accessed 31.10.13.

Pierson, Paul (2004): Politics in Time: History, Institutions, and Social Analysis. Princeton, NJ ua: Princeton Univ. Press, 2004.

Plehwe, Dieter (2010): "Brussels Think Tanks and Corporate PR", in: Helen Burley, William Dinan, Kenneth Haar, Olivier Hoedeman & Erik Wesselius (eds.), Bursting the Brussels Bubble. The battle to expose corporate lobbying at the heart of the EU.Brussels: Alter-EU, 53-61.

Plötz et al. (2013): Markthochlaufszenarien für Elektrofahrzeuge Langfassung. Studie im Auftrag der acatech – Deutsche Akademie der Technikwissenschaften und der Arbeitsgruppe 7 der Nationalen Plattform Elektromobilität (NPE). http://www.isi.fraunhofer.de/isi-de/e/projekte/316741_Markthochlaufszenarien-E-Fahrzeuge_Wi2014.php, accessed: 15/12/2014.

Prätorius, Gerhard & Frank Lehrach (1998): Operation of Electric Road Vehicles in Germany. Investigation of Selected Examples. A Case Study for the Project "Strategic Niche Management as a Tool for Transition to a Sustainable Transport System". Braunschweig: Reson.

Quandt, A. (2010): Voluntary Approaches in Climate Policy: Comparing European and Swiss Transport Legislation. Retrieved from http://www.cces.ethz.ch/projects/clench/CLIMPOL/Publications/D2

Razemon, Olivier (2013): "On a raté l'objectif. Autolib' ne supprime pas de voitures". 26/3/2013 in Le Monde Blogs, http://transports.blog.lemonde.fr/2013/03/26/on-a-rate-lobjectif-autolib-ne-supprime-pas-de-voitures/. Accessed 3.9.2014.

Reverdy, Thomas (2005): "Les Normes Environnementales En Entreprise : La Trajectoire Mouvementée D'une Mode Managériale." Sociologies pratiques 10(1): 97.http://www.cairn.info/revue-sociologies-pratiques-2005-1-page-97.htm (June 21, 2012). Accessed 12/08/2014.

Ruhrort, Lisa; Josephine Steiner, Andreas Graff, Daniel Hinkeldein, & Christian Hoffmann (2014): Carsharing with Electric Vehicles in the Context of Users' Mobility Needs – Results from User-Centred Research from the Be-Mobility Field Trial (Berlin). Int. J. Automotive Technology and Management, Vol. 14, Nos. 3/4, 2014. pp. 286-305.

Schensul, Stephen L. Jean J. Schensul, Margaret D. LeCompte (1999): Essential Ethnographic Methods: Observations, Interviews, and Questionnaires (Book 2 in Ethnographer's Toolkit). Walnut Creek, CA: AltaMira Press.

Schmidt, Vivian A. (2002): The Futures of European Capitalism (1. publ). Oxford [u.a.]: Oxford Univ. Press.

Schönduwe, R., Bock, B. & Deibel, I. (2012): Alles wie immer, nur irgendwie anders? Trends und Thesen zu veränderten Mobilitätsmustern junger Menschen (No. 10), InnoZ Baustein. Innovationszentrum für Mobilität und Gesellschaft (InnoZ) GmbH, Berlin.

Scott, W.R. (2008): Approaching Adulthood: The Maturing of Institutional Theory. Theory&Society, 37, 427-442.

Scott, William Richard (1995): Institutions and Organizations. Thousand Oaks u.a: Sage.

Shaheen, S. & A. Cohen (2007): Worldwide Carsharing Growth: An International Comparison, Transportation Research Record, 2007, Vol. 1992, pp. 81-89.

Sheller, M. & Urry, J. (2002): 'The City and the Car', Int. J. Urban Reg. Res., Vol. 24, No. 4, pp.737–757.

Sheller, Mimi (2012): The Emergence of New Cultures of Mobility. Stability, Openings and Prospects. In: Geels, F. W., Kemp, R., Dudley, G. & Lyons, G (2012): Automobility in Transition?: A socio-technical analysis of sustainable transport. New York: Routledge. pp. 180-202.

Shnayerson, Michael (1996): The Car That Could. New York: Random House

Simon, Herbert (1959): Theories of Decision Making in Economics and Behavioural Science. American Economic Review, 49, 3, pp. 253 - 283.

Smith, Andy (2013): How the European Commission's Policies are made: Problematization, Instrumentation, Legitimization. Journal of European Integration. Published online: 4 July 2013.

Snow David & R. Benford (1988): Ideology, Frame Resonance, and Participant Mobilization. International Social Movement Research. pp. 197-218.

Snow, David & F. Benford (2000): Framing Processes and Social Movements. An Overview and Assessment. Annual Review of Sociology, 2000. 26:611–39.

Snow, David A., E. Burke. Steven Rochford, K Worden & Robert D Benford (1986): Frame Alignment Processes, Micromobilization, and Movement Participation. American Sociological Review 51(4):464–481.

Stone Sweet, Alec, Wayne Sandholtz, Neil Fligstein (eds). (2001): The Institutionalization of Europe. Oxford ; New York ; Auckland: Oxford university press.

Streeck, Wolfgang & Kathleen Thelen (2005): Beyond Continuity. Institutional Change in Advanced Political Economies. Oxford [a.o.]: Univ. Press.

Strübing, Jörg (2004): Grounded Theory. Zur sozialtheoretischen und epistemologischen Fundierung des Verfahrens der empirisch begründeten Theoriebildung (Reihe: Qualitative Sozialforschung Bd. 15). VS Verlag für Sozialwissenschaften.

Transport & Environment (2000): The Drive for Less Fuel. Will the European Motor Industry be Able to Honour its Commitment to the European Union? Written by Per Kageson, January 2000. http://www.transportenvironment.org/publications/drive-less-fuel-te-0001, accessed 28/7/2014.

Transport & Environment (2005a): Cleaner is Cheaper. Why European Climate Policy for Cars is Failing, and What Can be Done About it. Mai 2005. http://www.transportenvironment.org/publications/cleaner-cheaper. Accessed 28/7/2014.

Transport & Environment (2005b): Reducing CO^2 Emissions from New Cars. A progress report on the car industry's voluntary agreement and an assessment of potential policy instruments. Per Kågeson.

Transport & Environment (2005c): Reducing CO^2 Emissions from New Cars. A progress report on the car industry's voluntary agreement and an assessment of the need for policy instruments. http://www.transportenvironment.org/search/site/Reducing%20CO2%20Emissions%20from%20New%20Cars.

Transport & Environment (2007): Reducing CO^2 Emissions from New Cars: A Study of Major Car Manufacturers' Progress in 2006. https://www.transportenvironment.org/docs/Publications/2007/2007-11_car_company_co2_report.pdf

Transport & Environment (2013): Annual Report 2013. http://www.transportenvironment.org/publications/annual-report-2013. Accessed 28/7/2014.

Transport & Environment (2014): Electric Vehicles in 2013: A Progress Report. http://www.transportenvironment.org/sites/te/files/publications/Electric%20Vehicles%20in%202013_full%20report_final_final.pdf. Accessed 28/7/2014.

Transport & Environment and European Transport Safety Council (ETSC) (2005): Commission's New Car Industry Group "Lacks Expertise" Say Transport NGOs. Press release from January 13, 2005. http://www.transportenvironment.org/press/commissions-new-car-industry-group-lacks-expertise-say-transport-ngos. Accessed 13/08/2014.

VDA - Verband der Deutschen Automobilindustrie. (1998). Jahresbericht 1998. https://www.vda.de/de/publikationen/jahresberichte. Accessed 13/08/2014.

VDA (1998): Auto 1998. Jahresbericht/Annual Report. https://www.vda.de/de/services/Publikationen/Publikation.~489~.html. Accessed 9/4/2015.

VES (Verkehrswirtschaftliche Energiestrategie) (2007): 3. Statusbericht der Task-Force an das Steering-Committee, Internet: http://www.bmvbs.de/Anlage/original_1049739/3.-Statusbericht-VES-des-Jahres-2007-Langfassung.pdf, Zugriff: 27.05.2010

Villareal, Axel (2014): L'industrie automobile à l'épreuve des voitures électriques. Entre changement et continuité. Thèse de Doctorat : Sciences Po Bordeaux, Novembre, 462 pages, unpublished.

Volkswagen (1993): Umweltbericht. Wolfsburg.

Volkswagen (1995): Umweltbericht. Wolfsburg.

Volkswagen (2000): Umweltbericht 1999/2000. Wolfsburg. http://www.volkswagen.de/content/medialib/vwd4/de/Volkswagen/Nachhaltigkeit/service/download/umweltberichte/umweltbericht_19992000deutsch27mb/_jcr_content/renditions/rendition.file/umweltberichte_par_0012_file.pdf. Accessed 9/4/2015.

Volkswagen (2003/2004): Umweltbericht: Partnerschaft in Verantwortung. Wolfsburg. http://www.volkswagen.de/content/medialib/vwd4/de/Volkswagen/Nachhaltigkeit/service/download/umweltberichte/umweltbericht_20032004deutsch28mb/_j cr_content/renditions/rendition.file/umweltberichte_par_0004_file.pdf. Accessed 9/4/2015.

Volkswagen (2009) and Volkswagen (2010): Nachhaltigkeitsbericht 2009/2010. Wolfsburg. http://www.volkswagenag.com/content/vwcorp/info_center/de/themes/2009/09/sustainability_report_2009_2010.html. Accessed 9/4/2015.

Wang, H. & C. Kimble (2013). Innovation and Leapfrogging in the Chinese Automobile Industry : Examples From Geely , BYD , and Shifeng. Global Business and Organizational Excellence, 32(6), 6–17.

Weider, Marc (2007): Technology Forcing – Verkehrspolitik und Umweltinnovation. In: Oliver Schöller, Weert Canzler, Andreas Knie (ed.), Handbuch der Verkehrspolitik, Wiesbaden: VS Verlag für Sozialwissenschaften 2007, pp. 663-686.

Welch, Catherine, Rebecca Marschan-Piekkari,Heli Penttinen & Marja Tahvanainen (2002): Corporate Elites as Informants in Qualitative International Business Research. International Business Research Review, 11, pp. 611-628.

Wells, Peter (2010): The Automotive Industry in an Era of Eco-Austerity: Creating an Industry as If the Planet Mattered. Northampton, MA: Edward Elgar Pub.

Wells, Peter, Daniel Newman, Ceri Donovan,Paul Nieuwenhuis & Huw Davies (2014): Urban, Sub-Urban or Rural: Where is the Best Place for Electric Vehicles? In: Hildermeier, Julia & Weert Canzler (eds.) (2014) International Journal of Automotive Technology and Management, Vol. 14, Nos. 3/4, 2014, pp. 306-323.

WELT online, die (2014): Mobilitätsdienstleister statt Autohersteller, 3.3.2014. http://www.welt.de/motor/news/article125397001/Neue-Marke-Mercedes-Me.html. Accessed 9/4/2015.

White, Harrison C. 2005: Markets from Networks: Socioeconomic Models of Production. Princeton, NJ : Princeton Univ. Press.

Womack, James P, Daniel T. Jones & Daniel Roos (1990): The Machine that Changed the World. New York: Free Press.

Yin, Robert K. (2009): Case Study Research: Design and Methods. Thousand Oaks: Sage Publications.

Zeit, Die (2013): Trendforscher erwarten baldigen Durchbruch des Elektroautos. 5.11.2013. http://www.zeit.de/mobilitaet/2013-10/elektroauto-durchbruch-trendforscher. Accessed 9/4/2015.

Zucker, Lynne G. (1977): The Role of Institutionalization in Cultural Persistence. In: American Sociological Review, Volume 42, issue 5, Oct. 1977, pp. 726-743.

Annex

A. Timeline of events

Year	Event
1993	European Single Market
1998	Car Makers' Voluntary Agreement to reduce CO_2 emissions
2008	End of Voluntary Agreement
2008	Beginning of Economic Crisis
2008	European Green Cars Initiative
2009	Commission adopts CO_2 Emission Regulation
2011	European Strategy for Clean and Energy Efficient Vehicles

B. Table of Interviews

ID	Organisation	Function	Date	Registered	Duration	Language
			Automotive Industry			
1	BMW France	Director E-Mobility	26 March 2012	Yes	1:40	Fr
2	Bosch	Director E-Mobility	19 March 2012	Yes	2:27	Fr
3	ADA Location / ULPRO	executive manager	28 March 2012	Yes	1:58	Fr
4	Autolib'	executive manager	20 March 2012	Yes	0:45	Fr
			European Institutions			

5	EU Parliament	Advisor	12 January 2012	No	0:47	Fr
6	EU Commission DG Clima	Legal Officer	19 January 2012	Yes	0:35	En
7	EU Commission DG Employment	Policy Officer	18 January 2012	Yes	1:00	Fr
8	EU Commission DG Enterprise	Policy Officer	22 March 2012	Yes	0 :47	En
9	EU Commission DG Enterprise	Unit Director	17 January 2012	Yes	0 :59	Fr
10	EU Commission DG Environment	Policy Officer	18 January 2012	Yes	1 :03	En
11	EU Commission DG Infso	Research Programme Officer	18 January 2012	Yes	0 :43	En
12	EU Commission DG Move	Policy Officer	17 January 2012	Yes	1:01	Fr
13	EU Commission DG Research	Project Officer	16 January 2012	Yes	1:25	En
14	EU Commission DG Clima	Policy Officer	16 October 2012	Yes	1:09	En
15	EU Parliament	Legal Service	17 October 2013	Yes	2:37	Fr
16	EU Parliament	Advisor Transport Policy	18 October 2013	Yes	2:00	En

Interest Groups

19	Ertrac	Director	11 April 2012	No	1:40	Fr
20	Eurelectric	Policy Officer	11 April 2012	Yes	2:16	En
21	Clepa	Deputy CEO	12 April 2012	Yes	0:40	En
22	Clepa	RTD Director	12 April 2012	Yes	1:12	En
23	T&E	Programme Manager	1 April 2013	No	0:15	En
24	T&E	Policy Officer	1 October 2013	Yes	1:15	En
25	Committee of Regions	Permanent Delegate	13 April 2012	Yes	1:13	En
26	BEUC	Policy Officer	3 October 2013	Yes	2:01	Ger
27	Greenpeace	Policy Officer	2 October 2013	Yes	0:38	Ger
28	ACEA	Policy Officer	20 January 2014	Yes	1:00	En
29	BMW Europe	Director EU Affairs	18 October 2013	No		Ger
30	VW	Policy Officer	12 October 2013	No	0:22	Ger
31	FIA	Policy Officer	23 October 2013	Yes	0:50	En
32	CEPS	Researcher	18 October 2013	No	1:00	En
33	ETUC	Policy Officer	4 October 2013	Yes	1:18	En

National and regional actors

34	Sustainable Development Ministry France	Transport Officer	4 April 2012	Yes	1:11	Fr
35	Industry Ministry	Transport Officer	27 March 2012	No	1:15	Fr
36	Cnisf	Consultant	27 March 2012	Yes	2:05	Fr
37	City of Paris	E-Mobility Officer	17 April 2012	Yes	1:05	Fr
38	WZB Berlin	Researcher	22 April 2012	No	02:00	Ger
39	InnoZ Berlin	Director	12 October 2013	No	1:00	Ger
40	InnoZ Berlin	Researcher	14 October 2013	Yes	1:30	Ger
41	City of Berlin	E-Mobility Officer	14 October 2013	Yes	01:00	Ger